Tom Cox lives in Norfolk. He is the author of the *Sunday Times* bestselling *The Good, The Bad and The Furry* and the William Hill Sports Book longlisted *Bring Me the Head of Sergio Garcia*. *21st-Century Yokel* was longlisted for the Wainwright Prize, and the titular story of *Help the Witch* won a Shirley Jackson Award.

@cox_tom

Also by Tom Cox

Ring the Hill

TOM COX

unbound

First published in 2019
This paperback edition first published in 2020

Unbound
6th Floor Mutual House, 70 Conduit Street, London W1S 2GF

www.unbound.com

Text Design by Ellipsis, Glasgow

A CIP record for this book is available from the British Library

ISBN 978-1-78352-901-8 (paperback)
ISBN 978-1-78352-835-6 (hardback)
ISBN 978-1-78352-836-3 (ebook)

Printed and bound in the United States by Sheridan

1 3 5 7 9 8 6 4 2

CONTENTS

'For he conducted his life as
everyone does—by guessing at
the future'

> —Annie Proulx,
> *Accordion Crimes*

'The man the hare has met
will never be the better of it
except he lay down on the land
what he carries in his hand—
be it staff or be it bow—
and bless him with his elbow
and come out with this litany
with devotion and sincerity
to speak the praises of the hare.
Then the man will better fare.

'The hare, call him scotart,
big-fellow, bouchart,
the O'Hare, the jumper,
the rascal, the racer . . .
The creep-along, the sitter-still,
the pintail, the ring-the-hill . . .'

> —Anon,
> *The Names of the Hare*
> (Thirteenth century)

ISLAND-HOPPING

(2018–19)

When you arrive at my house – my current house, which might not be my house for very long, since that increasingly seems to be the way of things with me – something you will probably notice about it before long is that it is in the sea. Not the extreme bottom of the sea, low tide perhaps revealing a chimney pot and the weatherworn edge of a seventeenth-century gable, but certainly not what could be considered officially part of the mainland. It's a fact that makes itself more apparent on some days, and from some vantage points, than others. When the mist is heavy and you stand at the summit of one of the abrupt, isolated hills common to this part of Somerset, the realisation becomes stronger that, not all that many

I

centuries ago, all the low ground as far as the eye can see was underwater: first proper sea, then a sort of marshy half-sea, dotted with small, tall islands, where semi-feral humans lived off fish and a king could successfully hide in times of trouble. I am fascinated by this place, and like it more every day, although I did not fall instantly in love with it. As most people who have got any kind of living under their belt know, though, the kind of love that arrives at first sight is rarely the most fulfilling.

I moved here at the beginning of the crisp, golden, hazy days: the period when, after the scruffiness of late summer, nature gets the decorators back in. It was a time of year that I already associated with the heart of Somerset and now probably will forever: the season when the region shows off its long, cosmic sunsets, the intricate embroidery of its skies, to best effect. In August I had made the mistake of boasting about a long period of excellent health and been summarily punished for my smugness with a back injury and chest infection, but the golden days kept stretching on and I was determined to make the most of them, so I hobbled out into the dry sea, past its sparkling coppery trees, coughing my way to the top of the island lookout points, doing a commendable amount of exploring for an invalid. I'd ordered the map before I'd booked the removal van: one of the lovely personalised ones the OS do nowadays, with your house at the dead centre. You get the privilege of choosing the cover photo yourself. Mine was one I'd taken on my first visit to Glastonbury Tor, in autumn 2015, at dusk, of the silhouettes of two Danish women watching the sun fall into the sea just below Weston-super-Mare, seventeen miles to the west. In Somerset and Dorset, more than in other coastal counties, I always get the impression the sun takes its nightly rest in the sea: nowhere too far away, but not quite in a spot you could easily swim or row a small wooden boat to.

I came to live here in the other sea – the inland sea that is mostly, but not always, dry – by accident; and then again I didn't. Accidents are often an amalgamation of intentions, hopes, misfortunes and the knock-on effect of experiences, which arguably makes them not all that accidental at all. I impulsively left a part of the UK I love in order to live out a crazy, ambitious writing experiment in a brutally cold, topographically hostile spot; when I decided it was over, which was quite quickly, I ran back as soon as I could into the arms of part of the UK I loved but ended up in a house where I found it extremely difficult to work; I looked for a quieter, more private house to write in a couple of places which I thought might provide a balance between my social and working needs; I didn't find one, but I fell, in a subtle way, for a house in another area, not all that far away, an area I didn't know well at all. That all happened in under twelve months and accounts for why I am now in the sea. In other words, I am here as a direct result of being me. In this instance it has been expensive and tiring, being me, but I don't regret it.

Twenty one is the number of houses I have now lived in. I can't claim full responsibility for that total. My parents moved a lot when I was growing up. In my ancestry, on the Irish side, there is evidence of travelling salesmen, so maybe that's an additional explanation for the wanderlust.

I'm disturbingly good at moving now: the packing, the labelling, the sizing up, the prioritising and deprioritising of bullshit admin. I wouldn't say it gets easier, but doing stupid things during house moves in the past has, finally, after many years, made me marginally better at not doing stupid things during house moves. There is no better illustration of the human brain's ability to blank out bad experiences as a coping mechanism than that of moving house. 'Never again!' we say, after a move, feeling like we have been slowly backed over three times by a large tractor with tyres caked in hot manure. But after a while, the details of exactly why it was so traumatic fade. 'Maybe it wasn't so bad after all?' we think. But it was. Probably worse, in fact. Our memory is lying to us. If I was ever stuck for inspiration for writing, I would apply for a job as a removal man. It's not just that removal companies see the intimate, behind-the-scenes paraphernalia of strangers every day; moving – stressful enough on its own – often happens when at least one other big life event is taking place. Bereavement, a break-up, a change of job, a financial crisis. It's hard for people to keep their masks on when they're mid-move. Movers see people stretched and fraught. They see a full flame ignited under stories that have been left on simmer for years.

I suspect my movers thought me oddly phlegmatic, my packing amazingly orderly, when they took my stuff from the edge of Dartmoor to east Somerset, but they were dealing with a rumpled relocation veteran. It was ultimately just another day in my peripatetic recent life. But I know, even so, from overhearing their banter, that they found amusement and intrigue in the quirks of my possessions. Why would anyone go to the trouble of buying this many books and records yet not replace that filthy, dented car, with all the bits hanging off it, or own any furniture made after 1972? 'You've got a lot of lamps and plants, mate,' one mover told me. 'I have,' I replied. 'You've got a lot of lamps and plants, mate,' his colleague told me, an hour or so later. 'I have,' I replied. I love the plants, and wouldn't want to be without them, even though they don't make moving any easier, and merely living with them is a much finer art than you assume, at times feeling like hosting a party attended by fourteen quiet but oddly high-maintenance friends, all of which you must keep constantly happy. 'Jim needs a lot of encouragement to come out of himself but don't talk too loudly around Celia, and make sure Matilda always has a drink by her side even though her husband Bob is tee-total, and don't worry if Greg seems very down and colourless early in the evening: he doesn't really reach his best until 2 a.m. Also, don't dance too close to Bianca or open the curtains suddenly when she is nearby if it is a nice sunny morning.' The biggest of the lot – a vast Dracaena, taller than most rooms, which had lodged with me almost forever, in a huge pot full of earth and big pebbles, and which even the burliest of the removal men would not risk carrying alone – became very opinionated when I was experimenting with room arrangement, just when I thought I'd got through the move relatively unscathed. That's where the back injury came from. A deranged disc, necessitating hundreds of pounds of chiropractor treatment. It wasn't the Dracaena's fault, though. It was mine for being an idiot, and, without evidence, believing myself to be in possession of the strength of a man four times my size.

All the same, I can't deny that there is an awful lot I like about moving. I get obsessively excited about the idea of being out in a new area, exploring on foot. When I began to show small signs of nomadism in my twenties, it reignited an earlier worry of my mum and dad's: that their house troubles during my childhood might have had a lasting psychological effect on me. If this is true then I view it only as a positive one. The six moves I'd been a part of by the time of my nineteenth birthday, plus the weekend walking trips we made to escape houses and jobs that were making my dad unhappy, are probably part of the reason I am now such an enthusiastic minor explorer, well-travelled in a small and unglamorous way. What a visit to the Harry Potter studios probably is to others, a visit to the headquarters of the Ordnance Survey – such as the one I took last summer – is to me. Discussions of the OS are probably the only time when I become truly patriotic. It is a place palpably full of love. All the employees seem to have been there forever – in some cases marginally longer. Martin Jones, a draughts-man I met, had worked there long enough to remember the summer of 1976, when, arranging a landscape in the record-breaking heat, he would often realise he had a tiny copse or church stuck to his forearm. He didn't look nearly old enough to have been there that long. Clearly that was what working for the OS did for you. Now-adays, there is no need for miniature adhesive copses or churches, as everything is laid out and stored digitally: a rare instance in modern life where the transfer of an experience from three dimensions to two has not sapped it of nuance, perhaps has even furnished it with more nuance, since the zoom feature on the new digital OS maps allows an extra capacity for detail. Nonetheless, I stick evangelically with my paper versions, many of which are now flecked with farmyard mud or crimped by rainwater.

On the eve of my latest move, I spread a brand new, soon-to-be-mud-spattered OS map out before me, just as I had on the eve of my previous few moves. Immediately I could see plenty of intriguing stuff going on. Washing Stones Gully, less than a mile from my back door, caught my eye immediately. Over to the east, on the edge of thick woodland, there was something called Maggoty Paggoty. *What on earth was that?* Clearly it was mandatory that I soon walk the six and a half miles separating it from me and find out. I do not understand how anybody who loves art or language or detail can fail to love maps. What objects in everyday life are more endlessly magical, and more endlessly taken for granted? When it seems we are attempting to hastily cram more and more onto the surface of the land and blot out its mystery, maps offer solid evidence of something more permanent beneath all we have built in hurriedness and greed, something that will outlive our nonsense. Somerset, to me, especially at its heart, is the most map-like county to walk in. There are hills, but not so many that you can't see the land spooling out in front of you for long distances. You crest them and, although you might not be in the greenest place in the whole country, you sense how much green is still out there. It is here that the sense of living in a palimpsest is at its most apparent: petrol stations, telephone exchange boxes, unimaginative new blobs of executive housing, sewage plants, concrete smears of agribusiness, they all tend to fade away. All the reassuring patterns of the earth are still there but much of what we have daubed on top is not. The situation looks better than it did when you were down in it.

Easily the most striking and famous of the islands above the dry inland sea, and one of the best viewpoints in the whole county, is the Tor at Glastonbury: alleged birthplace of British Christianity, alleged burial place of King Arthur and home of the Holy Grail, alleged gateway to the faerie underworld and alleged site of many other alleged events. The contrast of the surrounding low, fairly sensible, agricultural ground makes the Tor look all the more otherworldly, sticking up 521 feet into the heavens, with its pointy stone finger at the top. You can't see it from my house because another less singularly shaped island is in the way, but it's visible from virtually everywhere else within a ten-mile radius. The extended stone middle finger, which is all that remains of the fourteenth-century church of St Michael, always beckons rather than insults. I became hypnotised by it and felt it was vital that I travelled to it on foot as soon as possible after settling in.

I planned my route on the personalised OS map: it should not be much more than six miles, across mostly flat ground. But everywhere I went, footpaths seemed to have been blocked off by the local farmers. Electric fences had been strung across fields a matter of inches beyond stiles, leaving no room to circumvent the intangible produce they were protecting. Some stiles were only retrospective suggestions of stiles. Paths clearly marked on the rigorously detailed map petered out, unannounced, into raging tangles of bramble and overripe blackberries. I picked a few sloes from a hedge and sat on some sandy stubble, hot, bothered, and flummoxed. I decided I should probably file a report to Paul, who I met at the OS, whose job it is to keep Britain's rights of way totally up to date. But then I remembered a story about an altercation between a farmer and a newcomer in a village near where I used to live – the details of the exact offence were blurred by time, but the image of a coffin set alight and left outside the front door remained in my mind – and I thought better of it. In the end, I was not totally unable to see the farmers' point. Who precisely were they obstructing? Who actually walked around here, for fun? From the information I could gather, the answer was essentially just me. I could not help but appreciate the irony of the fact that I'd spent the last nine months living in two of England's last remaining upland wildernesses – the Peak District and the edge of Dartmoor – yet it was here in this apparently benign flatland where I was facing some of my biggest challenges as a hiker. I was now edging, zigzagging, hare-like, into the more geometrical area of flatness west of my house: an area of arguable, somewhat fluid borders referred to as the Somerset Levels or Sedgemoor. Being a Dartmoor evangelist – never happier than in clean, acid air, walking through clouds, or climbing lichen-splattered boulders – I had scoffed at this idea of the sunken part of the landscape being cited as 'moor', but it had its own tricksiness, a stark mathematical wildness. With dead ends and detours, my route to the Tor turned out to be closer to ten miles than six, and the amount of time lost zigzagging through the sea meant that my plan to walk back had been scuppered.

I didn't see the Tor at its best that evening. Dusk was coming on but the weather was a little drappy – a Somerset word I'd recently learned, which means 'starting to rain slightly'. Even without the benefit of one of its legendary sunsets, the view from the top pushed you back onto your heels, opening the world's mouth and allowing you to see humblingly down its throat. It is no surprise that people have been coming to this place on pilgrimages for thousands of years. Even if the bodies of King Arthur and Guinevere were not really found in the grounds of the ruined abbey down the hill in town, even if Joseph of Arimathea, great uncle and undertaker of Jesus, did not allegedly plant his staff across the valley in the earth of Wearyall Hill, causing the Glastonbury Thorn – and, by extension, British Christianity – to grow, travellers would have been seduced and summoned by this tall island: a green ladder to the heavens which seems much closer to the celestial threshold than hills two or three times its height. Tonight there were the usual two dozen people milling about the doorless church at the summit and a man in the doorway, meditating. Few words were spoken. I counted three foreign accents, which was not at all unusual, and nine shawls, which was less unusual still. The view, though muted by weather, was vast and silencing. To the south-west, flanking the Polden Hills, the Levels stretched out, with their cross-hatching rhines: ribbons of water used to drain the marshy sea, where in the past a hungry person might annihilate an eel using a fork-like implement known as an eel prong, waiting, ideally, until the eel was asleep in the peaty side of the ditch, to make the task easier. To the north was the darkening grand-stand of the Mendips. It was from their direction that in November 1539 the last Abbot of Glastonbury, Richard Whiting, was brought with two of his monks, on the orders of Henry VIII's chief minister, Thomas Cromwell, fastened to a hurdle and dragged to the top of the Tor by horses, before being hanged, drawn and quartered where I now stood. As the light faded, above Wells (Britain's fourth smallest city, where some of Whiting's body parts were exhibited) the giant, glowing-red telephone mast began a dialogue with the Tor. There were other towers on hills nearby – the Hood Monument above Butleigh, the Pynsent Monument at Curry Rivel – but these two were the ones who had the big stuff to say to each other. 'I am the now, and I'm what's coming,' said the telephone mast, 'and I have no respect for any of this. Nothing that went before me matters.' 'You are taller in stature,' replied the Tor, 'I'll give you that. But that is only one kind of size. I dwarf you in every other way. You would not even begin to be able to guess at the multitudes I contain.'

Long before that mast could help you send a text to your cousin to tell them Sunday's barbecue had been put

back an hour or Snapchat a stranger a photo of your naked body, I came here, only semi-knowing where I was in any historical sense, and listened to some live music in some fields four miles up the road. I'd just turned nineteen and it was my first Glastonbury Festival. When it was all over, my girlfriend and I walked through the gate and along a small country lane, passing hundreds of queuing cars, down a hill, until – at the bottom of the steep part of the hill, just where the ground began to flatten out and a smattering of cottages appeared – we reached the car containing my dad, who kindly drove us home to Nottinghamshire. Remembering this, standing on the Tor, I found two aspects of it remarkable. First: how illustrative it was of the faith people had in the times and vague meeting points they'd arranged, in the days before mobile phones. Second: the fact that the point where we found my dad's car in the long queue was quite possibly directly outside the house where I now lived. I looked out from the island across the cow pastures and rhines and sham footpaths I'd negotiated to get to the Tor, back towards the house, and noticed smoke billowing from its roof. The smoke reached for the sky, then danced north on the breeze, diminished slightly by the drappy rain, in the direction of Worthy Farm, where the festival's organiser, Michael Eavis, would already be making plans for next summer's event, for which tickets would cost almost precisely five times what my girlfriend and I paid for ours in 1994, and which, unlike 1994's festival, would not feature a succession of drug dealers crawling through holes in the fence then waking you up to try to sell you Benzedrine.

It didn't look like the fire brigade had arrived yet but no doubt they would soon. Someone in the village would have raised the alarm. Maybe Eavis would assist in getting the blaze extinguished. In 1963, when the fourteenth-century tithe barn at Pilton, three miles away, was struck by lightning and caught fire, Eavis – then just twenty-seven and not yet in possession of his world-famous music festival – was one of the first to raise the alarm. But it was presumptuous to rely solely on Eavis. He was far busier now, I expected, than he had been then. I'd heard he liked to turn up in pubs around here and, uninvited, sing 'My Way', and it was getting on for seven. There was not much I could do. I didn't yet have a number for my next-door neighbours. I could call my landlady but she was in Spain. Less than a month earlier, in a pub in Bristol, somebody had stolen my rucksack, which contained my wallet, my journal, my phone, a Lush bath bar and my car keys. The following morning, using some cash that a friend had kindly loaned me, I'd caught an early train back to Devon. I had felt anxious, since I could not remember for sure if my spare car keys were at home or in a jacket in my locked car parked near the pub in Bristol, but also very freed, having been materially reduced to nothing more than the clothes on my back, a return train ticket and £31.30. It was as if many of the complexities of my life had floated away, and I was realising my essential core being for the first time, which was just a transient collection of experiences and opinions and hopes, blundering along to the next destination, maybe picking up a few more along the way.

You could say there were similarities in my current predicament. Certainly, I liked my books, my records, my plants and my furniture, but undertaking the next house move without them would be much easier. My main worry was my two cats, but I knew them well and felt confident that they would have fled well clear of the house as soon as the fire began and, when the smoke had gone, would return – although I would surely find them cowering in a field long before that anyway. From here I could just pick out, across the dry sea in the gathering gloom, the field I suspected they were most likely to retreat to, but it looked different to the way I remembered. The wood abutting it was gone and I couldn't see the farm on the slope where the hill begins to get steep, in the direction of Washing Stones Gully. Had it burned down too? Precisely how much damage were I and my fire responsible for? I swung my vision gradually thirty degrees anticlockwise where, a mile north, I re-orientated myself and found the spot containing my actual house, which appeared to be smoke-free. I set off down the slope, reburdened by the clutter of material life, but genuinely relieved about the cats, who would been ill-suited to a life solely on the road.

All day, HGVs bump and bang along the road below the Tor, staining dark cottages darker with their exhaust fumes. Signs in the cottage windows offer cartomancy readings and beg for the road to be diverted. PLEASE SLOW DOWN. SACRED SITES AHEAD, asked a notice tied to the leg of a pavement mannequin, as I reached the foot of the Tor. She looked quite smart, with her flower headband, blue anorak, fluorescent tabard, long hippie skirt and wellies, but in a couple of weeks' time, in a period of high winds, I would drive past and notice her upside-down legs sticking out from a hedge; an incident from which she would partially recover before vanishing for ever six months later during Storm Gareth. I decided to pop into her local, The Rifleman's Arms. A lady with a busy sleeve of tattoos was telling a friend about another friend who had fallen out with her because the friend claimed she 'didn't text regularly enough'. The lady with the busy sleeve of tattoos said she had done nothing wrong apart from not wanting to be on her phone all day. 'Exactly!' I thought, already over-involved. My intention was to have a quick drink, without getting carried away and becoming what the Somerset drinkers of the nineteenth-century called 'overtookt', then call a taxi. I've only taken the taxi option once during a walk, and, even when circumstances made it the only option, it felt like the lamest kind of chickening out. This, however, wasn't to be a sequel: of the six local taxi companies I called, only one came close to agreeing to pick me up. 'I'm having my tea but I could do it after, maybe,' said the driver. I asked him how long his tea would take him to eat. 'A couple of hours or so,' he said. I imagined him on a high dining chair with a mesh of wooden beads beneath him, looking regal and entitled as a doting wife brought out each successive course, each one a little larger than the last: prawn cocktail, jellied eels, sturgeon, beef bourguignon, trifle, a really massive apple.

If you make your way back to my house from the Tor via the lanes, avoiding the main roads and unreliable truncated footpaths, you take the lowest ground: the deepest part of the reclaimed sea, threaded with the rhines the monks of the Middle Ages dug to drain it. Arguably nobody enjoys a better view of the Tor than the travellers who have constructed their own small, easily dismantleable neighbourhood along here. I passed about two dozen of their caravans in total. A couple were

empty, their innards appearing recently ransacked, their doors gone or hanging by a single hinge. The occupied ones glowed with light, music and the aroma of weed, and maximised the luxury potential of their rhine-side locations. One announced itself with an appropriated AREA UNDER SURVEILLANCE sign. Another had constructed a hammock by wedging a mattress into the crook of a willow overhanging the water. A couple of hundred yards away, on the River Brue, whose surface solemnly reflected dark silver sky, a plank had been nailed into a board submerged in the bank, for diving.

Crooked tents and parasols and tarpaulins had been shoved together outside caravans, haphazardly: Franken-stein's awnings. I startled a couple of herons and they made their escape on big hushed wings the same colour as the river, charting a path between realities.

On the skyline to the north, Whiting's death church and the glowing red telephone mast, symbols of the old and new religions, continued their debate, until night gradually snuffed out the former. Looking towards the long, blurring wall of the Mendips, taking in the commanding hills and flatlands, it struck me that I had in my haphazard way ended up living in a landscape that was a composite of the two very different places on opposite margins of the country that I had loved most deeply and chosen to spend most of my adult life in: Norfolk and Devon. It was not twee or manicured but it was definitely not rugged, either. It was anti-rugged. In this light, from this perspective, it was like looking at a scene concocted by an imagination obsessed with a time that will never be. Not much could be added, atmospherically speaking, besides perhaps an eel crying through the dark. Maybe it was because I was tired and emotional and still five miles from a place where I could rest my aching back but I couldn't stop thinking about the poor eels, the image of them sleeping innocently in their peat hideaways and waking to the horror of being pronged. I'd once met a man who used to catch and sell them for a living in Cornwall. He'd even briefly had a pet one, which lodged alternately in a large tank in his house and the leat that flowed beside it. The eel went missing from the tank at a particularly lively party he and his wife held and was found over twenty-four hours later under a sofa cushion, caked in fluff and, miraculously, alive. It went to live outdoors permanently after that. The former eel catcher, who confessed he'd never been very good at catching eels, told me about the noise the eels would make as he stalked the Cornish rivers, searching for them: a bark-moan that seemed to come from the most unfathomable well of loss and despair. It was a noise, he said, that still haunted him now in his less robust moments, over a decade after he'd quit his job as an eel catcher.

I did not hear the noise of an eel as I negotiated the dark, early autumn lanes beside the rhines here, in the dry sea, but I did stumble across something no less outlandish or liminal. A mile from my house, I rounded a corner beside a large orchard – a sleepy, houseless stretch of lane – and realised that I was being flanked by fairy lights, dozens of tiny bioluminescent spots of green. After mentally replaying my time in the pub – with an awareness of Glastonbury's reputation – and assuring myself that at no point had my drink been left unattended, I realised that I was staring directly at a vast colony of glow-worms, the first I'd ever seen, and active here in the hedges, a place where I'd never expected to see them, two months after what I'd been assured was glow-worm time. Had I not had all the problems with the footpaths earlier and arrived at the Tor so much later than expected and failed to find a taxi, I would not have been here to witness them. It was indicative of a lesson I had learned about walking: that a mistake or a wrong turn was something to be embraced, an experience not always synonymous with only failure and frustration. I can think of no stronger example of this than a walk I'd done two summers previously on the fringes of the Stourhead estate, twenty miles east of here, where Somerset, Dorset and Wiltshire intersect. A moment of lackadaisical navigation had led me into thick woodland past a shag rug of foxgloves and, in trying to find my way back to the correct path, which would lead me to my destination, King Alfred's Tower, I'd become hopelessly disorientated in a series of wildflower-heavy clearings. It was not so much that I had lost my natural compass, more that the entire concept of compasses had evaporated, and I became under the impression this would now be my habitat forever more: a psychedelic space walled in by trees on all sides. It was early June, the exact time, maybe even the exact hour, when everything had reached the apex of its growth for the year, and I stumbled and tripped over tussocks and difficult boggy ground, warmed by a beating sun, with poppies and foxgloves and ox-eye daisies all around, until I felt like I was spinning in a dream, and flopped onto the ground, exhausted, contentedly defeated. A cloud of holly blue butterflies gathered above me and instinct told me that the right thing to do was wait. I let myself slip into the delight of a half-nap, until a potential way out suggested itself in the wood fifty yards down the hill directly below my left big toe. I walked back to my car along lanes where large flocks of unseen sheep could be heard shouting together at the tops of their voices, a noise that from an individual sheep can seem to smack of the most terrible depression but in chorus sounded totally joyous, as if rows and rows of hearty pensioners were behind the hedges all saying 'Yeah!' over and over again. I never found the tower.

A few weeks after my experience with the glow-worms, I retraced the Stourhead walk, and could not see how I had got it so drastically wrong on my first attempt. Horse chestnuts were scattered on the quieter lanes through the woods, sealed and spiky. If goblins had a game of bowls, then abandoned it in a hurry, it would look like this. In drappy rain, I followed the route I'd planned on my OS map, took a few simple twists and turns, climbed past fresh log piles to the top of Kingsettle Hill, turned left onto a wide grassy path and watched the sun crash through the clouds as Alfred's Tower materialised ahead of me. The entry fee for the tower is cash-only, and all I had in my wallet was seven pence, a bank card and an old Gnasher the Dog *Beano* fan-club button badge missing its pin, but I managed to sweet talk Chas on the door to let me up for what I described as research purposes. I was not telling an untruth: everything is research, if you want it to be.

County borders are rarely denoted by very sudden marked changes in terrain but, from the top of the 160-foot folly, the different characters of farmy, verdant Somerset (west and north-west), bald, yellow Wiltshire (east and north east) and furry, ridgey Dorset (south, south-east and south-west) were very discernible, especially with the clarifyingly abrupt sunlight. The tower was built by the banker Henry Hoare in 1772 as a showy commemoration of King Alfred's victory over the Danes in 879, which Alfred purportedly initiated from this spot after hiding out on the Somerset Levels in the house of a peasant woman and burning her cakes. The word 'folly' refers to a building with no purposes other than to demonstrate the indulgent eccentricity of the person who decided to build it, but people seem strangely reluctant to use the term for big buildings. Few people I have spoken to about Alfred's Tower have called it a folly, whereas the dovecote above Bruton, four miles to the west, is often called a folly, even though it's not one. For over two centuries the dovecote, which also once belonged to the Hoare family, has been specifically used to house pigeons and doves, which, if you climb through the hole in the wall like I did,

can still be witnessed above you, cooing from various slots in the brickwork, like furry singing packages in a pre-Reformation Royal Mail sorting office.

In the days of late autumn, as the last of the gold disappeared from the treetops and hedges, the starker aspects of living in the sea became more apparent, and I found myself frequently popping over to the Bruton area and asking it for a little hug, which it always offered unconditionally. It had the same spellbinding mists and long sunsets as Avalon but its hills were not such loners, and were struck through with rumpled coombes and wooded holloways that gave me a small, gentle fix of the Devon walks I missed, without any accompanying belief that I was settling for Devon lite. The Brue, such a minimalist, geometric river from the coast to Glastonbury, underwent an almost total character change here, becoming paintable and cuddly. John Steinbeck and his wife Elaine lived in a cottage on the edge of Bruton in the spring and summer of 1959. Nine years later, when Steinbeck was dying, they both stated independently that their period here was the happiest of their lives. I wonder if they were able to suppress a chuckle at Sexey's Hospital, in the centre of town – or, for that matter, Sexey's School, located on a lane called Lusty Gardens – unlike literally every other person I took to Bruton ('Which hospital are you going to? I'm going to the sexy hospital.') Like ordering a pint of Butcombe ale, if you can talk about it without giggling it probably means you're properly entrenched as a Somerset resident.

Bruton is all art and secret backways and artisan baking and well-spoken children and – a mark of its past as a wool town – stone ram carvings. Many speak of the increasing house prices, the 'down from London' aspect of the population, but if you listen to Pentangle's brilliant interpretation of the old murder ballad 'The Bramble Briar', renamed 'Bruton Town', you might conclude it has never been a place where the peasantry have blossomed. In the song, which prior to my first visit had been the source of pretty much all my information on Bruton, one of the two sons of a wealthy farmer finds out his sister is indulging in relations with the family's serving boy. The brothers take the lad on a spurious hunting trip, kill him and hurl his body in a thicket, all of which their dad seems to have no problem with. When their sister finds out, she sits with her lover's blood-soaked body for three days and three nights, until finally she gets hungry, heads home, and life resumes. The name of the farm is not specified in the song but something tells me it's not the one on top of Creech Hill, which is notable for its silage lake, in which the wrecks of boats and vehicles rot away, half submerged. From here, near the site of a former Roman temple, the town looks so tiny and perfectly placed in the valley bottom that its buildings might have been painted on fine cardboard then carefully placed by the hands of surgeons or nineteenth-century draughtsmen. I recommend the view this spot offers not only of Bruton but of the head and shoulders of Alfred's Tower, poking up above the woods at the top of the horizon. I also recommend the unusually furry, eerily silent German shepherd who crept up on me from behind as I gazed across the valley, and

slowly, calmly stared at me: a rare farm dog more interested in mind games than bluster or violence. Nearby was
a large barn, where cows were listening to thumping
1990s R&B on what I at first thought was a radio but
on further evidence could only have been a mix CD or
Spotify playlist devoted specifically to the genre. The last
bee of the year followed me a few yards down the valley,
back in the direction of town.

   In my garden, the leaves on the back hedge fell away,
revealing that my neighbour was a horse. A strikingly
handsome cock pheasant began to pay me visits, twice
daily and more; an isolated flash of colour on an increasingly grey scene. The crisp, misty punctual days had ended,
replaced by graceless dishwater ones that didn't fully
happen, if they did happen at all, until gone 11 a.m., by
which point at this time of the year, let's face it, it was
essentially evening, and you were already wondering
about what to have for tea and what book to read and
whether that bit of damp kindling you'd found was going
to be enough to get the woodburner going. In an attempt
to add some sparkle to a December morning I filled my
bird feeders to overflowing and sat back to watch the
action. The pheasant, I realised, was the one my landlady
had told me about, whom she called Clarence. She talked
about what a mystery his singleness was, especially in
view of his appearance, and when I saw him I puzzled
over the matter too, but then I realised this made me one
of those people who assume that everyone who is single
is desperately looking for love, without taking into
account that some enjoy their own company, are very

content in a single state and don't view it as a position of intrinsic sadness.

When the feeder was full, it meant more robins, dunnocks, blackbirds and blue tits dropping seeds on the grass for Clarence to vacuum up, along with the flakes of last night's poppadum I'd left out for him. He had become quite bold, for a creature who had been bred to exist in a constant state of terror. Sometimes he'd see me through the picture window in my living room and, so long as I avoided sudden movements, carry on pecking about, maybe let out a triumphant 'ch-kauwck!' and fluff out his feathers a bit. I told myself I was providing a refuge from the people who wanted to kill him but all I was really doing was making sure he had a constant supply of food and taking care not to be boisterous in his vicinity. As I was leaving the house late one day, I noticed he was in the back field, and, fearing for his safety, shouted 'Clllaaarrrrence!', but then remembered he had no idea he was named Clarence, and was a pheasant. He did a little run, in the way he did, which as with all pheasants looked like he was saying 'Shit shit shit!' His 'ch-kauwck!' joined the undersong of the day. Other ingredients in the undersong included the clop of three horses farther along the lane and a succession of gunshots two or three fields away. The undersmell, meanwhile, was cow. In truth, it was more of an oversmell – fairly constant since my arrival. There had been plenty of cattle close to the two Devon houses where I'd lived, but their aroma never pervaded the air in the way it did here in the reclaimed sea.

Beside the A303 – the road into the west, the ancient road, a big road that is something of a big-road anomaly in that it often acts like a secretary to landscape rather than like landscape's pissy, inconsiderate boss – men in green semi-camouflage attire were shooting Clarence's contemporaries in the fields. There might have been women too, I can't say for sure. I only saw men. Presumably the camouflage gear was in case they encountered an unusually pecky and violent pheasant who crept up on them from behind and tried to fuck them up. They would no doubt argue that what they were doing was traditional and historical as opposed to, say, a grand act of cowardice taken out on a defenceless animal bred purely to indulge their bloodthirsty twattery. I suspect it is unlikely that these men, so in thrall to tradition and history, would practise the even more historical art of dressing only in a loin cloth, starving themselves for a while, then attempting to bring down an animal five times their size while unarmed.

Not far past the turning for Warminster, I noticed a dead hare on the verge: soggy and half-black and sinewy. A few miles on from here, as you head east, the land turns sinewy too. I am interested in this terrain but, unlike Bruton's, it's not one I could imagine offering me a hug when I needed it. Strangely, for a county best known for Stonehenge, a landmark so closely associated with summer solstice, Wiltshire always feels like winter to me. Maybe that is partly because winter is when I have most frequently walked in it. But each time I go, I look in vain for the places where summer might happen. I love soaking up the Neolithic ambience on the Wiltshire Downs but I can't shake a stronger feeling that I'm walking around a film set: a balder, one-colour, parallel Britain, underpeopled, overthatched. The book I had just finished reading – also set in Wiltshire – was not about winter, but it was overwhelmingly wintry. A book well-known at the time of its publication but now a little bit overlooked, by a dead writer, in which nearly everyone either dies or seems to be in some kind of bucolic yet austere antechamber for death. Perhaps more of an antegreenhouse for death. Greenhouses crop up in the book a lot.

I plan some of my walks in advance but an increasing number get scheduled on the day they happen, in a burst of scattershot inspiration, like the walk is a verse I'd been waiting to write but couldn't, until inspiration struck. Were I a session musician, I'd probably be a nightmare to collaborate with on a group project. 'Where is Tom?' 'Oh.

He's at another recording studio, sixty miles away. He decided at the last minute that he wasn't in the mood for country rock today and that he would record with another band instead. They play funk.' Today, for example, I was meant to be doing something completely different, but I found myself driving to Wiltshire, propelled spontaneously eastwards by the vivid pictures created by the book by the dead writer, which was called *The Enigma of Arrival*. It had been written during the mid-eighties, by the former Booker Prize winner V. S. Naipaul. Naipaul describes Wiltshire almost as you expect an alien might and to an extent that is what he is, as someone who spent the first two decades of his life in Trinidad, even though he'd already lived in the UK for several years before he relocated to Wilsford cum Lake, near Stonehenge. He disguises the location to an extent, but it's not hard to work it out, just as it's not hard to work out that his reclusive neighbour and landlord was Stephen Tennant, former cherubic Bright Young Person of the Bloomsbury Set and inspiration for Sebastian Flyte in Evelyn Waugh's *Brideshead Revisited*. Even though it's at the commercial end of the county, you can see why it was a good place to escape, both for Tennant, whom Naipaul never spoke to and only saw twice in the whole of his decade of living there, and for Naipaul himself, who was in a quiet period of 'withdrawal' during his time there. It seems impossible that the tourist bustle of Stonehenge is only a couple of miles away. As I climbed out of the village, I got a decent view of the landmark from a ridge at the highest point of a farm track. It looked like a little green birthday cake in the distance topped with grey candles. Another part of the film set.

Being here felt like walking onto a film set in a different way, too. There are days when you choose your place and time well as a walker and it can take you so vividly and swiftly inside a legend, or a piece of history, that it feels a little illegal, like someone ought to come along any moment to check you have the appropriate wristband. To finish a book I'd been mesmerised by – albeit in a slow-motion, almost banal way – from start to finish, then drive an hour from my house and be deep inside its setting, alone and free to explore, all for the price of quarter of a tank of petrol, left me giddy, which was an incongruous sensation on a route frequently redolent of death. I'm not sure where the death ambience came from most: the barren vegetation, or the realisation that every major character in the book – the gardeners Naipaul befriended, Tennant, Tennant's housekeepers, the local farmworkers and electricians, the neighbour whose husband murdered her, Naipaul himself – was now dead. But this aura of death, of the emptiness that death leaves, also made the universe that Naipaul described more present. I saw just one other walker on my seven-mile route: a Barbour-jacketed, Labrador-walking man of about seventy, who looked more like a Barbour-jacketed, Labrador-walking man of seventy might have done in 1985. When I drove out of the village, two small children in identical pink bathrobes, very 1980s bathrobes, rose from behind a hedge to wave to my car, like children in 1980s villages used to wave at cars before they had more exciting pursuits to occupy their attention. Did they read my lips as I shouted 'Fucking hell!' and almost careened across a water meadow into a cob wall in fright?

The walking route criss-crossed the River Avon several times, a shallow-banked but full river whose tributaries were often clogged with dead trees, the kind of river you feel might whisper about you behind your back, and I thought of what Naipaul had written about Tennant's love for ivy, and how he refused to allow it to be cut off the trees behind Wilsford Manor, causing the little inlets nearby to get congested. Unlike Tennant's biographer, Philip Hoare, who was permitted to wander around the manor as a stranger, not long before Tennant's death, and heard Tennant talking and laughing to himself in his room, I could not get a proper glimpse of the grounds. Close to the border, I was chased by a bitter but ineffectual poodle, who was soon gathered up by a youth in wellies with an aristocratic, cherubic, not un-Tennant-like face. I walked past the pub which Naipaul's gardening neighbour Jack had soldiered to for a last drink, the night before his death. It was closed but I got the impression it wouldn't have looked a great deal livelier if it had been open. On the quietest paths, farther from the villages, in the final part of the walk, a soft sunset briefly threatened to warm the earth, but didn't. The big skies were brasher characters than Somerset's, unkeen to listen to anyone's nonsense. Spindly clouds appeared to reflect the bare branches of the trees, not unlike the way the Avon did. Naipaul learned to identify tree types while living here and described it as 'learning a language, after living amongst its sounds'. The cow undersmell of home was replaced by a sweet, horsey one, which was apt, as all the horses I met on the walk came across as very sweet. One added self-grown loon pants to a nice jacket and scarf to complete his look. It was the most fetching horse outfit I'd seen out and about since the matching checked jackets two horses had shown off for me on my way to see a much bigger horse: the prehistoric Uffington one, above Compton Beauchamp in Oxfordshire, which might in fact be not a horse at all, but a dragon, depending whose theory you believe.

Every year, the Uffington Horse is spruced up by National Trust volunteers equipped with hammers and tubs of chalk. Its chalk gleams much more impressively than the Cerne Abbas Giant, Britain's most pornographic hill figure, whose erect thirty-five-foot member has looked in need of some TLC on both the recent times I have visited it. The giant's penis – bigger than it once was, since incorporating what was originally the giant's navel – is well-known for imbuing those who spend time on it with magic fertility. It is fenced off nowadays, but I once met a shaman on Dartmoor whose fifty-something friend had just slept on the giant's penis, unaccompanied, and enjoyed what she described as 'the most erotic night of her life'. When I walked there for the first time it was April, the earth was frisky and I was with my friend Lucy, who is in possession of what must surely be one of the planet's three or four sexiest voices. In the Giant Inn in Cerne Abbas village at the foot of the hill, a party of a dozen or so women of varying ages crashed through the door, breaking the sleepy midday atmosphere of the place, apparently still drunk from the night before, which, from all we could gather, had involved some form of

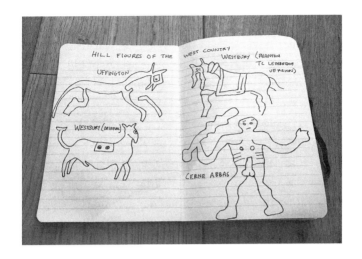

hedonistic pilgrimage to the hillside. I remember thinking how the treadmarks of the footpath leading past the figure resembled the footprints of an actual giant, feeling the wind turning my face and hair wild on the way up, and spotting an unidentifiable creature marching industriously through a cornfield at the summit, badger-shaped but fox-coloured.

Wiltshire's most famous hill figure, the white horse above the village of Bratton, near Westbury, famously depicted in watercolour in the 1930s by Eric Ravilious, lacks the wild pagan nature of the figures at Uffington and Cerne Abbas. But the Bratton horse might well have once been more feral, if you believe the theories of either Richard Gough (1772) or T. C. Lethbridge (1957) about the original shadow horse pre-dating it. Gough's drawing shows a smaller, jollier-looking horse, potentially of a clumsy nature, whose slightly exposed penis and solitary eye fail to add any threat to its character; Lethbridge's, meanwhile, is downright terrifying: a war-ready beast with tusks instead of a face, also Cyclopean, but in a much more ominous way. A slight anticlimax upon getting up close to the Bratton horse comes from the realisation that it's largely made of concrete, not chalk. This gives it the appearance of a modest yet extreme skatepark. The vantage point from the horse is more commanding than from above the Cerne Abbas Giant, however. Above it, with the weather the way it was, I had the luxury of seeing for entire yards.

As I explored this still slightly unfamiliar part of the West Country, the almost cold, drab dishwater days continued: mornings that never really started, afternoons where you

thought it was getting dark then realised you were just looking at the colour of the day. I'm not a winter person and, while I am fine with the concept of Christmas as an approximately forty-eight-hour period concomitant with a generally agreeable set of warm family feelings and the natural world turning over, December steadfastly maintains its status as my least favourite month. I missed Devon, but I checked myself, as I knew my judgement could traditionally become impaired on such matters around now. I often get a strong sensation of missing stuff at this time of year – people, places – but I know a large amount of it is often an illusion and what I'm really missing is colourful petals and birdsong and days that aren't like living inside a cup of tea you left to brew five hours ago and forgot about. December is like no other month when it comes to realising how many people and cars and butchered animals and bad songs there are in the world and if you find this, combined with the lack of natural light, all a bit much, some of the lesser-known footpaths in Somerset, Dorset and Wiltshire aren't bad places to retreat to.

A six-mile circle of Ilminster took me into the peculiar quiet spots you find only next to a big, important road: neglected, sluicey edgeplaces, part industrial, part arable – not hiking country. Gates on the north side of town were stiff, suggesting I was one of, say, nine people to have used them since June. The trig point above town was half-hidden and shy, as if it knew there were more famous and cocksure hills nearby whose summits it had missed out on. A riverside path took me past ribbed, oxidised iron posts and an open but deserted warehouse full of machinery with purposes I was oblivious to but wanted to learn, then past rusty barrels full of miscellaneous everything, ready for burning. I poked my head into the warehouse, unable to resist a lungful of oil. Over the course of a decade this had become something of a Christmas tradition. Others went carol singing or drunkenly snogged someone from their office; I walked along the banks of small, slightly polluted rivers, sniffing fumes and admiring arcane rusty ironwork. I remembered I had almost zero food in the fridge and that I needed to get to a supermarket then made a hypothesis regarding the chances of being asked if I was all ready for The Big Day and remembered I did still have some crisps and a banana and one can of tonic water at home and drove directly there instead. My timing was all out anyway: I wasn't hungry and, as anybody who has accrued any life wisdom knows, you should never go to a supermarket when you're either very hungry or not hungry at all. Supermarkets are to be negotiated only when experiencing a medium level of hunger.

Pheasants were ubiquitous, particularly on the walks I embarked on farther east, in Wiltshire and north Dorset. Why wouldn't they be? English shooting estates now rear 20 million of them per year, meaning the weight of pheasants in England is now greater than the total weight of wild birds in England. In the fields around the Dorset–Wiltshire border the only thing I saw more of than pheasants were flints: big ones, like old chipped bones once belonging to knees, feet and hips. Damp weather had brought the softer chalk to the surface too, mushed it up attractively. I could imagine popping up a hillside with a spade and pickaxe and sketching a quick figure. A protest image: The Long Pheasant Of The A303. Historians in the twenty-fifth century would puzzle and theorise over its meaning. Except they wouldn't, because, the way everything was going, it would all be long over by then. The evidence was all here, in your face, despite the denials of those in power: the statistics on the vastly reduced numbers of birds and insects, just in the space of my lifetime; the way the seasons were starting to blend together. I'd seen blossom in Bristol in early December and lambs in the dry sea before the year was out. A hornet flew into my living room in January, excitable and confused. A week after heavy snow, February decided it was May and soared to nineteen degrees. There was a sense that nature was rubbing its eyes and waking up but in the way that you might wake up with the first day-light, only to realise it's not daylight at all but a new streetlamp that has been installed needlessly by the council on the pavement outside your bedroom window. Under a sky of thick blue, slightly redolent of chemicals, I walked from Ham Hill to Montacute, quickly stripping down to a t-shirt, and saw buff-tailed bumblebees, a cockchafer beetle and dozens of red admiral butterflies. It was bliss-ful, but slightly wrong, tinged with guilt. In the woods on Ham Hill a tiny female child walked past me, alone, pulling a plastic crate on some rope, full of fluffy toys, talking to herself. It was only later that it occurred to me she could have been a ghost, blown in on the breeze of fake spring. I walked on through the golden soil of Hamdon, above stone the same colour, which stonemasons say is as easy to cut as cheese. At the foot of the valley the houses of the village of Montacute are made of the same stuff: perfect little cheese homes. A cat in the churchyard rolled on tombs, headbutted me passionately, begged me to take him home, using every bargaining technique in his arsenal, which was vast. Whoever lived with this cat was lucky, but also must have been constantly worried about his potential infidelity. I decided he was the best cat ever, but aren't they all?

Montacute is the perfect name for Montacute: a village somehow both sweet and haughty. The name in fact comes from the abrupt conical hill above it – 'mount acute' – which is crowned with an eighteenth-century tower. The tower was deserted when I reached it. I climbed its spiral stairs, which were covered in broken glass, to a prison-like space entirely covered in the graffiti of the youth population of Greater Yeovil. The graffiti created a pleasing wallpaper whose aesthetic appeal was entirely democratic, nothing to do with the quality of any individual art. Pretty much all of Somerset was below, to the north, hypnotic in the thinning blue haze at the cusp of dusk, enhanced by the fact that from this distance you couldn't pick out the badger, pheasant and fox carcasses currently lining the A37 at sixteen-yard intervals. Nobody appeared to have informed the sky that it was Monday. My back was finally better and I felt I could have continued walking indefinitely. I noted that only a mile to the south was Odcombe, birthplace of Thomas Coryat, known as the Odcombe Leg-Stretcher and often thought of as the patron saint of hikers, who set out to explore Europe on foot in 1608 and walked all the way from Venice to Somerset in the same pair of shoes. Upon his return, inspired by Italian dining culture, Coryat popularised the table fork in the UK, and donated the shoes to the village church, where they were displayed for many years until they rotted away and were replaced with replicas that remain there to this day.

My landlady got in touch with some important news: Clarence was named Lawrence, not Clarence. I decided this was absurd. He was quite patently a Clarence, so that is what I continued to call him. One day he turned up with a lady friend, and from that point his visits were a little less regular. Studying his perfect feather jacket had made me more aware of pheasants as individuals, suddenly ashamedly aware that previously I had been a pheasant racist of sorts. How had I ever believed that, notwithstanding the obvious distinction between the sexes, pheasants all looked alike? My parents' regular garden pheasant, for example, had a much cheekier face than Clarence and a wattle that looked prosthetic, very obviously made from felt. When a replacement for Clarence arrived in my garden to take over his shift in March, I noticed he was less robust, nervier, and that the pattern on his underside was more leopardlike. 'Is that Clarence?' asked a visiting friend. 'No, that's Jeremy,' I replied. 'He's nothing like Clarence at all.' Many pheasants I spotted on walks now appeared a little undersized or scruffy. I'd never been so critical of the appearance of pheasants in the past but Clarence had raised my standards. He was permanently resplendent: a cosmic chicken in a perennial state of glow up, as if ready not just to go out, but to go what the young people of today call 'out

out'. One day a couple of months earlier, I had tried on a nice new black cape in the living room and had been feeling pretty good about it, until I spotted Clarence strutting about behind me through the window, and became starkly aware of all my sartorial shortcomings. No outfit could make me look as dashing as him.

I have never purchased a cape but there must be a natural ambience of cape about me, since people keep donating capes to me. 'I saw this and thought of you straight away,' they will say, handing me a cape. In a surprising development, I had discovered that the actor Nicolas Cage lived in the neighbouring village to mine, close to the curiously named Teapot Lane (Worms Lane). Neighbours told me he was often seen walking the local footpaths, wearing a cape. From this information, a fantasy had emerged: me walking across a field in one of my capes and bumping into Nicolas Cage in one of his capes and stopping to discuss the various problems we had experienced with footpaths in the area that had been blocked off by farmers, me at all times being careful to steer our dialogue away from any situation where I might be asked for my honest opinion of the remake of *The Wicker Man* because, although I wouldn't want to lie to Nicolas Cage, I wouldn't want to hurt him either. 'Do you sometimes get your cape snagged on brambles or barbed wire when you cross a little-used stile that has become slightly overgrown?' I would ask. 'I do, a lot,' he would say. 'Me too!' I would reply.

In truth, I had only been walking in a cape once: in 2015, at Burrow Mump, another island in Somerset's dry sea crowned with a ruined church that looks like Glastonbury Tor's lonelier nephew. On 1 May the sun rises on a direct line between the two hills and both, it is said, form part of the St Michael ley line, which stretches from Land's End in Cornwall all the way to Lowestoft, 452 miles away in Suffolk. Burrow Mump – which translates as 'Hill Hill' – was used by Alfred as a lookout spot during his wars with the Danes, and it was close to where he incurred the wrath of the peasant woman who had entrusted him with watching her cakes, which were actually not cakes at all but bread. The church on top of the mump was used as a garrison during the Civil War. If you were going to choose one place in Somerset to walk in an emerald-green cape and witchy hat, you probably couldn't do much better. In the late-afternoon autumn light, I had become increasingly aware of my status as an accidental human mimic of the hill itself, being a high triangle of soft, lush green with a dark, man-made structure at my summit. As I strode down the west side of the mound, my Darth Vader-meets-Vincent Price shadow stretched out before me, engulfing the hillside, and an estate car passed on the road below. The woman perched on the back seat, probably well into her eighties, turned in my direction, her eyes and mouth slowly widening. The middle-aged couple in front of her kept their eyes on the road ahead. I imagined the whispered conversation that would take place later that evening, in a troubled kitchen: the concerns for Jean, with her talk of ghosts, of puritans and the New Republic, her ever-increasing jabber and delusions.

If, from here, you head a few miles north you hit the Polden Hills, the long ridge that splits the dry sea in two, from where, at the end of a clear day, in the long pauses between the trees, you can watch the sun guillotine ochre and blood-red slits in the entire universe. On the way you'll pass Somerton, where in a pub in 2016 a stranger introduced herself by lifting up my t-shirt, uninvited, to check if I had 'a hairy chest', and, satisfied at answering the question herself, grabbed at it in approval, until her friend remonstrated with her with the words 'Doreen, you can't just go around touching young men when you feel like it!', leaving me with the not quite ambivalent feelings of a person who has been lightly mauled against his wishes and complimented on a state of youth for which there is no statistical support. Carry on in the direction of my house from Somerton and you arrive at Dundon Beacon, with its dark and hidden grass roof, where I found an ash tree throttled by a riot of dead ivy resembling an orgy of serpents. On the eastern slopes I saw a flock of sheep had been set loose on a field of kale. One sheep was on its back, on its way to what appeared to be a kale coma, yet still mustering enough energy to take a last few lazy bites at the stalks it was able to reach without compromising its horizontal position.

Using my now dog-eared personalised OS map, across the valley in the woods above Butleigh, another site on the St Michael ley line, I finally located Maggoty Paggoty. It was attractive but slightly underwhelming, after all the hype I'd attached to it: just some trees and nascent bluebells, to all initial appearances both maggot- and paggot-free. But that was OK. Of the intriguingly named features of the area, I'd become far more interested in Teapot Lane (Worms Lane). I sensed it had a story to tell. Why had the history of teapots associated with the lane superseded the history of worms associated with the lane? And who had decreed that the worms still got an acknowledgement, rather than being totally consigned to the compost of local history? The lane was very close to where I'd seen the hedge lit up with bioluminescent green dots in September, which suggested that perhaps the worms in question were the glowing kind, rather than the soil-enriching kind. Through my neighbour, Jane, I tracked down an elderly local historian in another nearby village, Allen Cotton, who agreed that my glow-worms theory was a definite possibility, although he had previous believed the name to be derived from the nearby Big Warms Field, and that 'Warms' was a possible Somerset mangling of the word 'worms'. He could, however, clear up the issue of the teapots. Two cottages on the then-Worms Lane, known collectively as Solomon's Temple, had once been the poorhouses for the village of Baltonsborough, and were occupied by two widows who were known for going into the village to collect used tea leaves. The widows always had a teapot on the hob and, because of this, people began to call the lane Teapot Lane. Early this century, when updating the lane signs in the area, Mendip District Council decided to acknowledge this but consulted Allen, due to his knowledge on the matter, and he insisted 'Worms' remain on there too.

Teapot Lane (Worms Lane) is the point where the Tor asserts its pre-eminence again, after being blocked out by the beefy weightlifter's shoulder of Pennard Hill. Primroses and dandelions grow more riotously on the verges of Teapot Lane than they do on the lanes in Pennard's shadow. Pennard is where the cowy smell that pervades the area is most pervasive of all and if you're cresting it in winter from the direction of Wells, it's an idea to avoid the time when the Friesians get taken along the road to bed at Hill Farm, as bed is a few hundred yards down the lane and they are not cows who move quickly for anyone. A hundred yards farther up the hill from them is a garden where a giant goose lives. Walking from the direction of my house, a right turn just before the giant goose will take you to the fringe of the festival site, where the Pyramid Stage remains up all year round. Turning left at the giant goose will take you to Withial Combe and Washing Stones Gully, which you descend to find a lonely steel barn, not far from a house with an unseen angry dog with preternaturally good hearing. The dog will hear your footfall from more than half a mile away and whirl itself into a high-pitched rage, as if irked by the slightest shadow idea of your core – or maybe it's just me. In high winds, a rip in the thick steel wall of the barn twangs repeatedly back on itself, and always reminds me of a flap of skin that hung from my finger after I hacked deep into it while chopping lime with a wandering mind. Horses clop regularly along the road below, in twos and threes, and are one of the ingredients that make these country lanes far more perilous than the much steeper, narrower ones where I lived in Devon, along with endless tractors and dimensions just wide enough to invite risk from the renegades of the highway, including the local taxi drivers, whose penchant for speed almost rivals their penchant for not picking up the phone.

In 1934, the artist Katharine Maltwood devised the theory that the whole Glastonbury area formed a zodiac, the shapes of the fields and ditches and hills exactly mirroring the patterns in the stars above, and that the features were created in 2700 BC by the people of Southern Mesopotamia, who, it should be noted, already had plenty of experience of draining marshes in their own region. If this theory is to be believed, the area at the foot of Pennard Hill is Sagittarius, the half-horse, half-man creature. My house is in the human bit of him, not the horse bit. Go over the hill, past the giant goose, and you soon reach Capricorn, the horned goat. Poetically, I would have preferred to discover that Capricorn was a few miles farther on in the same direction, at Cheddar Gorge, where on a wind-ripped day in March I met numerous horned goats. The goats were introduced to Cheddar not long after the turn of the millennium to help reduce scrub on the east side of the gorge and their home is officially there but they roam precisely where they like, owing to the fact that they are goats. On the west side of the gorge, where it is technically illegal to be a goat, I watched two pygmy goats bashing horns, a gentle, playful battle that, with time, I suspected was less about any genuine acrimony and more about the satisfying sound their horns made as they clashed. It ignited in me the passing wish that I and some of my closest friends could have horns too. Cheddar cheese is still made at the gorge, as it has been for centuries, although in texture it no longer resembles the rough, pockmarked limestone cliffs of its namesake, as it once did. The biggest cheese made at Cheddar during the nineteenth century was the one that the village presented to Queen Victoria on her wedding day, which was more than nine feet in circumference, two feet high and necessitated the milk of 737 cows.

I chose a good day to walk the gorge, a Wednesday just after the apex of Storm Gareth, when everything flapped and, in the windy light, from the highest point the lakes of the region looked like magic puddles. Visit on a sunny weekend, though, and being in the valley bottom, close to the village, is like being in a giant service station that sells cheese instead of petrol. It's a classic example of one of the rules of the twenty-first-century British countryside, which is that 90 per cent of the general public go only where they are loudly instructed to go. Nobody gets loudly instructed to go to Ebbor Gorge, a few miles south-east, so on a similar day it will typically be close to deserted, yet its natural beauty is every bit as staggering, if not more so. 'Mini Cheddar Gorge' is the name my closest Somerset friend Michelle – a known snack aficionado – prefers to call it.

The space between my house and Wells and Ebbor, the last part of the sea before Mendip Country begins, is where my natural map-nerd's sense of direction goes awry. I think I am going west when I am going east. Two lanes, in opposite directions, somehow lead to the same place, without offering anywhere near enough bends to quantify the enigma. I turned my satnav on in this lost land behind Pennard and it took me somewhere three miles from where I wanted to be. 'That will be the zodiac,'

a couple of Glastonbury residents told me. Michelle's best friend Sara is an estate agent who has lived in the area for nearly five decades, and conducted viewings on hundreds of houses, but she still sometimes gets lost in that same space where you sense that, if the sea was real, and not just dry sea, you would vanish forever, without a trace, Bermuda Triangle-style.

When Sara is not being an estate agent, she also works in a pub and conducts ghost tours in the now defunct prison at Shepton Mallet, an outlier on the zodiac's borderland. On a bright, almost warm day in late March, which felt like a less hysterical second beginning to spring, she kindly gave Michelle and me a one-on-two personal tour of the prison, which, before its closure in 2013, was the UK's oldest working jail and is notorious in ghost-hunting circles as a hotbed of paranormal activity. It more than lived up to the preview Sara had given us in the pub a week earlier. We'd been in the building, which originally dates from 1610, less than half an hour when I received the privilege of having my hair touched by Mike. I thought what had touched my hair was some furry dust that had gathered into a kind of dirt stalactite, which you often find hanging from the deep recessed window frames in the prison, but it turned out to be Mike. 'They are always touching my hair,' Emma, an employee of the prison for eighteen years – for twelve of which it still contained inmates – would tell me later. By 'they' she meant, well, *they*. When Mike touched my hair, I was having my first half-decent hair day after a run of bad ones, although I have no idea if this influenced Mike's decision to be bold and make the first move. Michelle and Sara and I were climbing the narrow, dark staircase up to the prison's gatehouse at the time, a dank, claustrophobic space with a large hole in the floor that probably doesn't even quite edge into the list of the top ten most atmospheric or terrifying parts of the building. Mike had been making his presence felt in here several times recently, to paranormal experts and Ouija board owners, although nobody knows exactly who he is or when he died. If you make a recording while you're in the gatehouse you won't hear him at the time, but you might on playback, if you slow it down. A few weeks previously, Sara had had her hair touched by him too.

There are a few scattered bits of information and photos gathered by ghost hunters around the prison, plus a few historical recreations in the cells of C Wing – the smartest of the penitentiary's three sections of cells – but it could be argued that they are superfluous. The building speaks for itself. It's the kind of place you suspect could be reduced to rubble, its foundations entirely rewilded, and would still radiate its dark history pungently into the air. It was, in its later years, a place for lifers: murderers, rapists, child-killers. It's a building of quiet alcoves reeking of evil, sudden astonishing drops in temperature, half-revealed secrets. Across the road is a crypt, for which the prison does not have a key. During construction work a few years ago, a sinkhole opened up between B Wing and C Wing, unveiling a horse skeleton. Seven executions by hanging took place at the prison between 1889 and 1926. '1926!' I thought. 'That was pretty much last week.' If you are feeling a bit low about living in the era that you do, I'd highly recommend the perspective-enhancing properties of a visit. The summer before last, on a country walk, in a state of mild hiker's delirium, I'd stolen four corn on the cobs from a field. Had I done that in the 1700s and been caught, I could have easily ended up here, doomed to die of smallpox, picking apart tarry rope for oakum with festering, diseased hands. The one chink of light in my day would have been an hour in the exercise yard with a bag on my head, forced to walk anticlockwise in an attempt to symbolically turn back time and erase the wrongs I had inflicted on society with my clinical and ruthless corn-stealing. For the first 200 years of Shepton's existence as a prison, the average life expectancy of an inmate was between three and four months.

When I had first been looking into the possibility of moving to Somerset, Shepton was the town I was most frequently warned away from. As far back as 1912, in his book *Highways and Byways in Somerset*, Edward Hutton was describing it as 'a singularly unfortunate town', 'very irregularly built', 'a town gone mad' and 'dreadful to live in'. I will concede this, on the side of the naysayers: it's the hardest place to get a good cheese and onion pasty in the whole of the West Country. The one I finally found, after nearly an hour of searching, tasted of toes. It is a town of efficient tyre-fitting centres, frightening dogs and Babycham, except nobody drinks Babycham any more, so the Babycham has had to adapt and become cider. Shepton is like the civic equivalent of a pair of cargo pants: hugely unfashionable and not very aesthetically pleasing at first glance, but full of unexpected pockets, many of which contain interesting stuff. The architecture around the prison end of town is especially attractive, and I include the facility's seventy-foot-high walls in that. Before meeting Sara, I did five miles of exploring on foot in and around the town. After passing a vast cider factory which used to be a Babycham factory and telling a man searching for his lost pit bull that I hadn't seen his lost pit bull, I rounded a corner and discovered spring under a disused railway viaduct in a flurry of sharp blue sky, blackbirds, fresh running water and forsythia.

In mid-afternoon it was barely jumper weather, but once inside the prison I was very glad of the padded high-vis jacket Sara loaned to me. Just how cold was this place in actual winter? Not that the prison's cold is a cold that can be compared to outdoor cold. It's a very different cold, that goes straight into your mind, via a steel rod up your spine. The chill was noticeably fiercer in some rooms than others, and all across the bottom level of B Wing, which is haunted by the ghost of a woman wearing a wedding dress who died of a broken heart here after murdering her fiancé. I couldn't help but note how many of the super-cold rooms corresponded with a gruesome or eerie detail related to us by Sara. In a malignantly chilly cell which was once the quarters of one of 1970s Britain's most infamous child-murderers, people have often seen an unknown man's disembodied face in the mirror above the sink. I approached the mirror with my phone and risked a selfie. I didn't see an extra face on the photo, but I did see my own. It looked terrifying, and not just in that way that most selfies are terrifying. I did not recognise myself. I looked angry. I didn't feel angry. I had rarely, in fact, felt less angry in my life. The face was me, but it mostly wasn't, at all. Confused and unsettled, I deleted the face, forever.

You hear distant echoing sounds as you're wandering around the vast spaces of the prison: footsteps on sturdy metal stairs, the clang of a door. They might be the sound of other visitors – less than a handful come through the doors in the three and a quarter hours we are there – or one of the two other employees on duty, or they might not. There are three ways to visit: you go on one of Sara's ghost tours, a guided history tour, or you explore freely in the daytime on your own. Sara is the perfect host for such a tour: an impressive retainer of information who clearly loves her job and is able to pinpoint the deeply fascinating in the ostensibly banal. As a commentator on the supernatural, she's just the right balance of sceptical and fascinated. Until recently, she drove a car with its own ghost, known to her as Dead Susan, who would enhance her life with small posthumous acts of kindness, such as helping her avoid a speeding ticket. When she and Michelle were last here and listened back to one of the slowed-down recordings Sara had made in one of the cells, they could clearly hear a voice saying 'Saaaaaaave meeeee.' When they put it back to normal speed, though, they realised it was just a recording of Michelle inquiring, with reference to the ghosts, 'I wonder if any of them will say anything.' Sara said that none of the employees of the prison are ever in any rush to go home. The building has a strange power that locks you to the spot, while you simultaneously yearn to flee its mould-pocked walls, psychotic smells and impossible cold. It was not unknown for inmates here to commit suicide on the verge of their release. The last escape occurred in 1993, when three prisoners used knotted bedsheets to scale the walls. Two were recaptured very quickly near their old homes in Bristol. Another went directly for a pint in the Dusthole, the pub most local to the prison, where – upon drinking a second pint – he was recognised and apprehended by two prison guards who'd gone there for after-work refreshment. Three years later, toilets were finally added to cells, although out of habit many longer term inmates preferred to continue defecating in newspaper, which they then threw into the yard, as tradition dictated.

By the time we were in C Wing, the final segment of our visit, I was keen to leave, feeling to an extent that I had been serving an actual sentence here and had a fresh appreciation of all of the life I had taken for granted. Strangely, though, I found myself not acting on this impulse. I stood rooted to the cold hard floor, imagining life here in 1940, when the building was repurposed as an American Military Prison. During this period, C Wing remained as English soil, housing various not insignificant historical documents, including the Domesday Book and the Magna Carta, since nobody suspected Shepton would be high on Hitler's 'must-bomb' list. A man called Mr Johnson was tasked with looking after the documents, and his son – now in his eighties – recently revisited the prison. He recalled riding his tricycle around C Wing, as gospel singing floated over from A and B Wings. If that sounds quaint and idyllic, it is worth bearing in mind that sixteen US soldiers were hanged in the prison during the Second World War. Thirteen of the hangings were carried out by the famous Nottinghamshire-born executioner Thomas Pierrepoint, who legally killed a total of 294 people between 1906 and 1946, but was morally opposed to capital punishment and liked to farm in his spare time. The execution chamber and the drop room are not among the coldest places in Shepton prison, but the corridor leading to them definitely is.

A few months ago, a laminated photo of a young GI had been left in a cell by an anonymous visitor, without explanation: a smiling, brightly toothsome face that could only have been American. You won't find prisoners' possessions in the cells, but the aura of recent occupation is palpable, in the mould and dirt and graffiti, in the small sections of coloured tiles that a few prisoners grouted in to make life more bearable. Old smells are still here. The morgue reeks of burning hair. An aroma of perfume not emanating from any of the three of us wafted through the bottom of the gatehouse as we reached it, just after Mike had stroked my hair. In B Wing, three vast paintings, all by the same prisoner, still hang in the corridors. One shows a train puttering through classically English countryside. Another is a fantasy coastal scene: Tolkien and Cornish cliffs rolled into one. The third shows a woodland in spring, full of roe deer and bluebells, with a gypsy camp in the foreground: an unshackled, happy way of life. We studied the paintings more closely. In the fantasy coastal scene, two hanged figures, possibly armless, were visible on a bridge. In front of the bluebell wood, on a table, attended by gamblers, there was a red wine stain that seemed to coagulate, as it hit the floor, into blood. A woman standing behind the gamblers, viewed from a distance, might have been happily watching the game, but on closer inspection she looked thoroughly anguished. Off to the left, a man was approaching, wielding what might have been a machete but was probably more likely a cudgel, and apparently looking for a way to use it.

Did Shepton's severe-sounding name make Shepton a severe place? Or did being a severe place nudge Shepton towards its choice of a severe-sounding name? The 'Mallet' derives from the Malet family, who settled the area at the beginning of the twelfth century. Before that, the place was just called Sceaptun, which translates from Old English as 'sheep farm'. In the pub after we'd left the prison, Sara told us that her great-great-granddad had been a sheep farmer. 'A dead sheep killed him,' she added. 'He was loading it onto a trailer, he didn't push it quite far enough and it fell back on him and broke his neck.' The unfortunate incident had taken place in rural Surrey, although Sara's family had been in the Glastonbury area since 1970, when Sara was three. In 1974, she and her sister Marion joined in the Spring Equinox celebrations on the Tor. A gale was stirring up a dust storm and the ceremony's head druid sheltered them under his huge cloak. The legends surrounding the Tor were a constant background to her childhood. There were endless tunnels and staircases inside the hill. Children, she was told, disappeared in them. Under the opposing Wearyall Hill, beneath where the famous Glastonbury Thorn grew, a vast silver fish lived in the earth. Why shouldn't it live there? This was the sea, after all. In 1993, Sara's dad penned a book called *The Avalonians*, still to this day viewed as a classic of Glastonbury literature, detailing the early-twentieth-century influx to the town of artists and occultists – such as Dion Fortune and Wellesley Tudor Pole – that went a long way towards shaping what is still its current character. That character is a complex one. With its profusion of Victorian red-brick houses, Glastonbury doesn't look like any other Somerset town, nor does it feel like any other one. In discussions about rural hippie meccas, it's often mentioned in the same breath as Totnes, in Devon, but, having lived within eleven and a half minutes' drive of both places, I can report that they are very different, despite being connected by big promises of community and laid-back lifestyle, elements of under-reported penury, a large amount of politicised yoga and that same purported ley line that stops at Burrow Mump on its way south. Glastonbury is tattier around the edges than Totnes, gaudier in its retail outlook, less affluent and picturesque, its tourist economy driven more by daytrips than long B&B and glamping weekends, less uniform in its dress sense, less foody and foragey, a place where you will find it decidedly easier to locate a straight-forward sandwich. In Totnes, I feel acutely aware of my peasant heritage. In Glastonbury, I don't. Both towns talk about themselves a lot but Glastonbury does so with more open-eyed wonder.

During a succession of phenomenal sunsets as March became April, I found the Tor, if not the town, asserting an increasing influence on my life. The change in light, combined with the lack of leaf coverage, made it even more omnipresent, appearing in new spots closer to my house than before. In the evenings, I raced up to it, or to a spot on another island directly across from it, some-times getting there before the sun had fallen into the sea, sometimes not. Through trial and error, I found the best spot on Pennard Hill to photograph the sunset – the big-gest of the errors being when I ended up getting lost on a dirt track, phoneless and dressed in pyjama bottoms, and the biggest of the trials being when I got the back wheel of my car briefly stuck in a ditch as I tried to make a seven-point turn and escape. Pennard surprised me with its largeness and wildness, its loose deer and lonely coombes. The thick grey behind the windows of an abandoned farmhouse on its northern slopes, the forlorn look in the eyes of the dead pheasants draped around the door handles of its cottages, the constant gunshots and the vagueness of the footpaths combined to give it a feral agricultural quality that was a little different to any patch of countryside I'd known. It contrasted with the part of the sea that bled into the more arid ground to the east, which now offered more comfort, with spring's arrival.

Under the Tor's watchful gaze, I walked south down Teapot Lane (Worms Lane), away from Pennard, crossed through Baltonsborough onto Mulcheney Hill – barely a hill at all – and saw a large, freshly dead badger, apparently unblemished, on the verge, upside down, its paws raised in surrender. Land owners, I was aware, often killed badgers then dumped them at the side of the road to give the illusion that they'd been hit by cars. But, to

offer them the benefit of the doubt, early spring was prime roadkill season, and I'd been almost run over by the same Porsche Boxster twice in the last week. The speed and dust of major roads insulates us from the reality of roadkill, makes its victims easier to write off as non-animals. Here, on a quiet country lane, under a bluer than blue sky, the badger was astoundingly real. I had not seen Clarence for over a month, not heard the bassy beat of his wings, or his 'ch-kauwck!', which I had learned to isolate from the 'ch-kauwck!' of different pheasants. I had to accept that the badger's fate – whichever one of the two possible fates it had been – could very likely have been his too. Spring felt bittersweet today, light and gentle on top, dark underneath: confetti sprinkled on bloody earth. Orchards were coming to life. The mistletoe that had dominated the trees for months, like big organic Christmas baubles someone had forgotten to take down, would soon be hidden again. I walked and walked, taking little detours involving curiously named footpaths and meadows I'd previously missed: Harepits (no hares), Oddway (quite odd), Maggoty Paggoty (still no maggots or paggots). On clear days like this I always felt a little like I was in a shallow pasta dish on the paths south of my house: the front rim being the downland spine of Dorset, the back rim of the dish being the Mendips. In Barton St David, on an unmarked footpath, I asked a young, bald, Eavis-like farmer mending a tractor if the way I was proceeding across his farmyard was correct. He sighed a sigh that sounded like it had been sighed before and said it wasn't. In the pub in the same village, a few weeks previously, after watching the performance of an Elvis impersonator who didn't sing any Elvis songs, I'd met a poet called Wes. Wes had recently moved away, to London, but grew up on a farm behind the Tor which had its own modern stone circle. Until a year ago, he had occupied the official post of Bard of Glastonbury: a position gained by winning a competition held annually on St Dunstan's Day, open to poets, storytellers and songwriters who live within what, with beautiful, carbon-resistant Glastonbury looseness, is defined as 'a day's walk of the Tor'. Wes's Bardic duties included carrying the Silver Branch of Ynys Witrin – also known as 'The Wiggly Stick' – wearing a red cape, infusing a fool's hat with mirth, and supporting pan-Celtic culture, spirituality and creativity within the local community. During periods when Wes has been away from Glastonbury, people have often been adamant that they have seen him around town and will not believe him when he assures them otherwise.

Wes has climbed the Tor hundreds of times but has only once been alone at the summit. On the weekday evenings I spent up there, the median amount of people at the summit was around twenty: a roughly even mix of tourists and locals, which was unusual for a famous landmark. People meditated and sang. A couple in their early twenties collaborated shyly on a song as the sun set, reading lyrics off the singer's phone. A humming, beaming woman who was all knitwear asked a man in a football shirt whom she'd just met if she could hug him and he let her. One night, amidst the total acceptance of everyone in the vicinity, a man chanted to himself inside the ruined church, in bellowed Latin. The sound echoed out, far down the hillside. On my descent, I followed a wild-looking, seaweed-haired woman who held three full carrier bags and farted explosively with every other step. The farts also echoed out down the hillside, but not as far. As I walked or drove the higher lanes, the Tor hovered like a distant cake, made for somebody's first birthday, with just the one candle on top. I had somehow been living in Avalon eight months already. In no time at all our first anniversary would have arrived.

In addition to the most jaw-dropping sunsets I had seen in my life, from the Tor I saw a couple of the pinkest, fullest moons. One evening in April, in heavy rain, a week before the pinkest, fullest moon of all, I began the climb to St Michael's church again and met Johanna, who has climbed the Tor almost every day in the eleven years she has lived here, and her partner Steve, who has been doing the same for many, many years longer. 'It's our version of the gym,' Johanna, who is from Holland, told me. Steve set eyes on it for the first time on the summer solstice of 1972 – his first of many solstices spent on the Tor – after driving down from Bristol with a gang of friends. Just three years before, in 1969, the year of the moon landings, a series of inexplicable events had occurred on top of the hill. One of a group of visiting Buddhists was hurled several feet in the air by an elemental force from the ruined tower, and balls of light curved halfway around the dry island's circumference. Not long after, Glastonbury residents spotted saucer-shaped objects hovering over the town and a fiery red ball appeared, which was not the sun. More people than ever visited during the big days on the pagan calendar. Steve didn't arrive until gone 11 p.m. on the solstice of 1972, but stayed up there all night, wide awake, with what he described as some pharmaceutical assistance. 'I decided right then that one day I was going to get a job at the bottom of the hill,' he told me. Seven years later, he did exactly that, securing work teaching mathematics at Millfield Prep School, situated on Edgarley Road at the Tor's foot.

Steve and Johanna first met on the south-west coast path, where they were both walking east towards Lyme Regis. 'We wild camped, in our separate tents, and talked and talked and talked about everything,' Johanna told me. 'We were on the Undercliff, and there were glow-worms everywhere and a meteor shower was happening. Steve told me that if I was ever anywhere near Glaston-bury I should pop in for a cup of tea. Being Dutch, I didn't realise that British people say that kind of thing without meaning it, so a week later, that's what I did.' They climbed the Tor. It felt to Johanna like there was light and energy everywhere, brightness coming up through the earth. 'In all these years, I have never seen it quite like that again,' she said. The date was 11 August 1988. Johanna talked about her intention to go on a walking pilgrimage from The Hague to Jerusalem but said she knew it was an unrealistic ambition, with two small children to look after and a full-time job. When she returned to Holland, Steve sent her a chunk of the novel he was working on. Johanna replied with a mixture of critical and positive comments. She received no reply. The months, then the years, scrolled on. She worried she had offended Steve by being too harsh.

Fourteen years later, Johanna finally walked from The Hague to Jerusalem. It took her eleven months and the stress on her feet meant that forever after she would need to wear orthopaedic shoes. When she returned, Steve was prominent in her mind. She felt a need to get in touch and tell him that she'd finally actually done the walk, all 2,200 miles of it, all on her own. But so much time had passed. Was he even still alive? She wrote to him at his old address and they began to correspond again and, via their letters, fell in love. When they met up, the old chemistry and common interests that had kept them up into the night talking on the coast path, all that time ago, were still there. In the intervening time, Steve had not walked from The Hague to Jerusalem, but he had set himself his own very impressive walking project. After a heart operation in 1999, he decided that, as part of his recovery, he would ascend the Tor sixty times. This, he had worked out, amounted to roughly the height of Mount Everest, with the Tor being 523 feet high and Steve's house being around twenty feet above sea level. 'After that, I just kept on walking,' he told me. One year, he ascended the Tor a total of 525 times, including twelve times in just one day. He estimates that he has walked up it at least 5,000 times in total.

In time, Steve and Johanna would complete their own joint pilgrim walk: a six-week journey along the whole of the St Michael ley line, from Land's End to Lowestoft, passing through St Michael's doorless church along the way. Both retired, they now live together in a flat on the first floor of a red-brick Victorian house a couple of hundred yards west of the Tor, below Chalice Hill, where some claim that the Holy Grail remains buried. Steve told me that, whatever mood he has been in, he has never felt it dip as a result of a walk up the Tor. Johanna said it had an energy you could feel, pushing up through you: 'All hills do, but especially this one.' Sometimes she comes up to the top of the Tor or Chalice and sings. 'You can do exactly what you like up here, be who you want to be, and nobody will say a thing against it,' she said. 'People who have come away from organised religion come up here because they want to still feel part of something bigger, because that's a human need. It's a strange thing but as humans we need to feel insignificant. It makes us feel better.' She sees the Tor as having its own force field, which is constantly spinning, spinning stories, many of which are apocryphal, but can become slightly real with enough retelling. She and Steve disagree about some of them: Johanna thinks the story about Arthur and Guinevere's bodies being found in the abbey grounds in 1191 could well be true; Steve thinks it was a ruse by the Church to raise money, at a time when pilgrim visits had fallen and they badly needed it.

There was no sunset this evening, no spaces for it between the rain. I realised the smattering of other people around Abbot Richard Whiting's death church – an Italian teenager and her mum, a middle-aged dog walker, a tall, elderly man in a dress – had descended the hill, leaving just the three of us alone on the summit. Below us rabbits hopped along the strip lynchets, which might or might not be an ancient maze and not strip lynchets at all, and into burrows, which might or might not lead to a labyrinth and the faerie underworld. So much of

Glastonbury was about speculation: it had been that way for centuries, long before the shops had signs outside offering 'Free Vibes' and people went there to buy black onyx crystals and a guidebook on how to practise palmistry on a child. We looked across to the north, towards the two old oak trees known locally as Gog and Magog, and the farm where Wes grew up. Gog had been narrowly saved from destruction by fire a couple of years ago, when a tealight candle left in its branches had set it ablaze. Some claimed the two trees were 2,000 years old, but, as Johanna and Steve pointed out, that was more classic Glastonbury spin, as it's well known that oaks do not live that long and the oldest in Britain, the Bowthorpe Oak, in Lincolnshire, is not far past its thousandth birthday.

I decided Steve and Johanna were very Glastonbury in the best way: they weren't totally ensnared by New Age thinking, mocked themselves frequently, liked to read widely, ask questions and think stuff out, but they were simultaneously very open to magic and the unknown, and without that openness their own story could surely never have been the lovely thing it was. I accepted their invitation to drink some Avalonian cider at their flat. On the way down the back of the Tor, where the death church peeks back over the shoulder of the hill to check you aren't up to no good, the rain prompted us all to recall the last drastically wet winter, five years ago. It was the winter that ended with me relocating from the dry far east of the UK to the West Country, when nearly every house I visited in Somerset, Dorset or Devon had sandbags around its threshold: the last time the Levels, the

Great Low Moor, had severely flooded. 'It was terrible for a lot of people and they lost a lot of possessions and had to leave their homes,' remembered Johanna. 'But from up here it looked magical. There was water everywhere below. You really did feel like you were on an island in an ancient sea.'

JENNY DOESN'T
LIVE HERE
(2014–19)

The lunar eclipse had just happened and people in town were saying it had been having a dramatic effect on everyone's sleep, infiltrating dreams in troubling, vivid ways. Always a bit out of step with town, I'd slept soundly during the eclipse and got my weird dreams out of the way a week earlier. In one dream, my washing machine, which already displayed a tendency towards nomadism, totally broke free of my house to start a new life on the road, performing for coins. In perhaps the most disturbing dream, I dream-woke on my back, floating in deep water, having made the error of falling asleep in the sea. I sort of assumed in the dream that I was somewhere a few hundred yards off the shore of the hard-to-get-to Devon cove where I had done most of my recent swimming, but in truth there was no landmark to suggest I was actually near that cove, apart from the sea, which, while undoubtedly a very distinctive landmark, is a landmark only specific enough to tell you that you are somewhere on 70 per cent of the planet's surface. I did get a sense that it was the particular kind of sea you get near that cove, but I couldn't be sure. I woke up again, and realised that this was a proper waking and that I was in my bed and hadn't really woken up in the sea at all.

It probably makes sense that I'd dream such a dream – a dream combining freedom, homeliness, comfort and danger – about my favourite Devon cove. I had been going to the cove regularly for over four years and developed a relationship with it that had, at times, bordered on addiction. Through the cove, I could to an extent tell the recent story of my life: the books I had read, the books I had failed to read, the changes to my body, the little shifts in life philosophy. I had fallen in love at first sight twice on the cove – quite a high ratio when you compare it to the same period inland, where I had only fallen in love at first sight once. In my garden there are a small selection of stones from the cove, including a chunk of smoothed tarmac, which looks like a conglomerate puddingstone but on closer inspection is almost certainly a former part of the road a couple of miles away beside Slapton Ley, which was violently ripped apart by Storm Emma in early 2018, in an astonishing reminder of the brute force of nature the likes of which you don't see often in the UK. I have been physically attacked at the cove on fifteen occasions that I can pinpoint: fourteen of them by jellyfish, and once by a black Labrador, which swam over to me and climbed on my back, leaving my ribs covered in scratches. I doubt any of these attacks can be considered malicious: the jellyfish were just defending space that is rightfully more theirs than mine, and I think the Labrador – which was owned by a semi-oblivious Dutch man – just wanted a nice, big, wet cuddle. At least the salt water quickly went to work on my injuries, as it has done on pretty much every injury I have had upon my arrival at the beach, magically curing small patches of eczema, cuts and bites.

Down at the far end of the cove is a small, unofficial nudist section. I could probably join its ranks, as I feel increasingly relaxed about the idea of being naked in public and in the water, but something stops me – maybe it's the memory of those jellyfish stings. The nudists are nearly all 65-plus and uniformly almond-brown. Clothed people arrive, have barbecues, throw balls for dogs, get in the water and yelp about the cold, then leave, but the nudists abide: sleeping a bit, swimming a bit, sleeping some more. I have seen no evidence that they ever leave the cove. I would not be surprised at all to venture into the caves beneath the cliffs and find the hobs where they cook their fresh mackerel breakfasts, the beds where they sleep and have surprisingly agile pensioner sex, and the showers where they scrub the pebbles and salt off their wiry old bodies. Maybe people who have visited the cove a few times think not dissimilar thoughts about me. 'That hippie with all the dog scratches on his chest is here again,' they might say. 'I wonder which subterranean part of these cliffs is his home.'

I don't think the cove is the best cove in Devon and Cornwall for swimming – there are warmer coves, with clearer, more benevolent water and better rocks to leap from – but in an equation which weighs up ease-of-swim and proximity to the two houses in Devon where I've lived, it has worked out as the logical choice. I have grown to trust the cove, without in any way making the mistake of taking it for granted. While swimming there, I often starfish out and let myself float. It's my sea-swimming equivalent of the time you might take for a breather between lengths at a pool, and doubles as a version of meditation for someone who always intends to meditate but rarely does. I am very relaxed when I'm in this state, my mind a fuzzy blank, preoccupied only by the tiny noises beneath the surface, which, like everything at the cove, are always subtly changing. I doubt I could fall asleep in this state, I am not complacent enough to fully give myself over to a state in which I could – unlike in my dream. This lack of complacency might be a result of the period during my childhood when my dad would regularly convince himself that my mum was going to fall asleep in the bath. 'TOM, ARE YOU UPSTAIRS?' my dad would ask. 'Yeah,' I would reply. 'CAN YOU CHECK YOUR MUM HASN'T FALLEN ASLEEP IN THE BATH?' Following which I would knock on the bath-room door and ask my mum if she had fallen asleep in the bath and my mum would confirm that she had not fallen asleep in the bath.

A lot of people in south-west Devon call the cove 'Jenny's Cove' but that's not what it's called. Jenny's Cove is much smaller and directly next door and anyone who enjoys studying maps would know that, but a fact of life I have slowly and reluctantly come to accept is that most people don't enjoy studying maps. People have a tendency to hear a name being used by somebody else and start using it too, unquestioningly. It's not dissimilar to the recent trend of people adding 's' to the word 'vinyl' just because they have heard others doing it – a phenomenon I find baffling, especially considering that when I tried to start a trend for calling cattle 'cattles' it didn't catch on at all. It is entirely possible that one day so many people will call Not Jenny's Cove 'Jenny's Cove' that the Ordnance Survey, with a deep, defeated sigh, will rename it. In May 2018, on my birthday weekend, I visited it with a group of friends, including my friend Jenny, which you might consider apt, if you lie down and accept that we are living in a post-truth world. The tide was in, making it very difficult for Jenny to swim around the corner to her actual cove, and we were in an un-pedantic mood so agreed to let her hang out with us in the cove that is only designated hers because of modern gossip and hearsay.

Jenny, her boyfriend Pat, and our other friends Jim, Neal and Amy sunbathed and swam a little. Meanwhile, having been acclimatising myself to the temperature of the water over several weeks, I threw myself in and did a couple of lengths of the cove. A few people, such as Jim, who is from Sheffield and had last seen the sea during the 1890s, looked at me like I was mad, but nobody was bold enough to point it out, unlike on a far colder day a month earlier, when a paddleboarder had rowed past me in the same place and remarked, 'Look at you! You're crazy!' Not Jenny's Cove is known for having the most mysteriously cold water on the whole of the south Devon coast, but craziness is all relative. I probably seem bold and hardcore to some by doing long swims in nine-degree water, without a wetsuit, fairly early in the year, but a single encounter with a serious outdoor swimmer who lives in the Lake District or Scotland will disabuse you of this notion. In swimming, as in life, it doesn't matter how hardcore you are, there is always somebody out there more hardcore than you. My friend James is amazing to me, as he can swim two lengths of the local lido entirely underwater. But what is he, ultimately, compared to Elise Wallenda, who was famous in Victorian times for being able to undress, sew, write, eat and drink underwater, and in 1898 managed to stay submerged for a record four minutes and forty-five and two-fifths seconds?

On that day in May when my friends and I visited Not Jenny's Cove, the temperature was about twenty degrees, there was a light breeze and the water was the colour of used bathwater into which somebody had spilt half a glass of milk. I would estimate that I have visited the cove around a hundred times over the last five years and each time it has been a slightly different place. One day in late summer 2018, the sea was full of dead wasps. The week before, large waves drove diagonally towards the east side of the beach and, swimming back against them, into the wind and sun, my eyes burned with salt and the journey took almost three times as long as usual. A month earlier I'd arrived and the water had been so placid and clear I could almost pick out every individual jellyfish and driftwood chunk from the top of the cliff, around a hundred feet above the surface. I swam out to my friend Nick's boat, ate half a melon, jumped in a couple of times, and briefly forgot I wasn't in a big lake. One day in August the previous year the beach was covered in thousands of dead whitebait, glinting in the sun – a mass suicide pact, voted a preferable alternative to being eaten by a shoal of hungry mackerel. The place stank so pungently, I cut my swim short. The sea teemed with debris, like overly herby soup. The pebbles, which at the west end of the beach teeter on the line that separates

stone from sand, had a tired look and the untidy melancholy of summer's conclusion was apparent.

If I were to see footage of myself in 2014, the first time I stood high on the cliffs before my maiden descent to Not Jenny's Cove, I'd probably be a little taken aback at what a different physical being I was in comparison to the one I am now. I certainly wasn't overweight at that point but since then swimming has transformed my body into a collection of angles. I'm broader, lighter, sharper at the edges, more upright. A swimmer's body is light years away from the body that has become the cliched goal of the twenty-first-century gym junkie. Look at footage of Mark Spitz in the 1972 Munich Olympics, as he gets ready to dive, on the way to one of the record seven gold medals he won that year: he's not at all beefy; he's a bronzed javelin. To my mind no high-profile sportsman has ever looked cooler. Spitz was asked by a Russian journalist whether the moustache he grew for that Olympics – against the wishes of the American team coach – slowed him down. He replied that, on the contrary, it deflected the water from his mouth, allowing him to get into a lower, more dynamic position while racing (Spitz claims the article resulting from this immediately prompted every male professional swimmer in Russia to grow a moustache). It is when I'm at my most swimming-obsessed that I come closest to shaving off my beard for the first time in aeons and taming my hair's customary seaweed wildness. I get into a borderline trance state and swimming is all that matters. 'Might this small personal change help me swim more pleasurably?' I wonder. It is pointless: I am not a technically adept outdoor swimmer and, although I am improving, even if I one day become a technically excellent swimmer I am too old to do anything useful with it. But it is the pointlessness that's a big part of the appeal. I am not swimming for my livelihood, or to impress anyone; I'm not even doing it primarily to improve my body (although that has been a not unpleasant by-product). I'm doing it for the way it makes me feel.

Swimming has taught me a lot about the true chemistry of feeling good. It's very easy to believe that levels of personal happiness are entirely reliant on all the exterior factors impinging on your life at that time – financial fortunes, friendships, relationships, ups and downs with work – but being in the water, particularly being in a large natural body of water, brings you away from that line of thinking, makes you realise how many of these influencing factors are beyond your control, and ultimately unsolvable, and that at any time your happiness can be primarily down to your immediate environment at that exact moment, if you let go and allow it. Over each successive summer, I've come to value the cove more and more as an admin-free space, away from all the clutter and spiritual luggage, where you don't have to 'sort it all out'; you just have to exist. I have done some of my best thinking there. It might be the root of the reason that, when I am creatively blocked, my first response is often to take a bath. As Annette Kellermann, the champion Australian swimmer of the early twentieth century said: 'Swimming cultivates imagination; the man with the most is he who can swim his solitary course night or day and forget a black earth full of people that push.' The history of swimming is full of inspiring, heroic, outsider figures, few more so than Kellermann, who was a vegetarian all her life (before it was fashionable), became the first major actress to appear nude in a mainstream film, and during her career in Hollywood performed all her own stunts, including diving from over ninety feet into a pool full of crocodiles.

I see much more clearly since I've been a regular swimmer, and one of the things I see is that I have always loved being in water, that my binge swimming of the last five years is a kind of coming back to myself. When I used to go to the local swimming pool with my mum and dad I'd be so impatient to get in that, while they were still getting into their costumes, I'd paddle in the footbath at the threshold of the changing rooms. The first time I moved to a house beside a river, I immediately stripped down to my underwear and leaped in, before the van was even unpacked, with no premeditation, in much the way an unruly dog might. I did the first truly addictive swimming of my life alongside my dad, the two of us repeatedly diving into an Italian pool in the summers of 1982, 1983 and 1984, more child and child than father and son; on a couple of the same holidays my cousin Fay and I did the same off the back of a pedalo in the tranquil harbour at Menton, just across the French border. But I have no recollection of being taught to swim properly, only that my early school swimming lessons were taken in a dingy pool in an insalubrious part of Nottingham with an instructor independent of the school itself who had a reputation for being very stern, and for flicking his bogeys into the water.

In the early months of 2019 I began swimming lessons with Charlie Loram, who teaches the Shaw

Method, a style of swimming originated by former champion swimmer Steven Shaw which uses elements of Alexander technique to create a more effortless stroke and a greater general sense of well-being. Charlie shot a video of me doing front crawl and what primarily emerged from this was solid evidence that in the water I am less dolphin and more spaniel. I am not alone in this, apparently. In many other regions of the planet, humans adapt themselves to their environment. In Western society, by contrast, we have adapted our environment to us. This has plenty of downsides, one being that we don't use our bodies as effectively as we could. With Charlie, I began not just relearning how to swim, but unlearning decades of bad habits: mainly bad posture caused by too much time in cars, too much time in front of screens, too much time sitting in awkward positions. An additional reason for the very non-dynamic head position I had adopted for many years is no doubt the recurring ear infections I suffered for most of my twenties: a searing pain and occasional bleeding in both ears that led me, on my doctor's advice, to forgo swimming for a long time and then, when I began again, only with ear plugs and extreme caution.

Now ear-infection-free, I do most of my swimming in the sea or rivers or open-air pools, but in winter I do retreat, reluctantly, beneath a roof. I ruled out the public pool closest to my current house in Somerset since it's very dark and as you navigate the deep end, there is a palpable sense that you might be swimming over a section of abandoned car, its interior now inhabited by a family of mutant three-headed fish and the occasional eel. Instead I drive twenty-five minutes to another, lighter pool, which is decent enough as public pools go, although not devoid of acts of passive aggressive backstroke. Here, in the medium ability lane, I have attempted to work a more dynamic posture into my stroke, getting more intimate with the water, which allows me more speed although conversely gives me a clearer view of the occasional thick clump of black hair as it floats up from the depths into my shoulder. Charlie's teaching makes swimming the opposite of a vicious circle: you swim with less effort, which stretches your spine and makes you longer and thinner and fitter, which makes you swim with less effort, which stretches out your spine and makes you longer and thinner and fitter.

You could say I left it all quite late to do this. I'm forty-three. All attempts to feel and look better must now naturally be set against the downhill physical slope that eventually leads to life's off ramp. I am sometimes tempted to speculate about how different the years between twenty-four and thirty-four might have been for me if I'd exercised more and not shovelled so much rubbish into my body, but that is a moot point since the very fact that I didn't exercise much between twenty-four and thirty-four and ate and drank a lot of rubbish is an intrinsic part of why I am getting so much pleasure out of doing the opposite now. Besides, I have always had a preference for going about life the difficult way. Long cuts don't get anywhere near enough credit in this age of the short cut, this age of the spurious 'life hack'. Life cannot be hacked; not in any meaningful or lasting sense. I've worked hard on my swimming. Fifty lengths of a twenty-five-metre pool felt like an achievement at one point. Now, fifty feels like chickening out; seventy or eighty feels more like the mark. There is a point during one of these long swims – usually a little after halfway – where it all becomes much easier, but only after it's become much harder first. I have noticed that if I look at my fellow swimmers and measure myself against them, my swimming deteriorates. This makes total sense because it's a microcosm of that bigger lesson that swimming will eventually teach you, about happiness coming from being inside your own space and not trying to control separate ones that are out of your reach.

Public swimming pools nearly always have a finely nuanced, low-lying drama to them, as if something very important is about to happen but never quite does. Tension appears to build over the hour or so I spend at mine – yet when I emerge from the pool the tension level is somehow the same as it was at the start. The large number of lifeguards no doubt assists in the creation of such an atmosphere. I would be totally fine being a lifeguard if I could read a book on duty, but I am guessing that's not allowed, and I assume the job must be deeply boring. One day last winter there was a major crisis for the lifeguards at the pool when a large amount of shower gel was spilt on the floor of the men's showers. More and more lifeguards gathered around the head lifeguard and a plan was strategically formed to defuse the situation. Below the lifeguards, four men in their fifties were ploughing through the water with a fair amount of violence. The men share a friendship – maybe originating in the pool itself, or prior to that, I can't tell – and I don't go in the Fast Lane when they are there: not just because

I'm nowhere near as fast as them but because the whole lane assumes a different character when they are in it, and I hail from the Medium Lane, which is a whole other continent. Also, one of them – the one with the most calm, commanding aura, whom the others listen to attentively – is a police officer, and for much of last January mud was obscuring my rear registration plate, the treads on my front left tyre were quite low and my bumper had fallen off twice in two days in the same spot just outside Ilchester. When the men swim they do so in a splashy maelstrom that creates a kind of unison, and it is impossible to tell where anyone is. I don't get the impression they're people who swim the way that they drive, though, in the way that I do with some of the more aggressive and selfish swimmers at the pool. In their breaks, the men chat about the quality of the water. 'Is it me or is it a bit more choppy today?' the large, bald one asked one day.

My dad formed a gang at his own local public pool in Nottinghamshire and I had long wondered how that could happen, but witnessing these men as they go about their ritual has made me more aware of how the process might work. I've never been to my dad's local swimming pool, but the cast of characters who populate the male changing rooms there for the early swim on weekdays are so familiar to me they seem like old friends. There's Pat, a retired mining geologist my dad once enlisted to identify an old bit of stone he'd brought to the swimming pool changing room, and Malcolm, whose clothes my dad will often hide while Malcolm is showering. There was also Andrew, who died last year, and who, in the advanced stages of his cancer when he could barely walk, still doggedly swam thirty lengths a day before crawling along the poolside to the changing room. My dad misses Andrew who, late in his illness, once kindly picked a bogey off my dad's cheek for him. 'The things I do for my friends!' Andrew said, as he removed the bogey. More occasional members of the gang include Underpants Sebastian, who, while standing naked in the changing room, likes to wave his Y-fronts about in an attempt to emphasise a strident political point he is making. When I see my dad, he brings each of these men with him in spirit, as they now represent the most eventful part of his social life, which could already be considered surprisingly eventful for a sixty-nine-year-old who professes to dislike pubs and multi-person gatherings.

When my parents drove down from Nottinghamshire to Devon to visit me in June 2017 I was coming off the back of a sociability overdose and all the invisible swimming men my dad had brought with him became a bit overwhelming. In the month since I'd finished my latest big writing project, six different sets of friends had stayed at my house and, as much as I'd enjoyed all the conversation, my brain was feeling like it had been left for too long under a heated lamp, like scrambled eggs you get at the buffet of a bad hotel. After four weeks of almost constant walking and talking, merely following the structure of a simple anecdote now made me feel like a cat chasing a laser pointer wielded by someone particularly vindictive. What I wanted to do more than anything was sit in a copse on top of a hill and take a week-long vow of silence. Having my parents in the house felt more like having thirteen people staying with me than two, my mum representing one of these and my dad representing the other twelve. I told my dad how tired I was, due to all the people I'd seen recently. 'THERE'S NOTHING WRONG WITH BEING SOCIABLE,' my dad replied. 'IT WILL STOP YOU GETTING ALZHEIMER'S. THEY'VE PROVED IT.'

I wished I could have given more attention to my dad's stories, as I hadn't seen him for several weeks and there was a lot to catch up on, very little of it not tinged with peril or excitement. 'DID I TELL YOU ABOUT THE HAIRDRESSER'S CAR?' he asked.

I searched the now extremely dry scrambled eggs inside my skull. I definitely remembered at least a couple of hairdresser-themed episodes he'd regaled me with recently – something about a double entendre, the multicultural tour of hairdressers he'd been on around Hyson Green in Nottingham where, after hearing how loudly my dad spoke, a young Jamaican girl had made the assumption he must be deaf and taken to repeating all the tour guide's comments for his benefit – but nothing about a car.

'I'm not sure,' I said.

'MY HAIRDRESSER HAS GOT THIS REALLY FLASH SPORTS CAR AND I SAW IT IN THE SUPERMARKET CAR PARK. IT'S WHITE AND IT WAS A BIT DIRTY SO I WENT OVER AND WROTE 'HAIRCUT' IN THE DIRT WITH MY FINGER, BECAUSE I NEEDED A HAIRCUT. SHE DIDN'T FIND OUT IT WAS ME UNTIL ABOUT TWO WEEKS LATER. SHE'D THOUGHT HER GRANDKIDS HAD DONE IT. SHE GAVE THEM A RIGHT BOLLOCKING.'

*

It rained for most of my mum and dad's stay at my house which meant that, unusually, my dad spent barely any time outside in my garden with his top off. Sometimes my dad and his swimming-pool friends complain about stuff their wives won't let them do. One of his friends at the pool had lately complained that his wife won't let him kiss her goodbye on the front doorstep if there are people in the street and he is wearing his pyjamas. My dad responded by complaining that my mum would not let him walk around with his top off when her friends come over for cake. Last time my mum's best friend Jane had dropped by my dad had tried to find a loophole in the rules by walking around the garden with his top off but with strips of gaffer tape over each of his nipples.

The weather improved on the third day of my parents' stay, which was also the eve of the general election. My dad went out into the garden early and bathed in what little gauzy sunlight there was, moving the deckchair every few minutes to chase the rays with precision. As I cleaned my teeth, I noticed his electric tooth-flosser on the sink. In the late morning, he and my mum went off to the beach to do some rock-pooling. Feeling bad that I hadn't gone with them, I walked down to the polling station at the village hall, where I voted, voting a bit harder than I had voted at points in the past. I then used my remaining solitary time to enjoy some silence, meditate and read, which is to say I replied to the messages I hadn't replied to while friends had been visiting, replied to some of the replies to those, got back to some other friends I was due to see in a week or so about exactly where and when I was supposed to see them, got sucked into a couple of online conversations about rare records, quarter-digested four pages of a book, then heard the click of my garden gate and my dad shouting 'EY?' at my mum.

'Did you have a good time?' I asked, when he arrived in the living room.

'YEAH. GER OUTSIDE AND HAVE A LOOK WHAT'S ON THE LAWN.'

My dad is a collector, but not of the conventional kind: you won't find rare records or complete sets of old maps in his house, but you might well find a dried hedgehog, a comically shaped cucumber or an esoteric piece of metal he has dug up while creating a new flowerbed. It was only about five paces from the middle of my living room to my lawn but in the time it took me to take those I hypothesised several possibilities relating to today's discovery. Would it be another dried snake, like the one he found a few years ago while walking in Norfolk, then stored in the pocket of his car's driver-seat visor? A bottle containing an ancient love note from overseas? Or maybe he had brought me a surprise impulse present? Another electric tooth-flosser, to add to the two he had purchased for me in the past, which I had never used? What I saw instead was a long fish, dappled, and of aerodynamic appearance. I'd seen a few dead animals on my lawn since living in Devon, but this was undoubtedly the most exotic.

'IT'S A SMALL-SPOTTED CATSHARK,' said my dad.

'It absolutely stunk up the car on the way here, but your dad insisted on bringing it back,' said my mum. 'We found it on the tideline, near the beach where you like to swim.'

'LOOK AT THAT HOOK IN ITS FACE,' my dad said. 'EVIL THING. SOME FOOKIN' BASTARD SPORTS FISHERMAN'S CAUGHT THAT THEN CHUCKED IT BACK IN WITHOUT TAKING THE HOOK OUT. SPORTS FISHERMEN ARE BASTARDS.'

I looked more closely at the catshark. The bit of curved steel in its cheek was nightmarish, more so for the miniature neatness of its design. It wasn't even nightmarish in a spooky way; it was precise and malevolent, gruesomely efficient. I estimated the fish had been dead a couple of days: three days too early to see the apparently foregone result of the general election and a future which would undoubtedly spell even more doom for it and its fellow wildlife on and around the British Isles. A couple of flies crawled out of its mouth, part of which had already rotted away. I marvelled that so recently it had been a factory of life, able to wriggle and twist and bite and digest.

'What are you thinking of doing tomorrow?' I asked my dad.

'BEING DEPRESSED BECAUSE THE TORIES HAVE WON.'

Above us, a jackdaw, who'd been sitting on the aptly Gothic chimney pot of my house, took a sudden dive towards my hedge, banking, rolling 360 degrees in the air then accelerating through a tunnel of buddleia; an outrageous move that would no doubt have received all sorts of international awards, had it been performed by a more conventionally attractive bird. I liked my local jackdaws a lot and had an arrangement with them and the local gulls. The arrangement was this: if I put anything edible or half edible out on the lawn, within less than an hour they would remove it. I had come to look at them as fondly as I would two competing sets of handsome bin men – industrious, environmentally scrupulous ones, who eschewed landfills and didn't mess with your mind by changing their schedule after bank holidays. But over the next couple of days they surprised me: not one so much as picked at the catshark, let alone carted it away. I had taken them for birds who had little care for 'best before' dates, but I had been wrong.

The day after my parents left, the temperature rose dramatically. The garden grew hazy and slow, like steam was being squirted into it from a vast unseen subway vent turned on its side. The gulls and jackdaws mysteriously vanished. Wood pigeons took over, getting randy and acting like drugged fools, ending up upside down in thick conifers looking confused. Holding my nose, I transported the catshark to the wild ground behind my house. St John's wort and teasels were beginning to run rampant here, where forget-me-nots had been a month earlier. I couldn't see the tiny predators moving through the heat towards the catshark as I walked away but I could sense them. An hour later, on the clifftop above Not Jenny's Cove, I stopped to escort a drinker moth caterpillar from the south-west coastal path, fearing for its safety. It showed no outward sign of appreciating my efforts.

Down in the cove, I swam out alone to the far side, where the water always mysteriously plummets in temperature. I starfished, sustained by the salt, drifting for a while and listening to the noise of industry on the ocean floor. Today it sounded like a significant electrical project taking place beneath me: a high-pitched sound, evoking the image of crabs wielding dental drills. My mind cleared and I closed my eyes and let myself drift. Where would I end up, if I stayed like this? What would the sea decide to do with me? A large body of natural water gangs up on you, without you quite realising it. Waves often look pretty mellow, but when they all get together they're a forceful cult: they can use their collective belief in themselves to do what they want with you. You have to watch out for rivers too, in a not dissimilar way. A river's current isn't always a bodybuilder showing off its pecs; sometimes it's strong in a calm way, but its power is still there. I have felt it sometimes on mellow evenings when I have swum upstream on the River Dart: the sunlight above me is gentle and sensual and the water seems to be bathing lazily in its touch but there are spots where, doing energetic breaststroke, I find myself barely advancing. It's like I'm on a flooded treadmill. All it would take is for someone to turn the treadmill up a notch and who knows where I'd end up?

Over the next ten days I visited the cove – and a couple of others – several times. It was the second summer in succession where doing so had crossed the line separating a hobby from an addiction. Winter had been an interminable, hard-working one for me. I'd waited a long time for summer and wanted to wring every bit of magic I could from it. The previous year I'd taken a few small risks, swam out too far alone. 'STOP BEING A TWAZZOCK WHEN YOU SWIM,' my dad told me. I do listen to him, despite what he thinks. Fortunately, the root of my swimming addiction is less about macho box-ticking and more about an intangible alchemy that happens when you combine exercise and drenching your body in something totally natural: water, yes, but the stuff around water, too. Sand, soil, even insects. The tingling, post-orgasmic feeling afterwards. I can neglect pretty much everything else in favour of it, run away from all the things I'm supposed to do as an adult. If my bank man-ager or the person in charge of my pension – if I actually had a pension – knew about my swimming habits, they'd be dragging me out of the water by the ear. But I was not feeling hugely interested in my future self. I had once been more interested in him, but that hadn't worked out all that well for my present self so, instead, right now I was choosing to be interested in sand and salt and wind and rain and sun and being in all of it as much as possible.

I lean towards sustaining this feeling, even when I am out of the sea. Not Jenny's Cove is a long walk from the nearest parking area, which is part of the reason why it's rarely busy. The walk out of the cove is very steep and climbing it after an energetic swim leaves you dizzy and exhilarated at the summit. My friend Hayley calls it Uterus Valley. You walk up from the sand, through a narrow vagina, and into the uterus. For much of 2017 a fallen log resembling a giant desiccated lizard sprawled in the first part of the uterus. By spring 2018, it was, bafflingly, gone. I can only think it was chopped into bits by someone with an electric saw and used for fires on the beach. As I passed the giant wooden lizard on my way back up the uterus in 2017, I was usually barefoot. Back in April, on the first warm day of the year, I'd exploded out my front door barefoot and almost immediately stood on some sharp broken wood, sustaining several splinters. I managed to get three out with tweezers, a couple worked their way out on their own, but the biggest one lodged firmly in a very painful place, on the nerve between two of my toes, and for a fortnight I could barely walk. After three weeks with barely any improvement I visited my doctor, who located the bit of wood and said he could attempt to cut it out, but it might be messy and make walking even harder for a while. I opted to wait. In the end the piece of wood moved to a less painful place, and gradually, I suppose, just rotted away inside me. Long before then, someone had described me as being 'part tree'. The way I saw it, the splinter just made that part a bit bigger.

I sometimes kid myself that I have accrued some hard-won wisdom in my four decades on the planet and learned from my mistakes, but at other times it's clear that's not true. I have burned my mouth on pizza innumerable times due to being too eager to bite into it, but I still burn my mouth on pizza due to being too eager to bite into it. I have sustained innumerable cuts, splinters and blisters from walking barefoot outside, but I still walk barefoot outside. As I walked out of the top of Not Jenny's Cove for the third time in a week and along a fallopian tube footpath back to my car, I thought about a BBC documentary I'd recently watched celebrating the fiftieth anniversary of the Summer of Love, in which Eric Burdon from The Animals got irrationally angry at the preponderance of hippie girls with dirty feet during the late sixties. If Eric Burdon from The Animals had seen my feet now, he'd have been livid. A lot of people can get livid if you talk about the pleasure of walking barefoot, how it puts you more in touch with the earth and where you come from. They think it is whimsical hippie drivel, but that's probably because they've never tried it and because they live in a reinforced box of steel rage, self-built on a strong foundation of sneering joylessness. This is a problem with a lot of modern attitudes to the pursuit of being in and respecting nature: they're easily written off as mystic nonsense, and in the long term, nature suffers as a result of that. Mystic nonsense does exist, of course – there is no denying that. The fine line between mystic nonsense and bona fide, near-hallucinatory earth-based wonder is one of life's most fascinating tightropes to walk: It's a place where you can learn a lot about yourself, and possibly even make a great double concept LP with an excellent gatefold sleeve design at the same time. The 1960s probably wouldn't have existed without it.

What *was* definitely whimsical drivel was the paragraph of ellipsis-heavy prose on the coconut-flavoured bath and shower gel my parents left in my bathroom after their visit. 'I'm going to a faraway place she said,' began the coconut-flavour bath and shower gel bottle, '. . . just for a while . . . her toes wriggled in the warm sand and a silly seagull laughed and danced in the sweet wind.'

'What on earth did you buy that for?' I asked my mum.

'It's your dad,' she replied. 'He never looks properly at anything he picks off the shelf when he does the shopping.'

I am not into this recent trend of needy bath products cosying up to you and telling you about their day, so I normally prefer an old-fashioned soap bar, but I didn't want to let the coconut bath and shower gel go to waste so after I'd been to Not Jenny's Cove yet again, I lathered up my body with it. Afterwards I inspected my feet and legs. Following four days of swimming and barefoot walking my skin was a latticework of cuts and stings, most of which I'd not noticed when they occurred. On my ankle I saw the entry wound of a long thin creature I'd picked out of it earlier: some kind of sand tick, totally new to me. Above it: two horsefly bites, three flea bites, a few more bites from various small insects. Below all of this, a graffiti of cuts on my feet, which sea salt had already gone some way towards healing. With my body all clean and fresh, it would have been ridiculous to walk straight down to the river and throw myself in and get all dirty again, so I walked straight down to the river and threw myself in and got all dirty again.

I tried to learn from the technique of teenagers I watched jump into a deep patch from a high tree, the way they made their bodies sharp and long in order to hit the water with the least impact. I resolved to do the same, from the rocks next to my favourite pool on the moor, tomorrow. I swam alongside an Egyptian goose, up to a weir, keeping exact pace with it. I walked home barefoot, following the river south as the sun dipped behind the trees on the opposite bank. I shivered a bit and bumped into my friend Emily on the way. She told me that when her Scottish gran would see her or her brothers shivering after swimming she'd give them what she called a 'shivery biscuit'.

'What's one of those?' I asked.

'It's a biscuit, for when you're shivery,' Emily said.

I had entered a new kind of swimming addict's waking dream state. A swirling, multicolour tunnel of swim, never quite ceasing. The way my skin felt from the water was electrifying and, as the sun got hotter, I wanted more. Each night I would go to bed physically exhausted, thinking, 'OK, that's enough. Give your body a rest tomorrow. You must get back to work.' Each morning I would wake up, see more great weather, and ask myself, 'OK, what shall I do now?' then answer, 'I know: let's go swimming!' Sometimes I swam in other coves, including a couple of hard-to-reach inlets in Cornwall, where the sea was greener. My hair felt different after swimming in these to the way it did after swimming in Not Jenny's Cove: greener, somehow. My seventh day of swimming was the hottest yet. I returned to Not Jenny's Cove and, as I swam, I thought about how the vastness of the sea is so ominous, but also how the same vastness can serve to dilute danger in our minds. I'm fairly relaxed about having most crawling or slimy or tentacled or pincered creatures near or even on my body but, at the same time, when I swim in the sea there's a delusion at work. My mum and dad found the catshark close to here, which meant there was a good chance at least one catshark lurked beneath me right now, as I swam, but when I swim I am never thinking 'I bet there are several catsharks here, right next to me'. It's the same kind of delusion that lets us block out suffering – of people, of animals. There is just so much of it. If we thought about all of it, we couldn't live. The size of the world dilutes it, enabling us to cope. That caterpillar I moved from the coastal path was another example. 'But why bother?' you might say. 'What about all the other caterpillars on the coastal path this week that you can't save, that people will probably tread on? What about all the insects you've trodden on without realising?' And you'd be right. But I don't think that's a reason not to bother. You should still be as nice as possible to insects. You should still go to the polling station and vote. Your tiny part of the ocean, or the drop you make in it as you opt out, counts.

Spending a lot of time in the sea has also made me much more aware of the damage we are doing to it. By saying this, I am not saying I swim in the sea and see fragments of plastic floating all around me; I am saying that if you're submerged in the sea frequently, you get a greater awareness of its importance – how much more important it is than you – and that makes you think about the vast ways in which we have abused it, just to make our lives fractionally more convenient. A bin isn't a magic portal that makes rubbish vanish forever, as many of us seemed to believe it was for much of the twentieth century. I had become conscientious about recycling before I swam a lot; now I'm pedantic about it. I avoid plastic where I can, would like to work towards avoiding it totally, and I have a metal water canister that I take everywhere. We can't be perfect, and so much terrifying, unrepairable damage is already done, but we can try so much harder than we have been doing for the last several decades. Not long after dawn on a Saturday morning earlier in 2017, I had arrived at the Thurlestone Sands Beach, ten miles west of Not Jenny's Cove, and began – with the help of two people named Penny, and nobody else – to clean the beach. I felt that the Penny who was in charge had given me, herself and the Penny who wasn't in charge a very easy beach to clean. Was there even any litter on it? As I began to venture out with my litter picker and old empty compost bag, however, I gradually began to attune my eyes to all the tiny fragments of plastic, the countless bottle bits and bottle tops and strips of crisp packet, to distinguish corporate detritus from seaweed. It felt like gradually peeling back a layer of faux reality. It made me, too, more conscious of the seaweed itself: the myriad different types that you originally thought merely two or three. By the end, we had filled five entire sacks to the brim with litter. And I had

decided, as I always do, but even more than ever, that anyone who bags up their dog's shit then abandons it in any part of the countryside, coastal or inland, should be fitted with some kind of electronic ankle tag that prevents them from ever going anywhere even vaguely attractive ever again.

Of course, our brains aren't designed to take it all in: the world's rubbish, the world's danger, the world's suffering. Our vision of our environment isn't clear, and that's a survival technique. But it also stops us seeing a lot of magic, right in front of us. In *The Doors of Perception*, his famous 1954 essay about mind-altering drugs, Aldous Huxley talks about the interfering neurotic within us – the one Huxley left behind when he sampled mescaline and began to see through the door in the wall. I'm far from the first to note that there's something very narcotic, very trance-like, about swimming – not just in the deep liquid calm of the act itself, but in what it enables you to see in a wider sense. Since swimming a lot – since not just swimming, but pushing myself as a swimmer, through that door where swimming becomes harder then much easier – I have felt like some Vaseline has been wiped off my lens. There is so much that I see in a more honest, present way than I did before: my own weaknesses and strengths, the true obscured agendas – positive and negative – behind my own behaviour and the behaviour of others, the distinction between how I want to spend my time and how some intangible societal pressure has made me think I want to spend my time. The wonder of a wild acrobatic bird feasting on some seed you put out for it two minutes earlier. The undersong of woodland on a bright spring day. Music.

'I swam two lengths of the sea today,' I would often say, on returning from the cove. I tried to be thorough each time and make sure I touched the rocks at each end. I like breaking rules but I hate cheating. On that last day of addictive swimming in 2017 – a period when swimming took on a new narcotic meaning for me, a period I would repeat in the summer of 2018, even more addictively – I swam four lengths of the sea. It was only as I got out onto the shingle and my knees buckled beneath me that I truly registered how tired I was. This little dream period could not last. I'd already pushed my luck. The weather was expected to break soon. Tomorrow I needed to become a responsible adult again. When I got home my friend Charlie got in touch to say she had tomorrow off work and fancied getting the train down to Devon from Bristol and going swimming. I told her in no uncertain terms I had to have a day of writing and catching up on jobs and couldn't join her. An hour later I sent her a second message. 'Fuck it,' it said. 'Let's swim!'

After my hectic social period, I'd had the period of solitude I needed. The one time I had not been alone during my swims was at Talland Bay in Cornwall when a muscular, heavily tattooed holidaying man from Frome had followed me out over the rocks in my attempt to reach a small remote cove that had been rendered even more remote due to the closure of part of the coast path. We hurdled and climbed stone together for half a mile, until we reached a sheer twenty-foot wall of slate and I let him go on alone, swimming into an inlet – gazpacho to the cloudy lemonade of Not Jenny's Cove – and watching as he waved and cheered to me from a distant pinnacle, having reached his destination. Besides that, I'd been largely alone for a whole week. 'Yes, I've done a lot of swimming, but I haven't done any social swimming, and I deserve that,' I told myself. You can argue a case for how deserving you are of any treat, if you approach it from the right angle.

I picked Charlie up from the train station in the later part of the morning and we drove to the moor, walking several miles through orange- and green-speckled woodland and swimming in two natural pools. We leapt off high rocks, javelin-style, and, in order to get photographs of us doing this from the best angle, I waded across the river with the water at chest height, balancing on slimy rocks and holding my camera precariously aloft. We walked back to the car with tingling skin, chatting relentlessly. I noticed how open our conversation was, inadvertently so. It was as if the water had varnished us in truth. The door in the wall was wide open.

Afterwards, at home, I glanced down at my right leg and noticed a tick feasting on my blood, just above my knee. I was going to try to remove it myself with tweezers but it was in quite an awkward spot and Charlie suggested it might be more sensible to let a doctor do the job. I decided she was right, remembering the night at the end of the previous summer, after a moorland adventure, when I'd woken up in pain and found a much larger, angrier purple tick in the back of my knee. I'd attempted to get that tick out but had left the head in, ultimately requiring the nurse at my local GP's to hack into the back of my leg and make a fair mess of it in a procedure that lasted twenty minutes or more. It was more painful than another tick a nurse had once removed from my nipple, but only by a slim margin.

The doctor's surgery was closed but Charlie and I headed to the minor injury unit at the nearby Community Hospital, in the bathroom of which I located six more ticks, on various other parts of my lower body. The receptionist told me there'd been a lot of it going on today. Charlie, by contrast, had zero ticks. The doctor, perhaps due to recently having removed so many ticks attached to other buffoons who walked around Dartmoor in swimming trunks, was short-tempered. I'd estimate he was about four years my junior but he talked to me as if I were a naughty child who had spent too long outside playing – which, in a way, was exactly what I was. As he teased arachnids out of my thighs, ankles and right buttock with a small plastic implement, I tried to lighten the atmosphere by asking questions about ticks. 'Are they easier to get out when they're a bit bigger than this?' I began to ask, but he cut me off after three words. 'Are they easier WHAT? Are they easier WHAT?' he said. I thought fondly back to the time when I was young, my body wasn't riddled with parasites and I perceived doctors as kind, reassuring figures who didn't hate me. He calmed down once he'd killed the final tick and told me about his visits to the vet with his cat and his wife, whenever his cat picked up a tick, which the doctor said was the only time they ever argued. I assumed he meant the only time he and his wife argued, not the only time he and his cat argued. 'But we get it done, and then – hey presto! – happy marriage again,' he said. I watched the doctor's tick-removal technique quite carefully and he gave me a tick remover as a going home present, which meant that when at around 8 p.m. I found one extra tick attached to my left testicle, I could remove it myself with a fair amount of precision. By this point Charlie – mercifully for her – had left.

Earlier that day, I'd said something on the Internet about insects, asking people to be kind to them. When I'd said it I'd arrogantly imagined insects looking at it and thinking, 'Look at this guy. I like him. He is cool. He's on our side.' But that probably wasn't true. Insects probably viewed my statement in the same way as I'd viewed the bottle of needy coconut bath gel. They didn't need anyone cosying up to them and trying to be their friend; they just wanted to get on with the practical business of the day. Thinking ahead to the next few days when I would be checking thoroughly for signs of Lyme disease, I reminded myself not to patronise insects in the future. But it felt nice to be tick-free and have a body that, while far from perfect, was tanned and strong from all the sun and exercise. Officially you're not supposed to be aware of your body when you are a man but I have noticed that all the times I've been most aware of my body have been when it has felt nicest to live inside.

I stood barefoot on the lawn, on this final evening of astonishing weather, in the failing light. The grass needed a cut and was getting a little damp under my toes. I felt very conscious of it, very much inside myself and inside summer, 2017, rather than anywhere else. I could still sense the wood inside my foot, but not in a majorly problematic way. I considered checking on the catshark but instead decided to trust that smaller creatures were doing their job on it and didn't need any extra supervision. It was bio-degradable, despite certain signs otherwise. It made me think for the first time in years of another sea creature: a large plaice someone had mysteriously left on the side of the A6002 in Nottingham, in 1989, not far from Bilbor-ough College – which, as anyone who has visited the area would no doubt agree, is no place for a big fish to hang out, dead or alive. There was a drought that summer and, in the ever-increasing heat, the plaice gave off such a stink that it would make my dad and I squint as we drove past it at fifty miles per hour with the windows open. 'THAT FOOKIN' PLAICE IS STILL THERE,' my dad would tell my mum, when we got home. We must have driven past it six times a week for three months and, each time, it got an infinitesimal bit smaller, but it was an amazingly resilient plaice: the deceased fish equivalent of Bruce Springsteen playing one of his concerts. 'This is crazy,' you'd think, seeing it again. 'Just how long can this fish keep going? Its stamina is amazing.' Then it would keep going some more, its reek not diminishing. Greyer each day, it clung on fiercely to the tarmac. Then, finally, the rain came, and it was gone, its final fragments dispersed into the huge world.

NEARLY NORTHERN

(2017–18)

'Where are you from?' said my mum. The two of us were talking about the North, as a concept, but also as a weather system and a place where people can sometimes live, out of choice. We'd been remembering the time during the 1980s when she and my dad and I and their friends Malcolm and Cheryl went on holiday to Dentdale in Cumbria and the bedsheets in the cottage where we stayed developed icicles and one night everyone watched my head slowly descend until I fell asleep with my face in my dinner, which happened because I was so tired from walking so far through the snow during the day. Even after all these years I could visualise how cold it was during that holiday, a cold that made you have to try really hard not to cry when you were six – and probably also when you were thirty-one – and these recollections reminded me that the North is a place suited to people with wintry skin and bones, whereas I am biologically constructed to be at my best in regions where lizards are at theirs. But I had also told my mum that I sometimes fancied living in the North since – with exceptions, of course, just as there are exceptions everywhere – I thought of it as friendly, and a bit like home, even though I had only lived in the proper bit of it once, many years ago, for a few months, in York, which many might not regard as hardcore northern living. There was so much of the North I was yet to explore, I said, and I also sometimes felt a desire to be back closer to where I was from. Which was what prompted my mum to ask where I was from.

My mum knows very well where I'm from, since she played a not insignificant part in making me from there, but I could see what she was prodding at. I have got around a bit, so maybe the truth is that I am from lots of places now. I am also not originally from a Place in the same way that my mum, a true northerner, is from a Place. Where I *am* from, if we are talking about the first two decades of my life, is an Almost Place: not the middle of the Middle, but the end of the Middle, not even conspicuous for its middleness. For people who live in southern Britain, the distinction might not be important; for me, or people from just north of where I'm from, it's crucial. All my mum and dad had to do in 1975 was buy a house twenty miles farther up the country's oesophagus, in an area that really didn't look all that different to ours, with a similarly large quota of pebble-dash terraces, spoil heaps, chip shops and miners' welfares, and it would all be so much more clear-cut. I don't quite feel like a card-carrying Midlander but if I claimed to be a north-erner to, say, my Sheffield friends, who live not much more than half an hour north of where I went to school, they'd laugh me out of the room. It's the same place, but it's also not. If you listen closely you can hear signs of it in my accent, such as the fact that it sounds like nails scraping on the walls of Yorkshire, asking to be let in. It's been softened a lot, sanded down by years of living in East Anglia and the South West, years of living with and around southerners, but it's still very much there. Posh people from anywhere south of Birmingham think I sound northern. Non-posh people from anywhere north of that think I don't. It's all part of the confusion of being from the End Of The Middle. It's also an aspect of the larger complexity of life on a small island where, won-derfully, you can drive ten minutes up a road and hear voices that sound like they're from a whole different bio-sphere. We joke about accents in Britain but they are a more heated topic than we admit. When we discuss them, we discover that we are essentially still the people we were two centuries ago, locked proudly into the culture of our own village and rarely leaving it.

I know what I used to sound like. I can have a listen and remind myself if I want, since what I used to sound like is preserved on a VHS tape recorded when I was six-teen. There is nothing more illustrative of the softening of my accent to me than meeting up with the Nottingham friends I still know from that period, who back then ripped the piss because I sounded 'Yorkshire' and 'like a farmer' to their ears, and realising that in the two decades I've been away someone has flipped the picture: to me, they are now the ones with the coal and strong milky tea in their voices. But there is a difference: their accents are undiluted Nottingham; mine is North Nottinghamshire, made less gritty by my time away. It's a disused colliery where grass and four or five trees have grown, masking the iron ore underneath. It also retains just the faintest hint of passive Merseyside, owing to the fact that it's where most of my blood relatives – my mum's side of the family – are from. My dad's accent is stronger than mine but it's a few miles more southern, more Nottingham, less North Nottinghamshire–Derbyshire border, more factory, less pit. Growing up, as he greeted me with phrases such as 'ALL RIGHT, YOTH?' and 'AYE LET'S 'AVE A GLEG', I was barely aware he had any accent at all. That's what will happen when you live in the End Of The Middle, and manage to reach your nineteenth birthday without meeting an upper middle-class, university-educated person from southern England. To me, Nottingham *was* the refined southern accent in my immediate life, with the exception of perhaps Leicester, but Leicester didn't really count, as it was way down south, over forty miles away, and you only went there on special occasions.

By my mid-twenties, I was obviously still sounding comically common and upcountry to some of the privately educated newspaper editors I was working for. "Ey up, Tum!' one would say in a slightly off parody of a Nearly Northern accent when he answered the phone to me: a joke that, if only to his ears, never got old. Prior to nervously recording a segment for an arts show on the

BBC, I was given an elocution lesson so listeners would find it easier to understand me. After the show was broadcast, I was told the presenter thought me a 'new and different voice'. What he meant, I now realise, is that unlike most of the other people who appeared on the show, I sounded a bit working class and northern in a hard-to-pinpoint way. I have never consciously tried to alter my accent and it makes me a little sad to think that when I was younger and less sure of myself any of these experiences might have had any insidious impact on the way I spoke. Ultimately, I don't feel that the old, missing parts of my accent have vanished; it's more that they're just napping. It usually only takes a couple of drinks, or time spent with people from my homeland, to wake them up.

Even before I moved from Devon to the Peak District in December, 2017, I could already feel my accent rush-ing back, doing a happy jig in my larynx at the know-ledge that it might soon be free again. I have no doubt that if I'd decided to stay in the Peak long term, it would have returned unabashed, perhaps even gaining a new overcoat in the process. I'd been in a year-long period of fixating on the Nearly North and its borderlands, com-ing up from Devon to see my mum and dad on the Nottinghamshire–Lincolnshire border, then driving an hour west, walking the dales and gritstone plateaus and twitchels and ginnels and jitties of Derbyshire, finding little old pieces of myself in them, turning the pieces over, staring at them with a gormless look on my face, then realising they fitted the gaps in a jigsaw I'd neglected. The places – Matlock, Wirksworth, Birchover, Nether

Haddon – were like a pile of good thick cable-knit jumpers you thought you'd only dreamed were yours then woke up and, assisted by bright daylight, found at the bottom of an old box. I lingered in bookshops and cafes, bathing in the exchanges of strangers: sometimes the words, always the sounds. These places weren't home. But where exactly was 'home'? There'd been so many, now. The definition of the word had splintered. Home – by the 'house where your parents live' definition – was a wonderful place but it wasn't a building where I'd ever been a resident. Home – by the 'house where you lived for the longest period during your childhood' definition – now had strangers living in it and some tyres and a rusty sink in the front garden. These north Derbyshire towns and villages I was passing through on my walking expeditions were not places where I'd ever lived, just places half an hour away from places I'd lived; places where I used to go with my family a lot. Yet the people who lived in them sounded like the people from my childhood. In fact, they sounded even more like them, as if 'home' had been turned up to eleven, so maybe that meant these places really were home. As you moved up the map, they were also the first towns and villages that could make the claim to being genuinely part of the North, so perhaps, I reasoned, that made me genuinely part of it too.

Accents never wrestle you to the ground in the South; they flick their expensive paint on you very subtly, until finally you're dappled with a thin spray of it. But a northern accent will openly smother you, pin you down and make you part of its cult. I can see now that the north Derbyshire accent was a big part of my move to the Peak

District. I was sucked in and seduced by it, entirely comfortable about the prospect of it freely having its way with me. It was an extra current beneath the main impetus for my relocation, which was that I had got the curious, unshakeable idea into my head that the region could write my next book for me. The period when my parents and I did most of our walking in Derbyshire, the period when we crossed the unofficial threshold between The End Of The Middle and the Early North, every school holiday or bank holiday or weekend, was the point in my life when I was most obsessed with ghosts. Ghost stories – those I'd read, and those I made up – were the central way I kept myself amused on our walks. I associated rural Derbyshire – particularly the winter version, with its thick fogs, lonely barns and rain-lashed stone crosses – indelibly with the supernatural, could not look at its gritstone ruins and possibly imagine that there weren't dead people moving silently within them. Now, writing my first collection of eerie fiction, it seemed only correct that I should be in the same place, letting its ambience wash over me: nearly ghost stories from the Nearly North. Stories set in many more regions than just the Peak District, but which had the Peak District drizzled all over them, from winter's highest height. I liked the idea that a place could infuse a work of art, be somehow preserved inside it forever. I thought of certain records I loved where, deep in the grooves, you could hear the actual buildings where they were made. I had no guarantee that I'd be able to achieve a similar effect in a book, or, even if I did, that anyone would notice, but I was determined to give it my best try. I would find a very north Derbyshire spot, a rugged and old and high place, where the distant, harsh past was touchable, take my pets and possessions there, and I would write, and see what happened. Not once did I let the financially damaging aspect of the move become a deterrent. Not once did I let myself become worried or nervous or calculating about it. I was excited, in a way you can only be when you are doing something you have wanted to do since you were seven.

I'm old enough to remember a time when house hunting was a dark art: to find what you were looking for involved talking to real living strangers, making manual trips into the unknown, calling on indefinable earth magic. These days the Internet has changed all that, and you can tailor a house search to your precise specifications at the push of a couple of buttons. By using the special Plague Filter function on the popular RightMove site, for example, I was able to find a house to rent on the outer edge of Derbyshire's most renowned plague village, Eyam, in the last miles of the White Peak before the Dark Peak takes over. The village was familiar to me from a couple of childhood weekends, but not so familiar that it would not feel like a new adventure. I knew a little of its dark history, but not a lot. In 1665, a box of infected clothes had arrived in Eyam from London. Within a year, four-fifths of the village's population were dead. Famously, the village's pastor, William Mompesson, gathered Eyam's residents and kept them contained and isolated from the rest of the world, so as not to spread the disease to the surrounding north Derbyshire and south Yorkshire villages and towns. These villages and towns did not always display a fitting gratitude. Even as the seventeenth century breathed its last breaths, long after the plague had passed, people suspected of being from Eyam who visited Sheffield were frequently pelted with stones and rough sticks until they retreated beyond the city's borders.

Eyam is a tourist trap in the summer months, and could even be described as a little chocolate boxy, in a no-nonsense Derbyshire gritstone way, but in December it feels high and half-deserted and ice-scolded, swirling in cold clouds of its bedevilled past, harassed by sideways snow and sleet: a spectral place clinging fiercely to the side of Eyam Edge, the even more towering summit above it, as if in perpetual fear of being blown off. The village's vertiginous fringes are zigzagged by treacherous frost-slick roads. The sounds as I walked the streets during a weekday afternoon would typically be nothing more than a lone slamming van door, the broken-toothed whistle of the Pennine wind, and – just to make me feel entirely, rather than just slightly, like I was in a low-budget horror film from 1974 – the shouts and songs of children from the primary school, which borders a churchyard of incongruous, metropolitan size. Here, legendarily, in a big hat, walks the ghost of Reverend Mompesson's wife Catherine, who chose to stay with her husband through the plague period but, unlike him, did not manage to escape the deadly virus.

There are monuments to seventeenth-century suffering all over the village, but on a midwinter's day none speak more powerfully of Eyam's hardship than the Riley Graves, the resting place of seven members of the Hancock family, out beyond a landslip on a hillside on the edge of town, near the out-of-use road to Grindleford. It was on this side of the hill, in the space of eight days in the Devil's Year, 1666, that, without assistance, an Eyam resident named Elizabeth Hancock buried her husband and her six children. Any comprehensive book on Derbyshire's history will speak of the overwhelming desolation and loneliness of the spot: the total lack of visible buildings, the solitary nearby ash tree, the huge and fierce view south beyond it, including the claustrophobic limestone wall of Middleton Dale and – on many days at this time of year – a daunting Satanic fog hanging over Curbar Edge. To offer a little perspective, the house I found was about 500 feet above that, in the less bustling bit of town. To the average visitor, the Riley Graves look like the corner of the hill at the End Of The Universe. To me, they would soon feel like the point where suburbia began.

In my house hunting, I had not been looking for a soft place and did not baulk at the prospect of isolation, but timing played a large part in my decision to rent a house as outlying as the one I did. Another, smaller and more practical place I'd been heading to see the same day, a few miles south, on a slightly less fearsome hill, had been snapped up twenty minutes before my viewing. The day had been the last mild one of autumn. Prior to being shown my house I walked nine miles on the opposite side of the Derwent, stripping down to my t-shirt and more or less skipping up to the top of Froggatt Edge and Curbar Edge, observing the wind gently agitating the pools in the rocks. As somebody who had spent a lot of time here between the ages of zero and fifteen, I logically knew this place wasn't Devon. It was more vast and vertiginous and there was no sea and it had a different smell: wood-smoky, like Devon, but tinged with manure and mournful old stone and a hint of Victorian industry. But, perhaps lulled by the cragginess and the unseasonably mellow weather and the similarities of the nearby River Derwent to the River Dart, and those Dartmooresque faerie pools in the rocks, some part of me believed I was about to bring more of Devon north with me than I feasibly could. It was a classic mover mistake: the blithe assumption that your new house would offer new benefits in addition to, rather than instead of, all the benefits you took for granted at your previous house. On that day, my head was full of the general scenery, the feeling that I was coming back to Almost Home, and the startling and pleasing revelation that Almost Home was *quite a wild and rugged place*. I gave comparatively little thought to the house itself. What I took in about the building was little more than the basic pluses that it had the gravitas of age (Victorian, late), light (the windows matched the scale of the scenery), character (once, it had been part of a farmhouse), a rent I could afford and was situated down a rutted track, a long way from anywhere. Clearly you couldn't mess around when you found a place like this, around here. 'I'll take it!' I said, six minutes after I walked through the front door. But I was still operating on Devon Rules, and one of the most important Devon Rules is Always Live Up A Hill So Your House Doesn't Get Flooded. But in the Peak District, in winter, Up A Hill can be the difficult place to live. Up A Hill is where it snows. Particularly if you move Up A Hill during the cruellest winter for over a decade.

If you pitched the events around my move to Derbyshire as the beginning of a horror film, it might be rejected for being overdone, too full of well-known haunted house tropes and rural life pitfalls. You have the central character, driving almost 300 miles through heavy snow, alone, in a fatigued and dented car, every possible inch of its interior stuffed with possessions and cats. He sniffs, and we see from the red around his eyes that he has a heavy cold. The car gives the impression of containing many hundreds of cats but in truth there are three and one is merely a kitten, more white than black, a recent addition and somewhat symbolic of the new start. Between Lickey End and Alvechurch, she vomits copiously. We cut back to a couple of weeks before the move, with the central character boasting about how impervious he is to fear in remote, unpopulated places, even at night. They're not what really scares him, he tells friends. What really scares him is filling in forms, the prospect of losing a loved one, or the idea that he might have inadvertently said something that hurt someone's feelings in a conversation seven years ago. Dark hills, smudgy figures on heathery bluffs, lonely forests with ice cracking in the branches above: he is not a victim of the terror more suburban humans find in these things. By Tamworth, the snow is heavier, so he reroutes east to near Ollerton where his parents live, and where he and the cats, who are called Roscoe, Clifton (the kitten) and Ralph, opt to spend the night. 'It was weird: last night I kept thinking I could hear someone crying "Help!" somewhere in the house,' says his mum, the next morning. 'That was Ralph, meowing his own name,' he replies. 'I WENT TO THE HARDWARE SHOP FOR A SCREWDRIVER THE OTHER DAY, AND THEY WERE SELLING SEX TOYS,' his dad says. OK, we can actually cut the bit near Ollerton with his parents. It's not integral to the plot. When the central character arrives in High Derbyshire the next day, a genuine blizzard is raging. He is lucky to get the car up the narrow lane to the top of the hill, above the village, which in Victorian guidebooks is known as 'the mountain village', even though the desolate plateau above it needs another 500 feet to fit the official UK government criteria for mountain status. From the top of the hill, the car slips and slides along the rutted track to the house, a looming, sooty looking building with something of the tomb about it. The camera pans in on a row of wool strips caught on some barbed wire, being stretched taut by the wind, and, behind it, four cold sheep who appear to harbour secrets in their cheeks. The man steps out of the car and immediately slips on the ice, narrowly keeping his balance by holding on to the rear windscreen wiper of his car, which snaps. The camera zooms in on a freaky-looking owl sign, next to the house's name. We see the man look at it and mouth the words 'Holy shit.'

For my first two nights in the house, the blizzard did not let up. Exhausted from weeks of packing and downsizing and lifting and driving on the first night, I collapsed on a bed of shirt and knitwear maelstrom at around 8 p.m. and fell instantly asleep. I woke again not long before

11 p.m., to the sound of Clifton making a mournful wibbling sound. I got up to check Clifton was OK. I found her, and my other two cats, in the kitchen, looking a little alarmed. All of them were silent. The mournful wibbling noise, however, continued. I sat awake for over two hours on the staircase, tracking the noise as it moved around the house, occasionally harmonising with the other chilling noises in and around the rooms: the whump-whump of the wind passing through the cooker extractor hood, the eerie tinkle of the resetting thermostat and the snow driving against the thick walls. So, so much snow. I pictured the bumpy, half-mile track leading up to the main road, getting more and more covered with it. Would I ever make it up it again? I made mental calculations about how long the small amount of food in my freezer and cupboards – some of it quite old – would last. Did a whole can of kidney beans from 2013 count as a meal?

Being cut off in my first days in Eyam, with a cold, was entirely appropriate, as being ill and cut off were the two things Eyam was historically best known for. It was an ideal situation, I assured myself. I was sick of car travel anyway. I was here to explore in the way that was most ancient and natural: on foot. I walked past the lonely well named after Reverend Mompesson, which sits below a row of stripped banshee trees and where a ghost child of a blue hue clad in seventeenth-century clothes has frequently been spotted, then skidded and shuffled down the ravine beyond it. More ravenous than I'd been for half a decade, I ate enormous lunches at the cafes in two of the nearest villages. I couldn't tell if all the portions were enormous here, or the owners thought I looked like I needed filling up, or the lack of trade in the bad weather meant they just had excess food. Possibly a bit of all three. After I'd paid, I told the waitress at one cafe that I'd just moved in up the top, where the snow was thickest. 'You should have said!' she replied. 'Locals get discount and a bit extra free.' My route took me past the Boundary Stone, an indented boulder marking the midpoint between Eyam and the neighbouring village of Stoney Middleton where coins – soaked in vinegar, as a rudimentary attempt at disinfection – were left by plague victims as payment for food from outsiders. Once, centuries ago, two lovers – Emmott Syddal from Eyam and Rowland Torre from Stoney – would meet here, just to stand at a safe distance and stare longingly at one another, until April 1666, when Emmott stopped arriving, forever. Two ruins are visible on the hill on either side of the footpath behind the boundary marker: buildings hundreds of yards from any road, long unoccupied, stuffed with colourless weeds and misery. I thought about the pain Emmott and Rowland might have felt on the days when they came to the spot, the aching space between them. It was easy to believe that aching space was still there: a patch of invisible three-and-a-half-century-old air too heavy with sadness to ever be blown away, even by the strongest Pennine gales. The whole ridge had a bad romantic history. A century later, another heartbroken woman, Hannah Baddaley, leapt off the rocks on the other side of it into Middleton Dale, after being jilted by her lover; but she was not even able to find the sweet release of death, since her petticoats spread out and acted as a parachute, transporting her safely to the ground.

Nearly all the villages and landmarks around here sounded like session guitarists in progressive blues bands. As well as the lanky Stoney Middleton, who was in high demand everywhere from Hastings to Aberdeen from 1969 to 1973 but suffered from cocaine bloat during the latter part of the decade, there was his nemesis Froggatt Edge, who sat in with Fleetwood Mac on occasion just after Peter Green left the band. To this day he remained on decent speaking terms with Hathersage Booths, despite stealing his wife in 1978. And who could forget Wardlow Mires, whose guitar genius was suffocated by eighties show-off slickness, and who still appears on the occasional rockumentary, speaking in an inexplicable transatlantic accent? Usually, before heading home, I would stop at the Spar in Calver for beer and pickled onion Space Raiders, then, to cover as much new ground as possible, loop back along the other side of the Derwent; sometimes, if there was enough daylight left, climbing Froggatt Edge, before hitting the edge of Grindleford, whose lone 1969 album will now fetch over £300 on eBay or Discogs, if you have the original pressing of it with the black ice rim.

The Derwent looked deathly cold and deep, with a malevolent lonely shine, no longer at all mistakable for the Dart. The river's folkloric ghost, Crooker, an obscure branch-handed creature, is thought to feed the water when it is hungry, plucking passing humans from the banks, but letting them pass if they have an offering of wildflowers. But where did you find wildflowers around here? It looked like they could never grow again. Leaving the river's side, I squeezed, snake-hipped, through narrow rocks into fields where the snow was mushier. The Peak District couldn't decide whether it wanted you fat or thin: the cafes and footpaths were at loggerheads about it. One marker rock had a smooth, hare-sized hole in its middle, thus evoking a millstone made by nature, or a giant hag stone. No doubt, like a hag stone, it could potentially serve as protection against evil in the home, but there was no way I was lugging it back up the hill to my mantelpiece. From the summit of Froggatt, I tried to pick out my house's position on the opposite side of the valley, but found it difficult. It was buried in the hill's deep wooded layers, in a place even higher than the place popularly known as The High Place.

Back in the valley I took a deep breath as I started the monumental climb for home. I passed Grindleford's pinfold, and was thankful for the small mercy that I was not a nineteenth-century resident of my house, collecting an escaped sheep or cow from the pinfold, then dragging it back up the hill to its godforsaken pasture. All I was dragging was me and my beer and my pickled onion Space Raiders. The epiphany that I was no longer in Devon redoubled as I reached the quarter point of the ascent, which would have been enough hill in itself for many hilly places. It was not uncommon to see a balletic car glide past, spinning in full serene circles in the big silence. Soon, I would begin to think of this route to the house as The Hill That Never Ends. When it did finally end, you couldn't call what happened relief, because by that point you were in a different, more scoured place, above the snow line, and something primordial and blunt had closed in, rebuffing all notions of comfort. The highest, toughest, least nurturing bits of Dartmoor were no match for it.

During my first weeks in the house, as the mournful, wibbling ghost cat moved within and through the cavities in the walls, the snow licked at the bricks, two pictures fell off the wall and my salt shaker moved four inches across my work surface of its own volition, in my sleep-deprived state I came to a conclusion: all the historical sorrow of this area, all its terrible suffering, had oozed up the gradient and settled within the walls of my house. It invaded my sleep every night. I woke repeatedly at exactly 3.44 a.m. from nightmares which often featured violence being inflicted on me, although the most unsettling of these did not quite involve violence; it involved me walking down an impossibly black corridor, reaching out hopefully for a wall to get my balance, and having my ribs frantically tickled by three fleshless hands. On another night, I dreamed I'd been spooning the cold body of a skinless 300-year-old herbalist. I decided that something very bad had once happened in the house, or in the place where this house now stood, at 3.44 a.m. On the plus side, a story for my new book had written itself, one which I soon realised was a perfect fit for the book's title, *Help the Witch*, which until then had just been a title, not relating to anything specific, simply a phrase and sentiment I liked. I'd been relishing the prospect of making the stories in the book anything but autobiographical, but there was too much going on right here to ignore. There was a lot of the narrator of the story that I decided to make very much *not* me – he was university-educated, academic, not very outdoorsy, born in the south, recently heartbroken – but there was a bit of me, or at least what I was experiencing, in there. On one particularly shaky morning, after a night when the ghost cat, which I had now decided was a ghost dog, had been particularly active, I phoned my editor with a progress report. He made little attempt to disguise a gleeful cackle, and over the hearing snow I thought I heard the sound of skin on skin, like some palms – I'm not definitely saying his – were being frantically rubbed together. What he didn't realise, what he couldn't have realised, because he couldn't see the barrier of dark white outside my window or hear the barn door creaking in the wind, was how genuinely scared I was.

I was starting to believe that I had moved to permanent winter, wondering if, in being what I thought was quite kind to myself as a writer, I had done something unkind to myself as a human. The whiteness of the days always seemed deeply dark and the blackness of the nights was a sharp blade. On rare windless afternoons the tyre swing in the garden still rocked from side to side, as if comforting itself after a traumatic experience. Ralph and Roscoe, who had loved living at our previous house, all but refused to go out, cowered on the stairwell and stared in apparent terror at invisible objects, which they had always done anyway to an extent, being cats, but never anywhere near as much as they did here. The only one of the four of us who appeared unfazed was Clifton. She waltzed out into the snow and trotted along beside me as I observed the ancient Peak District tradition of walking half a mile to the Saxon Cross on top of the hill to check phone messages. From the cross, on a clear day, we could see Chatsworth House, seven miles down the valley, where the Earl of Devonshire had once lived, assisting with provisions for Mompesson and the plague victims. Had the Earl of Devonshire grown complacent and mistaken Derbyshire for Devonshire? Was that why he had ended up here? And when he lived here did he ache for the sea, like I already did, despite having only been away from it for a few weeks?

One day, when Clifton had been gone for many, many hours in some of the worst of the snow and I was

walking up the track looking for her, I bumped into Richard, the farmer who worked for my landlord. I'd earlier asked Richard to look out for Clifton, since it was one of her habits to take a nap in the driver's seat of his tractor when it was not in use. 'Found cat?' he asked, now. I took a dive into Richard's voice every time he spoke. It was a familiar and comforting place to go, in the midst of an awful lot that wasn't. If you were from Kent or Berkshire and you asked someone if they'd located their lost pet by saying 'Found cat?' you'd sound curt and demented, but when you were from Derbyshire there was something rich and earthy in the dispensing of the surplus words in the sentence. Richard didn't even say 't'cat' as some from these parts might. I knew what he meant.

Richard was boyish with an instantly disarming grin, but after over twenty years of farming up here, the snow and rain and wind were scratched into his face. He told me I had come to live in part of a 'shit weather corridor'. The corridor was an extremely specific one: it came down from Bamford and Edale in the north, managing to totally miss Grindleford, yet hit us full on. It was bad, he said, worse than he'd seen it for a while, but it could get a lot worse. A few years ago, in the most devastating February in recent memory, Richard had walked out one morning into the field behind my house and found his sheep huddled against the wall, every one of their lambs frozen to death. Martin, who also helped out on the farm, told me that when Richard talked to you for the first time he liked to check out your hands, in case they were small and you might come in useful at lambing time. By late January, Richard had seen my hands several times but had not asked me to assist him with lambing, which was already beginning to happen. On more days than not, one or two of Richard's sheep – which are Swaledales, and look like the kind of sheep Vikings would keep as dogs, if Vikings still existed and kept sheep as dogs – wandered into my garden, which solved the mystery of what my landlord had meant when he told me I didn't need to worry about the lawn as it 'sort of got cut'. In the blizzards, Richard and Martin checked up on me, bringing me wood, always making me feel welcome. This was in contrast to my landlord, who grumbled about everything, cited the snow as evidence that climate change was a myth, and had refused to give my parents a lift down the track in his four-by-four on my first day, as they dropped in to bring Clifton and Roscoe down to the house, skidding on the ice and having to hang on to the fence not to slip over.

My dad fell in love at first sight with Richard and Martin and, when the snow cleared a bit and he and my mum were able to come and see me, impatiently dashed off to find them in much the same way a ten-year-old might go off to find some mates who were already up the park with a football. 'I'VE MET EVERYONE AND I'VE

GOT LOADS TO TELL YOU,' he announced, after disappearing for an hour on his second visit. 'IF RICHARD COMES OVER WITH A RAM'S SKULL, THAT'S FOR ME.' He was in his element, the central contradiction of his personality – a desire to be far away from humans, coupled with a blatant joy in befriending every one he met, talking their ear off and interrogating them about their entire life story – operating at full throttle. North Derbyshire used to be his favourite place in the whole country, possibly in the entire galaxy, and during my childhood he'd yearned to live in its dark heart in an old building with as little connection to the late twentieth century as possible. Me being here gave him a vicarious thrill. Driving past many of his and my mum's and my grandparents' Derbyshire haunts, he spoke nostalgically and lyrically about the region, while also ticking off fellow drivers for their misdemeanours and filling me in on a book he was reading about the Napoleonic Wars.

'YOUR MUM AND I WENT TO THAT CO-OP JUST AROUND THAT CORNER IN 1974 AND AN OLD MAN WET HIMSELF. IT'S NOT A CO-OP NOW. LOOK AT THOSE SHEEP. BRILL. SEE THAT? NO BLOODY SIGNAL. THAT WAS THE OTHER THING ABOUT NAPOLEON. PUT YOUR LIGHTS ON, YOU IDIOT. HIS SOLDIERS USED TO CUT OPEN THEIR HORSES WHEN IT WAS COLD AND SLEEP INSIDE THEM. THINK YOURSELF LUCKY.'

I told him I thought my new house might be haunted. 'DON'T BE FUCKING RIDICULOUS,' he replied. 'GHOSTS DON'T EXIST. YOU'RE JUST LIKE YOU WERE WHEN YOU WERE EIGHT. GROW UP.'

My mum, who also does not believe in ghosts, was less sure. She would later admit that she'd found the house deeply unsettling. On the first day, while my dad and I had been briefly out and she'd been in the kitchen alone, she had found the weirdly vast amount of space at the top of the room frightening; she'd had to put the radio on, just for the company of everyday voices. She'd investigated the bathroom and discovered that the black paint on its walls had been employed to cover up rampant black mould. Later, I opened the cistern to find more mould, old and viscous, and around two dozen slugs. A man came over to fix the sewer system, owing to the fact that some previous tenants at one of the other two cottages on the farm had sabotaged it by the bizarre act of stuffing multiple kitchen rolls into it, after falling out with the landlord. Next to the black wall, with the black mould underneath it, after long walks I would let hot water blast the snow off my head and stare at the temperature ring on the shower, which was the exact same Mira shower my mum and dad had got installed at their house in 1984. The Mira shower pulled me back into the past, along with some sheep and coal I could hear beginning to return to my accent, and the pile of newspapers in the village shop ready for residents to collect. It all rushed at me, like a strange vision of home, with almost none of home's reassurances.

A calf was born in the barn out the front, the weight-lifter moos of its mother creating a more frantic vibe to the spooky early hours chorus, like an overdub on top of the whump-whump of the wind in the cooker extractor hood, the sleet and snow howling down the Shit Weather

Corridor and the mournful wibbling of the ghost dog. In bed, after waking up at 3.44 a.m. from my nightmares, I listened to weather pelt the front wall of the house. I heard furniture move upstairs in a loft where there was no furniture and no people to move it, and thought about the people who built the house for weather like this, building the house, in weather like this. I did not see a ghost in the house, nor even turn and expect to see one, but I keenly felt a collection of wretched events stored there. Maybe they were stored in that higher part of the rooms my mum had found so disturbing, where there was space for a whole other floor, and which dissuaded me from a long-held belief that all high-ceilinged houses create an atmosphere of lightness and positivity. A plant, a Clivia, that had lived in five previous houses in many different positions – near windows, away from windows – and had always flowered explosively without fail between late January and early February, now decided not to. A set of friends en route to the Proper North visited and, through lightly gritted teeth, told me how lovely the place was. 'We lied,' they would admit later, after I'd moved out. 'It was fucking terrifying.' Another friend visited with his girlfriend. The weather cheered up to all of two degrees, and we were able to get out to a pub a few miles away. As we walked through the door someone thrust a stuffed fox into my friend's girlfriend's face, and a man of seventy-ish immediately moved in our direction, running a hand down her back and slurringly warning her, 'There'll be some inappropriate touching later.' A week later, I revisited the pub and the man was there again, drunkenly rebuking a Welsh singer for singing in her native language, rather than English. 'Who is that bloke?' I asked a regular. 'That's the landlord,' he replied. I walked into my study a few days later and noticed that the wooden fish I own, carved by my uncle Paul, was on the neighbouring window ledge to the one where I'd last seen it. The fish had also changed window ledges just after I'd moved in, and I'd assumed my mum had moved it, for some aesthetic reason known only to her. Something had stopped me from asking my mum if she'd moved the fish. Since I'd last seen the fish, in the second of its three positions, nobody had been in the house but me.

Clifton went missing again, for longer, in more severe snow. I called and called, walked and walked, whistled and whistled in the endless wild ground behind the house, a yawning secret valley all of its own, an extra valley before the official valley, walled in by staircases of dense woodland whose carpets were made impenetrable by scrub and eclectic stone coated in old moss: no place to even begin to find a lost cat. The snow began to drift and by the time she returned I had almost given her up for dead and was already beginning the process of looking for the situation's bright side, telling myself that at least, in her current masticated state in a fox's stomach, she was keeping a starving wild animal alive.

Clifton had not been seeing eye to eye with Roscoe, who was repeatedly chasing her out into the cold, but I doubted that was the only reason for her disappearances. She had a wild streak, barely less wild than the place I'd brought her to. She'd been spotted in countless micro regions around The Hill That Never Ends, up to a mile away, strutting along the drystone wall at the summit near the old fluorspar mine, in tractors and barns, in fields, having her head licked clean by farm dogs eight times her size. Just prior to leaving Devon, I'd adopted her in a weak moment, as a favour to a friend who worked at the local vet surgery, and to myself. I named her Clifton because she looked so similar to a cat I'd met on the Clifton Suspension Bridge in Bristol only a week earlier, and because I was moving to a house overlooking an inland cliff, and because she'd been initially found, as a stray, outside a bookshop run by my friend Cliff. She'd repeatedly run away from her previous home, and I'd thought it had been just due to the situation there, but it seemed a lot of it was just her.

The snow did not appear to trouble her in the slightest, and she often returned home totally white, as opposed to the mostly white she was the rest of the time. So much was white here, in the final furlongs of the White Peak: Clifton, the face of every human I saw, the snow, that dark piercing daylight, the surname of my landlord. When we moved in, Mr White had promised me and my two sets of neighbours that his vehicles would clear the track if it got too snowy to negotiate, but it never happened. There was one other farmhouse half a mile away, but, besides that and our little clutter of buildings, there wasn't another human in residence until you got a mile away and the houses of Eyam, in one direction, and Grindleford, in the other, started to materialise. My adjoining neighbours, Mr White's other tenants, were two middle-aged sisters who'd come here from the edge of Buxton, in the High Peak, but said they were finding the weather conditions very extreme, compared to their previous house. On the other side of them, in the final part of the farmhouse, were a younger couple who'd come to Eyam following a long stint in Norway. Then, across the courtyard, there was Mr White and his wife. By the beginning of March, they'd all be gone – even the ghost dog. All that would be left would be me, two cats, and the snow.

'It's far more complicated than that,' has become a bit of a catchphrase for me in recent times, albeit one I utter more often in my head than aloud. It's something I find myself wanting to say a lot, especially when I see the shouty, unresearched condemnations of the Internet zip by, the back-patting knee-jerk opinion factory of social media. 'It's far more complicated than that' would also be a fitting response to any attempt to neatly sum up why, in early 2018, I found myself alone, near the pinnacle of an almost mountain, snowed in, on the edge of a plague village which was not in one of the four main areas of the country where my friends and family lived. But who isn't guilty of falling into the trap of oversimplification from time to time? We search for easy rules, so life doesn't keep us awake at night with its contradictions, nuances and anomalies. I know, for example, that I have fallen into the trap, at least to an extent, of viewing the United Kingdom as a graph of empathy and meteorological remorselessness, all growing in a northerly direction. But, of course . . . it's far more complicated than that. I knew it was far more complicated than that before I moved to the Peak District, and I knew it more profoundly afterwards. In north Derbyshire I witnessed more racist conversations, more anecdotal accounts of animals being killed for pleasure, than I'd witnessed in two decades of living below the UK's midriff. I witnessed a significantly less hostile climate in the south, it was true, but it wasn't as if it kept getting worse the farther north you went. During the heaviest snow, I'd see real-time photos of North Yorkshire and Cumbria and the Scottish Highlands looking positively Mediterranean by comparison. But, to be fair, that could happen in the valley directly below me, too. Down by the Derwent, the weather was sometimes so different, you wouldn't even know it was white up at the top of The Hill That Never Ends, let alone white enough to make it impossible to leave your house by car. I had somehow managed to pinpoint the exact worst spot for winter weather in the whole of England, then go and live in it, 1,500 feet above reality. 'You won't find a driver who'll take you back up there until March at the earliest,' a taxi driver in Sheffield told me.

Checking the forecast – which was taken from a point 300 feet lower than the house, so always needed to be embellished with an extra crust of ice – became an obsession. If I could safely get out via car to explore, even for a few hours, I was determined to do so. Despite being incontrovertibly snowed in for over 50 per cent of my three and a bit months in Eyam, I covered a lot of ground as a walker in the parts of the county beyond my immediate reach: the drowned stepping stones of Chee Dale; the standing stones of Arbor Low; Wirksworth's Black Rocks with their timeline of lovers' graffiti; the limestone cavities beyond Tideswell; Little John's Grave at Hathersage; Kinder Scout, where I found two conjoined sycamores

resembling a man with branch hands – Crooker himself?
– raging at an unjust universe; the silent fields behind
Monsal Dale, where my friend Sophie and I mooched
around an abandoned cottage full of dead crows and
mice. I escaped to Norfolk to visit friends and my dad,
arriving at my house during another onslaught of snow,
left his car at the top of the track, and sledged down to
feed the cats and spend forty-eight hours shadowing
Richard and his work, gathering firewood in the lost
valley and living his 1980s fantasy life. He enjoyed the
sledge journey so much he went back up to the top a few
more times and zipped down again, for the pure pleasure

of it. In August he would be sixty-nine. That is, if August ever happened.

Spring and summer were barely rumours in Eyam in January and February. Nobody even mentioned them. On a rare day when the God of the Fields, John Barleycorn, peeked one eye out from behind the white curtain, I went walking a few miles away in the Moss Valley with Jim Ghedi. I had met Jim in a pub in Hathersage just before Christmas. He had been hungover, having been drinking the previous night with more than three blacksmiths. He couldn't remember exactly how many blacksmiths but knew it was more than three. Jim is young and tall and never-married, with long, dark, flowing hair, but when he opens his mouth to sing it is as if his body has been taken over by the spirit of a ninety-four-year-old, three-times-divorced miner. He has a singing voice that somehow manages to be rich peat and molten iron at the same time, but he possesses the restraint and confidence in his own musicianship to only use it sparingly. We walked past St John's Church in the village of Ridgeway and he noticed that the poster advertising his upcoming gig there had fallen half-down. I found some Blu-Tack which, having had a long and involved relationship with Blu-Tack, I arrogantly pledged to revive and use to re-affix the poster to the notice board, but it was no use: the Blu-Tack was old and could not be resuscitated. We walked downhill to an abandoned engine room and past a rope-swing Jim had attached to a tree back when he was in his teens. The songs he writes are entrenched in the working life and social history of the Moss Valley, where he has lived for most of his life. He told me about the packhorse mule which would bring tools down the valley from Ridgeway to a waterwheel near here, four times a day, all on its own, from Phoenix Works, a five-and-a-half-century-old scythe and sickle manufacturer that Jim celebrates in a stirring song of the same name.

To get to Jim's from my house you curved around the bottom of the clock face of Greater Sheffield, from ten to eight to quarter past five. It is different terrain: rolling in a bumpy way, a little blasted and rough, but less epic. 'Ordinary, working countryside,' is how Jim described it. Because the Peak District is not 'ordinary, working countryside', I had perhaps been guilty of underestimating it. Due to its National Park status I viewed it marginally as an unreal, themed place, and took its darker side less seriously. Spring was revoked shortly after I saw Jim, and the dark side returned, in all its frightening nude whiteness. I walked outside my front door to call Clifton, who had been driven out again by Roscoe, and I felt a natural hostility to the air unlike anything I'd ever felt around any house I'd ever made my bed in. My heart turned arrhythmic as I took it in. It was as if the night had fangs. The house loomed behind me, like two tall and ashen undertakers. Beyond the old barns I was peering at through the gloom, hoping that Clifton would skip out from a low wall that she sometimes sheltered under, was the lost valley: hundreds of acres of wild ground with no public access owned by my landlord and his wife, scattered with derelict buildings, streams, rocks and jagged remnants of walls whose purpose nobody living remembered. Beyond it: untold numbers of unmarked graves, filled with plague bones – old bones from a different universe, but bones that in fact did their growing only thirteen or fourteen generations ago. Next to a small lake, the tall scarecrow skeletons of last summer's giant hogweed stood strong, despite the snow. Martin told me a previous tenant once swam in the lake and almost froze to death. 'What time of year was that?' I asked. 'July,' he said.

Martin had been working on the farm for decades, and – being a vegetarian, and a thoroughly non-materialistic soul – feeling different to the culture around it for just as long. Unlike my landlord, he took a passionate interest in all the nature in the wild ground behind the farm; that was why he was really here. He often spotted stags down there in the lost valley. Confusing paw prints in the snow had been reported. There were rumours of a large creature, like

a cat, but not quite. It was unmanaged, elemental land: a taste of what will happen when we are all gone. When I was down there, I was astounded by the scale of it all, the way the trees and dead vegetation swallowed you. It pulsated as the sun fell. It was the kind of place where you could die a spectacular death of a morning and no-one would know. Besides Martin and me, nobody went down there apart from the foot hunts my landlord welcomed onto his property. I'd seen the hunters behind the garden, heading up from the lost valley: men with tight, mouth-like eyes. Hunting was part of the fabric here. Not long ago, my landlord's son-in-law had shot a prize stag down in the lost valley. Before I discovered this, I'd said a cheery hello to the son-in-law outside my house. He'd glanced at me, then walked on, wordless. While I sat up in bed in the minutes directly after 3.44 a.m., as the furniture moved in the loft where there wasn't furniture, it seemed that all the wild ground behind the house was breathing, under the ice.

Searching for light relief, I drove south west, just over the Derbyshire border into Staffordshire, to the Manifold Valley. The lightness wasn't as light as I'd hoped but the white was less dark. Thick upland fog. Scraggy, hardcase, shit-caked sheep. Viscous peat. A hint of comfort, knowing that the sea was only fifty-eight miles away, as opposed to seventy-three. Descending in the direction of Thor's Cave, where Bronze Age humans fashioned amber beads and pottery and a few years later a photographer shot the cover for the The Verve's *Storm in Heaven* album, I slipped on limestone and fell on my camera, amazingly breaking neither it nor me. In winter White Peak limestone is a glazed treadmill: it's always being pulled away from you underfoot. A couple of hundred paces farther on I passed through a gate, noting the top section of a freshly, neatly decapitated deer on the path in front of me: a sight that would not leave me for a long time.

When you have come directly from a few years of being a Devon walker, you notice a rhythm to walking in the Peak: you tend to do it on terrain that's either a lot more controlled than any walking terrain in Devon, or a lot more fierce. There's rarely an in-between. Having done an example of the safe, controlled bit down by the rivers Manifold and Hamps, I climbed the valley back in the direction of Grindon, passing king-sized yob crows, and arrived at a farmyard, where I was instructed by my map to take a path running through it to the left. As I did, a man with enormous dark grey sideburns emerged from the farmhouse and barked instructions at me to take a gate on the right-hand side of his garden instead. He complained about the National Park doing him 'no favours' and directing walkers to the place, which was called Oldfield Farm. He introduced himself as Graham Simpson and said there had been Simpsons at the house since the 1740s, when two of his ancestors, Jacobites on the run, had first built it. Its original outdoor privy remained standing. We began to talk about the weather and he told me about the winter of 1947, which was so cold that 'your coat would stand up when you took it off' and a plane flying over to drop supplies to the snow-bound villages in the area crashed. 'I remember listening to it go over – you could hear the ice cracking in the trees,' he said. He looked good for eighty-three and I suspect he had looked truly magnificent at sixty.

Two things Graham said he didn't have much time for were Romans and computers. The way he explained this suggested that the Romans had come along, got a bit too arrogant, messed stuff up, then everything had been all right for a few years until computers had come along to mess everything up all over again. He told me there was a code you could type into a computer now and see inside people's houses, including his. 'People are too far away from the real world nowadays,' he said. We talked for around three quarters of an hour and, thinking suddenly of my dad, I wondered how many times Graham had stopped other hikers and marshalled a similar conversation: these hikers whom the National Park directed across his land in a bothersome way but whom he patently loved to talk to. He wasn't a religious man but believed it to be a travesty than many babies were no longer christened. 'It's like us tagging our cows: you have to do it so you know who they are and where they belong,' he said. I did not tell him of my unchristened status. Was that why I'd had a little trouble deciding where I belonged lately, I wondered. It was a very different life, this one of Graham's staying in one place for so long, just like your dad before you, and his dad, and his dad, and his dad, and his dad, and his dad – and not one I craved, but I could see its pluses.

The fog had lifted, just slightly, and it felt like this

brief fog-raising of an hour or so was a harsh Peak District winter's equivalent of what might count in many other places as proper daytime. Snowdrops were scattered all around, lighting up the world more than anything presently in the sky. 'They're amazing things,' said Graham. 'They'll thrive under snow and ice but if it's warm and dry, they won't grow. You can't tell me that can be explained. That's not just nature. There's something more going on there.' As he said it, he swept with his brush at non-existent debris on his front path and a hen – the only one on his farm – pecked around him.

I asked him what the hen was called.

'Hen,' he said.

Graham, who'd always lived in the south-western corner of the Peak District, sounded easily as northern as an average native of the north-eastern corner of the Peak District. In the UK, accents rise in the west. The process begins long before the North's diagonal, much argued-over border. Birmingham has immeasurably more of an accent than Peterborough, which sits eighty miles east of and very slightly above it, and seems more tethered to the South. People feel comfortable in staking a claim to northernness more quickly on the west side of the country. My house in the Peak District only needed to be another ten miles north to be level with Liverpool, which is west of it, but Liverpool is far more unchallengeably northern, not least because of its accent. I was reminded of this when I drove from my house in Eyam to Liverpool, to perform a spoken word event. The journey was a risk, but my Liverpool events always sold out, and the crowds were the warmest and liveliest I'd ever had, and I didn't want to let anyone down. I'd never lived there but, because I'd grown up close to my mum, her two sisters and my nan, who were all Scousers, it seemed like another home from home. I narrowly made it up the iced track from the house then drove west, going via Snake Pass as the snow worsened. My stomach tangibly descended from my throat back into its rightful place as I saw the lights of Glossop emerge, marking the end of the Pass. The event sold out, two knitters in the front row heckled me and I was glad I'd braved the trip, but on the way back, a few miles past Stockport, with the snow redoubling, my car skidded off the road. I clung to the steering wheel and somehow managed to avoid every obstacle flashing in front of me: the car directly ahead, the car coming the other way, a drystone wall, the small ravine to my right. To this day I have no idea how I made it back onto the road, the rest of the way to Eyam and the top of The Hill That Never Ends and the secret part of it containing my bed. The following day, still a little dazed and glad to be alive, I walked down into the lost valley and took some pretty photos of the white trees and icicles and uploaded them to Instagram. 'It's so beautiful,' commented strangers. 'I hope you know how lucky you are.'

And they were right: I *was* lucky. I was not trapped in my car, down a ravine, bleeding to death, unbeknownst to the traffic above. I was at home, in a house with central heating, and still had a chance to complete my book, and – one day – to dance, to swim, to drink in sun-splashed

beer gardens, to experience relatively pleasant weather
once again. I had my friends Rob and Donna, who drove
over from Sheffield to the plague village and fed me restor-
ative home-made soup. My Achilles tendon was playing up
a bit, from all the snow hiking, but I did not have the
plague. It was not 1666 and I was not covered in buboes
nor confined to one of Eyam's pest houses, slumped
among the newly dead, cough-vomiting and staring
through a tiny mucus-smeared window towards a hillside
where, last week, I'd buried my wife and child. It was
2019 and the earth was doomed but life contained all the
convenience that had assisted in causing its doom.

*

When we escaped Eyam – him for good, me just for a day – both Reverend William Mompesson and I went a little over forty miles east in exactly the same direction. Had we been born in the same era, a stick or chunk of flint hurled by a plague-fearing peasant could have almost hit both of us on the same flight. Mompesson headed to a rectory at Eakring, in Nottinghamshire, where he stayed for a number of years, preaching to a slightly apprehensive new congregation in the village's church. I headed to a house a few fields away from where the restored 1800s incarnation of that very same church still stood, where upon my arrival, like a twenty-first-century, Tupperware-owning Earl of Devonshire, my mum gave me food to take back to the plague village. I loved this red-brick, pantile cottage I had never lived in, which rested easy in this gentle, unshowy corner of the north-east Midlands. It was always full of plants and food and music and art and amphibians and cats. Even more of the latter, now. Roscoe's bullying of Clifton had escalated, and to make her – and my – life easier, my mum and dad had offered, a little reluctantly, to take her in. She seemed to be settling OK, with one exception. Sarah, the friend who worked at the vet surgery in Devon and who'd initially given Clifton to me, had told me she was 'almost certain' Clifton had been spayed, but at Eyam Clifton had started to whine a lot at night and seemed increasingly interested in Ralph, going to various efforts to display her rear end to him. Ralph, who had last known what it was to have balls way back in 2001, had just looked confused, but my mum and dad's solid young cat George and his all-white, toilet-roll-obsessed friend from next door, Casper, were, despite both being sterilised, apparently much more open to her advances. I am not sure how this fitted in with George and Casper's own relationship, which had been very tactile for a long time, but they seemed to have come to an arrangement of some sort.

'George smells brilliant at the moment,' my mum told me. 'It's because he keeps rolling around in the coffee your dad spills on the kitchen floor every morning.'

Outside, I noticed a table had been set to display the three ram skulls my dad had received from Richard. He showed me his new pitchfork and posed with it for a photo in front of the beds where this year's lettuce, courgettes and pumpkins would grow. He pulled an impressive pitchfork face: the face, perhaps, of a person protecting his crop, or a member of a baying peasant mob, fearful of an intruder from a cursed village who he thought might infect him, or blight the season's squashes and alliums, or bring him generic bad luck. 'It's far more complicated than that,' you might have said to the member of the baying peasant mob, but he would not hear you. He had his simple beliefs and would not be swayed from them.

'THIS REMINDS ME OF THE TIME I STABBED ALAN TITCHMARSH IN B&Q,' said my dad.

'You stabbed Alan Titchmarsh in B&Q?' I said.

'ALMOST. IT WAS A LIFE-SIZE CARDBOARD CUT-OUT OF HIM ADVERTISING HIS GARDENING FORKS. I THOUGHT IT WOULD BE FUN TO STAB HIM WITH ONE OF HIS OWN FORKS BUT THEN I THOUGHT I MIGHT GET INTO TROUBLE SO

INSTEAD I WENT RIGHT UP CLOSE TO HIM AND WHISPERED "FUCK OFF, TITCHMARSH" IN HIS EAR.'

We walked back towards the house, past George, who had Clifton's neck locked tenderly in his mouth. 'CHECK THE OIL IN YOUR CAR,' said my dad. 'AREN'T STARLINGS BAD-TEMPERED?'

The garden would be coming to life in a few weeks, flourishing as it always did, save for one small patch, where trees and plants always mysteriously perished: a pear tree, a crab apple tree and a viburnum then two Himalayan birch. Once, many decades ago, pigs had lived and died in the garden. The grandson of the family who'd formerly lived here told my mum he remembered the area where the plants perished as being the same area where the pigs were killed then covered in salt. The theory was that the salt was still deep in the soil, so rife that when the roots of the trees went far enough down, they hit it and began to rot. Some of the trees my parents had planted in healthier patches of soil when they'd first moved here were tall now, which reminded me that this was no longer the new house in a new area that they'd bought a few years after I left home, no longer the two-bedroom wreck they were doing up. Next year would be their twentieth anniversary of living here. The elderly neighbours who'd lived next door to them on either side when they'd bought it were no longer of this universe: part of a whole generation of the village that no longer existed. A young family with an old English sheep-dog had moved into the converted windmill next door.

The old English sheepdog was named Shirley. Two Decembers ago my dad had taken a Christmas card out to deliver to a woman in the village who was also called Shirley, but forgotten to post it and, instead of going back, chosen to deliver it to Shirley the old English sheepdog instead. 'Happy Christmas, Shirley!' said the old English sheepdog's card. 'Love from Jo and Mick.'

Mick was more embedded in his environment than he had been during their first few years here, when the house seemed more Jo's project than his. The footpath which ran directly past the front door, which once might have seemed a potential nuisance, now just provided an extra, happy source of walkers, villagers and tradespeople for him to talk to about their life stories. He no longer spoke, as he had done regularly for my entire childhood and beyond, of how much better life would be in Derbyshire. I wondered if I might have been responsible for giving him a recent nudge a little further along that road. My house on the edge of Eyam reignited an old, dormant part of my dad and excited him with its romance, with its lack of twenty-first-century trappings, but now I'd been there almost three months and he had a fuller understanding of how difficult life was, up there on Witch Mountain in the ice – the dangers of the roads, the endless weather checking, the Achilles tendon injury sustained in the drifts, the huddling in the one warm room, all the tiring contingency plans – and what he and my mum might have let themselves in for had they fulfilled his dream and moved somewhere similar in the eighties. To some people I knew in the South, it was all the same, north Derbyshire, east Nottinghamshire: all just part of the same North or

Almost North, that place where it was grim and bleak and cold. But it was far more complicated than that. I lived closer to my parents than I ever had, in all the semi-itinerant years since I first moved away from them, but our homes had never seemed more like separate planets.

There were even more extreme weather reports that day I first visited Clifton in her new home, so, after I'd witnessed Casper mount her then shred a post-coital toilet roll, and my mum had called the vet, I took advantage of the remaining daylight to set off back to Eyam. Weather forecasters were calling it The Beast from the East. In a frantic and bustling supermarket in Chesterfield, people – people who probably mostly lived on genial urban and suburban streets – were talking about the importance of stocking up. At times like this, you realised how quickly British society would collapse and become totally feral should anything genuinely cause the country's infrastructure to buckle. Chesterfield marked the halfway point between my parents' house and mine. When I'd first moved, seeing the crooked spire of its church had fuzzed me up with warm childhood memories, making me tingle with anticipation me for the moment a few miles farther on where you enter the National Park and the big views open up. Some say the spire twisted with the force of a sneeze from the Devil, as he was passing. Others say he was leaning on it, and bent it after turning in shock to see a woman who'd just been married in the church and realising she was a virgin. The consensus is that, whatever the case, he was travelling from Nottinghamshire at the time.

Coming from the same direction, I began to associate my first glimpse of the spire with the melting away of the levity of my parents' house and garden, the return to the cold, uncharitable place, where an incomprehensibly gargantuan heating bill, handwritten by my landlord for his incomprehensible self-run biomass heating system, was waiting. The Devil was in the sky, and I was on my way back to the plague village – not even the plague village, but the less welcoming place above it – and it was about to snow. Again.

When I edged up to the house in renewed ice, the sisters next door were packing a van. 'It's too bleak for us,' they told me. They, too, could not understand how their heating bill was so high, and planned to dispute it. A few days earlier, the couple who'd come here from Norway had vacated the other cottage. My landlord, I was told, was on holiday abroad. The Clivia still hadn't flowered. I filled the bird feeder for the nuthatches, grabbed myself a warm cat, and stoked up the fire. The snow hadn't quite restarted yet but you could sense the night growing fangs again.

I'd already made my decision, although I wouldn't be able to act on it just yet. I hadn't initially wanted to let myself hear what my gut was telling me, as I didn't want to be knee-jerk about the weather, wanted to give everything a chance, write more of the book, then when I'd written more of the book and stayed in denial for long enough, it had hit me like a deferred realisation about a lost lover: the south-west was the region whose arms I want around me for the foreseeable future. Perhaps the only way to fully realise it had been to leave. I wanted to be back there with all my heart and saw clearly all it had given me. I took a square look at the face of the upheaval it would necessitate, so quickly after the last lot of up-heaval, to get back there, and felt entirely accepting of that upheaval. The only thing that really worried me about moving back to the south-west so quickly was the questions people would ask me about it and how exhausting it would be to explain all the nuances of my decision. 'It's far more complicated than that,' I could already hear myself saying.

But first there was the snow, more of it than ever before. It fell softer against the thick sooty walls than it had on other nights, but I knew something more immense was happening out there in the dark. In the morning, I could barely open the front door. My car was a memory. A small cat, stuck out in that in a lost valley, surely would never have negotiated her way back. Waking up, at 3.44 a.m. from a nightmare where disembodied hands had shot out of the headboard and throttled me, I'd sensed that the gossamer mooring that had been linking the house to civilisation had snapped, and I was floating away. There was no going out, not even on foot. On the plus side, I no longer had a ghost dog, having a fortnight earlier met a small pile of narrowly living hair belonging to the sisters next door: a seventeen-year-old, deaf, dumb, blind terrier of no discernible breed. That is to say, the dog who sounded like a ghost through a thick wall, and possibly soon would be a ghost, had moved out. The furniture in the loft quietened down too, the carved fish remained in position, and only one picture fell off the wall, but as the temperature slipped further below zero, the place – in a slightly wider sense – frightened me more than it ever had. 'Weather is ghosts,' a note in my journal from this period says. The ominous spaces at the top of the rooms became bigger. I had a living room full of records but, unlike almost any other time in my life, didn't want to play any of them. I huddled upstairs in the one warm room, worrying about my heating bill while sitting in bed in a woolly hat, repeatedly pressing refresh on property websites. On the fourth day, I ventured up the track to take the rubbish to the bin – a futile gesture, as the bin men hadn't been able to get up the Hill That Never Ends for over a fortnight – in what, with wind chill, amounted to minus seventeen degrees Celsius. The light had changed. You might have called it piss yellow, if piss had no connection to warmth. It was a colour and light I'd never seen before: totally washed out, stinging everything. *I am the last person left on earth*, I thought. The road remained ungritted. My Achilles tendon injury made me feel like my foot was hanging loose from my ankle. The food ran out the day after that. My dad hero-ically hired a four-by-four to bring me supplies. Then, after going into a fishtail on the ice and spinning back down The Hill That Never Ends, he discovered the four-by-four the hire company had given him wasn't a four-by-four at all. Luckily, a Peak District angel called Matt was passing at the time, in his old Land Rover. Matt trans-ferred the food to the Land Rover, then to me. There was more of it than I could have eaten in a month. I wouldn't have starved without it, but I definitely would have had to dive into at least one tin of out-of-date kidney beans, straight, no chaser.

I continued to press refresh on property websites. The moment meltwater started trickling down the track and as soon as a suitable and affordable house in Devon came up to rent, with a provision for cats in the tenancy contract, I drove 280 miles south. I applied for the house. I got the house – but only because I paid my astronomical, nonsensical heating bill, since Mr White refused to give me a reference unless I did. I was not repaid my deposit on the Eyam house despite me leaving the house in better condition than I'd found it (the slugs lived outside now), nor the extra month's rent I paid when, in my absent-mindedness, I forgot to cancel the standing order going from my account to Mr White's. It did not surprise me. Some people stay well-off for a reason. Other people will never get well-off for many reasons, one of which being that they move house so much. But most importantly, to me, I was free: the state in which I am happiest. A month after I left, I was swimming in the sea. A month after that, I was writing the final sentence of my book of not quite ghost stories in 24-degree heat on a beach. My new house had nothing palpably malevolent in it. The kitchen drawers were sticky, as if they'd been used solely for the storing of loose home-made syrup. One of the exterior doors didn't lock. The shed contained half-finished woodwork, a PlayStation and a scratched Prince record and smelt of sawdust and marijuana. The place oozed its past, like a boy-racer's former car oozes its past. It was all party. The Eyam house had been zero per cent party. I am convinced nobody had ever had a party, or even a good time, there. Maybe somebody laughed, once, but the spirit memory of it had been trounced by the cold, cold atmosphere beneath the watching walls.

Places change us more than we realise: not just their people or culture, but their air. The air in the house on the almost mountain made me uptight, blew away a mellowness the south-west had coated me in that I didn't even know had been there. My hair was different, my skin, the way I breathed. Ghosts? I cannot say for sure. Extreme tiredness and extreme weather can change your perception of your immediate environment a lot. Our interest in ghosts is slightly egotistic. We can't believe we won't be here any more. We want some evidence we will continue, even if it's in tortured, unresting form. The question becomes bigger as you get older. You stand there, this collection of experiences and opinions that's become more complex with every year you've been on the planet. You and your unique accent, stewed in all the places it's been. All that energy. It might not be in your body and mind any more when you die, but it has to go somewhere. Maybe the answer is that it goes into brick and stone, into woodland, valleys, rivers. Maybe it is in the wind, the rain, the snow. I am not a scientist, but I know this: every house, every valley, every copse, every hill speaks in its own particular voice.

There were times in late 2017 and early 2018, on one of the less brutal days, when I would be driving across the Peak District – a notably high, desolate bit – and look up to a ridge, about 500 feet farther above that and think, 'What crazy idiot would choose to live up there in winter?' then, with a jolt, realise the answer was me. I might have only lasted just over three months in the end, but it was the longest three months I can remember in my recent life: a period where time passed as slowly as it does in summer when you are ten, but without the fun, or the summer. The subsequent three months raced by, but, because of the happy and untethered way I spent them in the best weather I'd ever witnessed in Devon, put such a divide between me and my experiences in Eyam that, in their own way, they felt like a long time too.

By June, when I sat beside my parents' wild pond in the sun during my first trip back north, that unwelcoming house, that hilltop, felt as far away as a dream dreamed under a different monarchy. It felt far away enough for me, almost as if the whole winter had slipped my mind, to casually tell my mum that I'd perhaps like to try proper northern living, one day in the future. George and Casper were close by, napping, but Clifton was away on an adventure. She appeared to have a different concept of what home was to the other cats in my life. She disappeared a lot, my mum said, and had been found living in the village primary school for a spell, and in a couple of barns over in the direction of Mompesson's old church at Eakring, but she always came back. We talked a little about Eyam and my mum promised me, for the third time, that she had never moved the carved fish. From one of the house's open upstairs windows, we could hear my dad on the phone, loudly befriending an IT worker based in India. 'He didn't really need to phone them,' said my mum. 'He could probably have just shouted, and they'd have been able to hear.'

My mum went inside to prepare lunch and I napped on the grass, fractionally under the surface of consciousness, until I was woken by a gang of ducks, charging past me in the direction of the water, talking in their varying local duck voices.

MINOR ALPS

(2011–19)

I'm not scared of people in positions of power or authority, I no longer especially fear death, but what does trouble me is this: over the course of the remainder of my life, I will suffer more head injuries. You can try to be more careful, work on yourself all you like, live in houses with loftier architraves, rise more cautiously after squatting under open windows, but there's no way of getting around the bare facts: the future is coming, and it contains head pain. When you're taller than average, from a long genetic line of head-knockers, and dopey by nature, the odds are more steeply stacked against you. I'm trying not to get complacent, but I've been doing pretty well since my last head injury, which was a nasty one and could have been significantly worse – could even, in fact, have been my final head injury of all. When I suffered this head injury I'd not long moved to a cabin on the edge of Dartmoor and was about to set off to find my local trig point, which is something I like to do when I'm making friends with a new neighbourhood. I'd spotted a couple of horseshoes on the bench outside the cabin and, remembering a horseshoe I'd hung outside a previous house but which had somehow been lost in one of my other moves, I scouted around for a place to hang them. I thought it a bit premature to be banging a nail into the wooden exterior of my new rented accommodation, so instead I found a perfect ledge for the horseshoes to sit, side by side, directly above the front door. Ten minutes later, excitedly clutching my OS map, I set off, slamming the door firmly behind me. Then, after I had picked myself up from the ground, staggered a little, and regained my balance, I set off again.

I had been lucky: although the horseshoe that hit me had gained velocity over the course of four or five feet before making contact with my head, the part of my skull it hit was the toughest part, so the noise of the impact was far more alarming than the moderate amount of pain accompanying it. The shoe that struck me was the older and rustier of the two, and had a couple of bent, jagged nails sticking out of one side, but the side without the nails had been the side that hit me. What I had experienced was the horseshoe equivalent of dropping a slice of toast butter side up. Nonetheless, twenty minutes later, as I began to climb Ugborough Beacon, the 1,240-foot-high mound behind my house, I reached a hand up to wipe what I thought was some sweat out of my eyes, brought it back down in front of my face and discovered it was covered in watery red liquid. The Beacon was in a benign mood and, from its upper slopes, as I blinked the rest of the blood out of my eyes and looked south, I could pick out the Blackdown Rings earthworks and the Avon Valley, a secret, currently primrose-lined corridor where my tree-surgeon neighbour and his friends liked to fly their hot-air balloons down to the coast. Dartmoor began more abruptly here than it did farther east, where I had been more accustomed to entering it over the last four years. Once you reached the summit of the Beacon, it was just acid soil, gorse, tussocks, feldspar, bracken and ponies stretching for miles.

The cabin wasn't on the moor, but was close and high enough to get its weather: rain and wind and mud, and even a little snow, hurtling down from the hilltop and hammering at the back walls of the bedroom and bathroom, asking to be let in. My neighbour once told me he'd built the cabin – the second house I'd lived in under the moor's shadow – from giant redwood, but he'd been drinking gin and taking hits from his bong for at least a couple of hours when he said this. It was true he had built the cabin himself from trees, though: his very own, sliced and diced in his woodyard, eighty yards away. Now, the cabin sat in the middle of more of his trees, like a squat robot tree impostor, maturing but not growing. The trees sussed out its phoniness and jostled and mocked it, blocking out its light, with the result that a tenant only felt the benefit of the cabin's large windows in winter or right now, in early spring, just as the canopy was on the cusp of exploding. It was a nice building to be inside, but draughty and damp, though no doubt not nearly as draughty and damp as the smaller cabin that had preceded it on the same spot.

My neighbour had hosted parties at the old, smaller cabin in the 1970s, pulling his Triumph Stag up close to the building's door and playing the same rock and reggae compilation on the car's cassette player, over and over again, as people drank and smoked and danced and snogged. The trees around the cabin were just saplings back then. At one party a girl whom my neighbour had been trying to impress said she had a friend, a poet from a Mediterranean town, who was looking for somewhere to live and write. 'Tell him he can live here!' said my neighbour. By the time an Italian man, equipped with a single suitcase, arrived at my neighbour's front door a couple of weeks later, my neighbour had totally forgotten he'd ever extended the invitation. But the Italian poet went on to live in the cabin for over a year. My neighbour's family also owned a swimming lake a quarter of a mile down the valley. One day, in a search for inspiration, the poet spent an entire day by the lake, thinking, jotting down notes, observing his surroundings in great detail, thinking some more, jotting down more notes, before proudly presenting my neighbour with the fruits of his labour. 'This is for you,' he said, handing my neighbour a sheet of paper. The paper contained just two lines of verse:

> The lake
> It is beautiful

My neighbour had told me the story about the poet a couple of days before I was hit by the falling horseshoe. It had been early evening, with the sun descending through the canopy, inspiring leaf shadows to get up and dance on the cabin walls, and my neighbour had wandered over to my house, carrying a couple of bottles of beer. 'Here,' he'd said, handing one of the bottles to me, having casually twisted the metal top off the bottle using one of the horseshoes. After I'd returned the horseshoes to their original, safer spot on the bench outside the house, I sometimes looked at the older horseshoe and, when not haunted by the image of its rusty nails embedded in my skull, imagined the kind of horse that had once worn it. I liked to think it was a horse from centuries ago, maybe one that had done an important job on the moor, a transporting task connected with a tin mine, perhaps, but horseshoes acquire the look of age very quickly when they're out in the elements and no longer part of a horse, and the truth was that the horseshoe had probably been worn by one of my neighbour's horses, back in the seventies or eighties, or even as recently as the nineties. My neighbour liked to take his horses to the beach or the moor to ride in the evenings. He spoke frequently of Willow. 'We're taking Willow down to Bigbury' he would say, or 'Willow is outside' or 'Katie is bringing Willow back later'. It took me many weeks to realise that Willow was his daughter, and not one of his horses. In my defence, one of his horses did look an extraordinary amount like the kind of horse who might be called Willow.

My original horseshoe – the one I'd lost in one of my house moves – had been one I'd found on a walk a few miles north of here, on the way up to Piles Copse, which is one of Dartmoor's three ancient woodlands, along with Wistman's Wood and Black-a-Tor Copse. Piles has the lightest atmosphere of the three, although it's also the one that's most tricky to navigate to and where the prospect of being carried off to the lair of a tree sprite and drugged seems most likely. The first time I entered the copse I immediately saw the biggest southern migrant hawker dragonfly of my life then dangled my toes in the river and watched a huge unidentified fish swim beneath them, so afterwards when I found the horseshoe on the ridge above the copse it was easy to believe that it might belong to some giant spectral moor-horse, rather than just, say, a more everyday horse of around the same size as my neighbour's horse who wasn't called Willow.

The most huge and spectral horse I have seen on Dartmoor was also spotted just above one of the ancient woodlands, on the hill opposite Black-a-Tor, in January 2012. Night was drawing in, with an accompanying steaming drink of fog, and although my girlfriend and I could not see the horse's eyes we knew it was staring directly at us and were momentarily frozen in the awesome power of its gaze. We had just enough time to get back to the car before the daylight totally vanished but only if we took the correct one of three parallel paths, and I suggested that we followed the path the horse stood closest too. My girlfriend, who was generally fearless and used to delight in frightening me by balancing precariously on walls above Dartmoor's steep dams and other formidable West Country chasms, expressed serious worry that the horse meant us harm, but we took the horse path, and it turned out to be the right one. We kept the horse in our sights the whole time and did not at any point see it wander away, and yet by the time we reached the place where it had stood, it was gone.

I wasn't living in Devon that time, but I was driving over regularly, from Norfolk, to spend time with my girl-friend. While I waited for her to complete her shifts in a shop in Plymouth, I explored the moor. I followed a broken clay pipe along a ledge above the River Plym, where the Devil once handed a farmer a sack containing the farmer's dead infant son. In rain that probably could not have been scientifically wetter, rain that I embraced more than I'd ever embraced rain before, I introduced myself to the rivers: the long busy row of them, running down from the moor to the torn edge of the country. I listened to their dramatic rush and it sounded like the new thrilling state of my insides. Each walk mussed me up a little more, pulled my stuffing out. Some neatened parts of me began a gradual, elated process of vanishing.

A year later, just after I moved to within fifteen min-utes of the moor, on the south east side, my dad was talking to his uncle Ken, who reminded him that my dad's grandma – Ken's mum – had lived on Dartmoor until her early teens, when her family relocated to Not-tingham. To me, this was hugely exciting, unexpected news, which I was more than happy to allow to underpin the deep sense of belonging I felt when I was out on the moor. I strived to recall the face of my great-grandma, when I'd last seen it in person at the age of five. I didn't get much further than a big grin and some glasses. A look through some photographs from the 1970s brought the grin and glasses into sharper focus. They remained the dominating features of the face. It was a wild face, not neat, not a face you could imagine ever rebuking you for living in your own free and particular way. Kathleen: that was her name. Mother of Ted, my grandfather and the most renowned head-bumper of all the many head-bumpers of the head-bumping side of my family. Had Kathleen been a head-bumper too? It was likely. I couldn't help but fantasise about this new unsuspected strand of my lineage: all my ancestors before Kathleen, generations of Dartmoor people with un-neat faces, going right back to prehistoric times and the time of my most un-neat ancestors of all, who went around grinning and looking unkempt and bumping their heads on the low-hanging boughs of ancient oak trees and delighting in letting the rain wash over them and standing on enormous rocks and trying and not always succeeding in not banging their heads on the enormous rocks and ritualistically worshipping an old god with the face of a knowing sun and waving their sickles around. 'HER FAMILY WERE TENANT FARMWORKERS WHO MADE FOOD FOR DARTMOOR PRISON,' my dad told me, reeling me back in a few feet closer to earth. But pride still rushed through me. I'd walked and driven past that prison on several occasions. Conan Doyle had written about it, or a fiction-alised version of it, in *The Hound of the Baskervilles*. Frank Mitchell, an associate of the infamous British gang-sters the Krays, who had the strength to casually lift grand pianos high into the air without assistance, escaped from it in 1966. Napoleonic soldiers were detained there in the early 1800s. A baby owl once made the local news headlines after being rescued from the space between its inner and outer walls. It was a very charismatic and historically important prison.

I parked fairly close to the prison, just outside Princetown, and walked to Wistman's Wood, the best known of the moor's ancient oak woodlands, thinking myself into Kathleen's shoes. The exact position she and her parents and four brothers had lived on the moor was now lost to time, but it was logical to assume that their rented farmhouse might not have been far from here. I pictured hers as a life of cramped living quarters and great outdoor freedom. Weekend mornings began before dawn and were taken up by farm chores but after that she would wander, with a couple of other local children, far from home. Nobody minded, so long as they were home before dark. Their games were based on the legends they'd heard about the moor. The phantom pigs of nearby Merripit Hill, who set out to find a dead pony then, realising it is just some bones, dissolve into the mist, again and again, for all of eternity. The Wisht Hounds who ride here at nightfall, worked into a blood-eyed frenzy by their master, Old Crockern, the Spirit of the Moor, with his lichen hair, peat eyes and granite skin. It was easy to imagine Kathleen and her friends in the wood, scaring one another by leaping out from behind the dwarf oaks and mossy boulders. In Wistman's Wood, the lichen hangs heavy, like special tinsel for people who enjoy folk music. If you visit in May, caterpillars will divebomb you from it and, if your hair is at all nest-like, as mine is, you might find yourself still gently picking them out of it up to an hour later, as you negotiate your way back along the opposite bank of the River Dart. If you listen closely to the river, it is said you can hear it call 'Jan Coo', the name of an innocent cowhand the water once lured to his death, farther downstream at Rowbrook. I once fell in the river here, but only a leg got wet, and as far as I know the leg has not now coalesced with the water's spirit and joined its haunted chorus. When I walk on it, it feels just the same as it ever did.

Over the ridge, towards Crockern Tor, you will find the road to Postbridge, where the Hairy Hands used to cause their mischief. Having left Dartmoor for Nottinghamshire in 1913, Kathleen might not have been aware of the Hands, the most modern of Dartmoor's well-known ghosts, whose notoriety blossomed in the years directly following the First World War, as motorised travel grew more popular and the Hands began to pull more and more cars and motorcycles off the road, all in exactly the same spot. Horses mysterious bolted. A doctor from Princetown was killed when the engine of his motorcycle inexplicably detached itself. A young army officer told of how the hands closed over his much smaller ones on the handlebars of his bike, hurling him and his machine into a stone wall. The *Daily Mail* arrived, amidst growing hysteria, to report on and attempt to find the Hands. Logic prevailed and it was decided that the camber on the road was dangerous and needed to be levelled, but, when it had been, the Hands sporadically continued their work, simply moving a little farther down the road. In 1924 a woman in a caravan saw the Hands creeping their hirsute way along the window above her sleeping husband, but hers was an isolated example of the hairiness of the hands being visually witnessed. Usually people just experienced the hands as invisible but very pointedly hairy and huge. In the Forestry Commission land around here, there are red warning signs, in which a large hand struck through with a bold red line forbids walkers to follow paths where dangerous tree work is happening, but which I am unable to resist thinking of as signs telling me to beware of Hands.

A couple of miles north is the Warren House Inn, whose fire is said to have never gone out, although my friend Pete once met a man at the bar who refuted this, assuring Pete that, while drunk one Saturday night, he had 'pissed it out'. The pub is the highest in southern England, gets its electricity from its own generator and stands totally alone on the road between Postbridge and Moretonhampstead, with no other building in sight. The nearest village to it is one that hasn't been occupied since the Middle Bronze Age, Grimspound: a low stone wall enclosing twenty-four hut circles, where it's possible to stand in a palpable former living room and dream up your Stone Age self, untarnished by tourist signs or information kiosks. Grimspound is a lonely spot and when you walk the ridge above it, back towards Hameldown Beacon and Widecombe, in winter fog, with frost on the ground, blurry standing shapes materialise in front of you and you wait a few moments to find out if they are alive. Some turn out to be sheep. Others are ponies. Very occasionally, one turns out to be another walker. Some of the shapes are the long posts that were hammered into the ground by the Home Guard during the Second World War to make the process of landing more treacherous for

German parachutists. Some of the shapes never reveal what they are and vanish by the time you draw level with them. One traveller, negotiating weather not dissimilar to this during the nineteenth century, was relieved to reach the Warren House Inn and find a room for the night, but the relief only lasted until he opened a trunk in his room, where he discovered a corpse. 'That's feythur,' he was told by the Inn's owners. 'Us salted un down against when us can get along to Lydford.' The tale is retold in different ways in several old Devon folklore books: sometimes the Inn's owners are waiting to bury the body very nearby, when the frost abates, sometimes they are waiting for more clement weather so they can take him to the churchyard in Lydford, via the ancient Lychway running across the moor, which passes above Wistman's Wood, under Crockern's gaze. In it there is a pre-echo of the story of the artist Robert Lenkiewicz and Edwin McKenzie, the diminutive homeless man Lenkiewicz found living in a barrel on a rubbish tip, who went on to lodge with Lenkiewicz in his studio a few miles off the moor's edge in Plymouth, first as a living man renamed Diogenes, and then – according to McKenzie's own wishes – as an embalmed corpse, in a large drawer, where he remains to this day.

In the wide spaces of Dartmoor's heartlands, I believe unequivocally in the ongoing existence of the dead. If that ever scares me, it is usually in an oddly comforting, non-claustrophobic way. The one time I was genuinely terrified on the moor was at the hot and tangled end of a summer many years before I first moved to Devon, when I was staying in a friend's cottage where heavy locked doors crashed unaccountably open in the night and the air seemed thick with rising glitter and the sough of the stream under the building was like the lament of a wraith. It's easy to associate the moor with the cold stone gloom of its winters, but it does some of its eeriest work on hot days, when everything goes still and slow. It was on a day like this during the 1930s that a friend's great-grandparents became pixie-led in a field on the

moor, lost in sparkly mist for an entire day in one small rectangle, walking and walking but arriving again and again at the same padlocked gate. The trick, it is said, is to turn your pockets out, then the pixies leave you alone. I have never been sure if this means leaving what was in your pockets for the pixies, or just showing it to them. Do the pixies need to take your bank card, or merely note down its three-digit security code and expiry date?

On another summer day when there was similar glitter and hot weight to the air, in 2015, I drove to the village of North Bovey and, looking up from lacing my walking boots in the footwell of my car, almost passed out from fright upon seeing the faces of three children pressed against the driver-side window. Nervously, I pressed a button and reduced the glass by not more than a couple of inches. 'Hello sir!' said the tallest child, who appeared to be the leader. 'Would you like to purchase any refreshments?' On a table behind her, in the small, otherwise empty car park, sat a jug of orange cordial and a couple of packets of digestive biscuits. I don't drink orange cordial and had only just eaten but spent the next hour walking bridleways and woodland paths in a state of profound regret caused by my decision to decline their offer and not encourage their entrepreneurship. Later in the afternoon my route took me to the grave of Kitty Jay, an eighteenth-century workhouse girl who committed suicide after being treated poorly by her Dartmoor farmhand lover. Because Jay's death was self-administered, she could not be buried in consecrated ground and was instead interred here at the lonely entrance to a bridleway, beside a lane running in the direction of Buckland-in-the-Moor.

On top of the grave today there was a rusty dog-themed necklace, various coins and a jam jar containing forget-me-nots and honeysuckle. The legend is that fresh flowers appear on the grave every day, but nobody knows who puts them there. The truth is that this myth was generated by the romantic novelist Beatrice Chase, who began to place votive offerings on the grave after her move to Dartmoor in 1901. Pleasingly, walkers and locals have upheld the tradition since Chase's death in 1955 – the one exception being during the foot and mouth epidemic at the beginning of this century, when the area was sealed off. I have left various offerings on the grave myself, including coins, a golf tee peg, a charity supermarket tiddlywink and – when I could find nothing else of use – my Caffè Nero loyalty card, which at the time was still seven stamps away from a free coffee.

Standing beside the grave on this particular day, in the thick air, I could not help but think of Kirsty, another acquaintance who had once got lost on the moor in the mist, while trying to locate a house party, stopped to consult a map with a friend, and in her rear-view mirror seen a figure in a white robe, levitating six feet above the tarmac. Only later did Kirsty and her companion discover that, by chance, they had stopped the car precisely opposite the grave. I walked back to North Bovey through deep woodland whose sunburst gaps gave it the quality of a hall of mirrors where every shape was being reflected apart from my own. A brief wrong turn took me to a farmyard where animal skulls were piled on a large ball of barbed wire. When I reached my car I noticed that its right front tyre was ripped and deflated. It had been a long time ago, four hours or so, which is even longer in Dartmoor Time, but I now recalled my swerve into a hedged bank on my way to the village to avoid an oncoming car that was travelling too fast and too far over my side of the road. I remembered the sharp thud the tyre had made, as it had hit a piece of hidden granite in the bank: an impact I had felt in my own shins. I also remembered that my roadside cover had expired and I no longer had a spare tyre in the boot. Over in the dense woodland opposite, deep in the moss, Crockern shrugged. I looked at my phone, saw I was without any hint of reception, and wandered over to the Ring of Bells, the village's thirteenth-century pub, which at that point was still six months away from burning down. In the mid-1800s, North Bovey had a reputation for fostering some of Dartmoor's most ferocious women, several of whom were frequently known to fight in the home of the village's rector, the Reverend W. H. Thornton, pulling one another's hair and throwing crockery and stones as Thornton attempted to settle their quarrels. Bovey men were reputed to be heavy drinkers, and in 1868 one sold his wife for a quart of beer. But the atmosphere in the Ring of Bells was sober and calm, and an extremely accommodating barwoman let me use the phone and recommended a garage in Moretonhampstead, whose head mechanic came out and attended to my problem within the hour.

'Good luck!' Dartmoor residents will often say as a sign-off, I have noticed, after giving directions to their house. The 34,000 people who live on the moor tend not to drive new or expensive cars, and those they do drive always have much smarter paintwork on their right side than their left. My granddad Ted drove an old Wolseley on some of these lanes while down from Nottinghamshire on holidays in the 1960s: holidays which I now realise probably doubled as pilgrimages to Kathleen's birthplace. On the narrower lanes, when he met a vehicle coming in the other direction, he would have to stop, get out and sprint up to the driver of the other car and politely ask them to reverse to the nearest passing point, owing to the fact that the Wolseley did not have a functioning reverse gear. Being content to spend a large part of your day reversing down tight green corridors is a big part of living in rural Devon, and I have always been OK with that. It's on the slightly wider lanes where the problems tend to emerge. Three times now my front left tyre has exploded as a result of slamming into a hidden chunk of rock in a bank to avoid a collision with a large and plush car, aggressively driven by somebody travelling in the opposite direction who almost certainly wasn't a resident of the moor. The penultimate time my front left tyre exploded near the moor, it was necessary for safety purposes to drive for a couple of miles on the unprotected wheel then abandon my car for the evening. It was dark but fortunately the point where I abandoned the car was barely more than a mile from my cabin. I walked through the rain and the dark directly to my neighbour's house, where ghost stories were being told in front of crackling logs. The father of my neighbour's Personal Assistant talked about the time he stayed in The Smugglers Haunt hotel in Brixham, a fishing town seventeen miles away, and woke up in the night to watch his luggage being thrown about by two small girls, who had somehow broken into his room. Later, not knowing about the incident, his wife had found out that the hotel's famous ghost, Aggie, is a small girl who fell to her death from one of the windows in the 1920s, and now likes to disturb the bedclothes and luggage of the hotel's guests. As we took this in, the PA's pet husky – when it came right down to it, just a wolf with a good stylist – stretched out in front of the woodburner and eyed us balefully, with an apparent abundance of recondite knowledge. The evening was very south Devon – woodsy, affluent, laid-back, superstitious, and lightly salted – and I enjoyed being within it while also very much on the periphery of it.

Dartmoor is what divides north and south Devon, and is a big part of what makes them tangibly separate places. North Devon is cheaper, less trimmed, a region where the coombes and hollows growl at you with a less refined vocabulary, where there are fewer opportunities to shelter from nature's unforgiving side at a farmers' market or a Bikram yoga class or an open-air sound system set up by a dreadlocked man whose parents have just moved down from Brighton and own a paddock. There is something particularly, unapologetically country and pagan about the area where the north moor melts into the villages of mid-Devon. Dartmoor was granted National Park status in 1951 but Old Crockern had no personal say in that. The A30 and A38 dual carriageways are not boundaries he recognises, and sometimes his influence seems even more present in the villages above the moor on the north side than it does in those on the moor itself. In St Michael's Church in Spreyton, I stumbled across the most

chilling Green Man carving of all the many Green Man
carvings in the churches of Devon's heartlands: less a
Green Man than a king blinded and suffocated by the
thick stalks of foliage. The message was unequivocal: the
only true monarch is nature, and those who build themselves up into spurious positions of power and lord it
over the land would be wise not to forget that. More
unnerving still was the death's head on All Saints Church
in Winkleigh, a lichen-splattered stone skull in the sky
which must surely count as Britain's most frightening and
durable Halloween pumpkin. The timing of my walk was
apposite, with Samhain just two nights away. I'd just read
Earth to Earth, John Cornwell's unique and disturbing
book about the double murder-suicide of the Luxtons, a
Winkleigh farming family who cut themselves off from
the rest of their community during the 1970s, and
worked and lived in the manner of people in the 1870s,

to the extent that, in preference to going out and buying paint, they made their own. As I walked in search of the Luxton farmhouse there were few cars and motorbikes on roads at the edge of the village but each one that did pass me appeared thoroughly intent on mowing me down. A dazzling late afternoon sun shone on hedgerows bursting with the ripeness that can only directly presage decay. The moor was visible on the horizon but it had its back turned, as if preferring not to be counted as a witness.

To my mind, Dartmoor always faces in a southerly direction, training its severe gaze down upon the towns and villages of the rolling pre-sea lands of the South Hams. The sprites of the moor tend to remain in the uplands but something of their essence is carried downstream into the towns and villages of the southern sub-Dartmoor area. This pixie and faerie run-off is most potent in Totnes, where it mixes with tidal river water, patchouli oil and raw carrot juice to create the stock that the town stews in from day to day. In summer 2014 I walked into an occult art and stationery shop on the high street to find some moving leaves talking about cheese: an incident that surprised me less than it probably might, had I not been getting to know the town for several months by this point. Only a couple of minutes previously, I had walked past a white van with the words 'Unicorn Ambulance' stencilled on it.

'Never have incense burning while you're eating cheese,' announced the leaves, which were dry and white. 'It's always a disaster.'

Remembering the block of cheddar in my bag, I wondered if the leaves had somehow gained a clairvoyant knowledge of my plans for the weekend, until a man stepped out from behind a rack of cards and replied to the leaves. He told the leaves that Camembert was the worst because it 'really absorbs the vapours'. At this point the leaves shook more animatedly and revealed themselves to be Ralph, the shop's proprietor, who'd been fiddling with something under the counter under the protection of the leaves, which he told me were white sage and had strong cleansing properties, especially when it came to fixing negative houses. I decided not to purchase any leaves, as my house at the time was quite positive, although briefly considered some for my garden shed, which was prone to intermittent bouts of negativity. Ralph lived on the moor and on my first visit to the shop had told me about a witch's dolly that resided in a pub up there, the Tavistock Inn at Poundsgate. It wasn't quite as if I said, 'Hello! I'm Tom. I've newly moved to the area' and Ralph replied 'Did you know about the one-hundred-and-twenty-year-old witch's dolly they keep up at the Tavistock Inn?' – but we still got to this point in what might have seemed remarkably quick time to someone not quite so interested in obscure folklore artefacts of the late Victorian era. The next day I'd driven up to see the dolly and would have closely inspected it, but it was on a shelf behind a table where a family were eating scampi and chips and I had been leery of awkwardly resting an elbow in their tartar sauce.

*

In my early days of exploring the moor, this tended to be my route: the steep climb up New Bridge Hill, where I once found a rare Octopus Stinkhorn fungus, past Poundsgate and its dolly, towards Dartmeet, where the east and west branches of the Dart crash into each other and become one. On the north side of the valley was the former site of Snail House, where two old women allegedly lived in the early 1800s and ate nothing but snails. Beyond that is the ledge from which a cow once fell onto the car of my friend Mike, who works for the National Park. The cow succeeded in writing the car off but emerged unscathed and sauntered off into a field on the opposite side of the road as if comprehensively unmoved by the whole episode. Deep in the recesses of the hillside opposite was the spot where, in 2015, I assisted with the rescue of a wild pony which had rolled onto its back to enjoy the sun and become trapped in the narrow space between two rocks. For this, I can thank my Dartmoor OS map, which enabled me to give the pony's co-ordinates to Karla McKechnie, Dartmoor's Livestock Protection Officer, who arranged for a farmer to come out and un-wedge it. As I waited with the upturned pony, careful not to get too close to its kicking legs, other ponies mooched around it, chewing on heather, as if in the mindset of, 'Oh, there's Greg again, with his drama and pratfalls. I'm just going to try to get on, and not rise to it.' Greg turned out to be unhurt and, within an hour, had been carefully nudged out from between the rocks and flipped the correct way up, and was once again chewing on heather himself.

When Frank Mitchell was sprung from Dartmoor Prison by the Krays, the escape plot was a simple one: while in a work party of prisoners out on the moor, Mitchell asked permission to feed some ponies, then, having had it granted by a guard, walked to a lane where a getaway car was waiting for him. This seems surprisingly laissez-faire of the prison authorities, but perhaps might be viewed as less so upon consideration of their decision four years earlier to grant Mitchell permission to take a taxi up to Okehampton, more than twenty miles away, to buy himself a budgerigar. Nonetheless, you might have thought a prison guard would be more aware of an important rule of the moor, which is that the ponies shouldn't be fed by members of the general public, since it makes the ponies more likely to both stray into traffic and develop an attitude problem. I learned this in 2015, shortly after I'd helped to rescue Greg, when I was invited by Charlotte Faulkner to assist with the pony drift at Haytor Rocks. Charlotte, who is founder of the Dartmoor Hill Pony Association, said that by feeding the ponies tourists increase the risk of them being hit by a car, and make them harder to drift. What a lot of people don't know is that every pony on Dartmoor belongs to a specific farmer. The purpose of a drift is to round the ponies up so their health can be checked, the foals among them can be weaned, and those who've strayed can be returned to their correct area. Some of them are also subsequently sold in order to keep the number of ponies on each common in accordance with the rules set by the executive public body Natural England.

The Haytor drift is one of the simpler drifts, in the sense that it takes place over a relatively small area of ground, but one of the most difficult, in the sense that Haytor also has an unusually large amount of tourist traffic and is home to, in Charlotte's words, 'the most arsey ponies on the moor'. The people doing the hardest work rode a mixture of horses and quad bikes. Less significant members of the team such as me, meanwhile, served as peripheral foot soldiers, my main job being to stand halfway up Saddle Tor, about a quarter-mile southwest of the start point, and wave my arms and shout at the ponies if they hurtled past. An hour and a half into the drift four of them did just that, in spectacular fashion. This was probably the nearest I would ever come to living in the Black Hills of South Dakota in 1864. 'I'm getting quite emotional watching it,' Kerry, a watching hiker, told me. She gestured at the traffic and tourists below. 'Isn't it a disaster waiting to happen?'

Charlotte belted about from tor to tor with infectious energy, shouting instructions into her walkie-talkie, racing alongside the ponies in her Land Rover with me in the passenger seat, but by the end of the day less than half of the eighty targeted ponies had made it to the pen. The stretch of craggy, marshy ground between Haytor and Saddle Tor was a graveyard of half-sunk and abandoned quad bikes. With the danger of being returned to society gone, the loose ponies swaggered about and resumed their business. One who was queuing for ice cream in the car park gave me a little nip on the ribs when I had the temerity to come between him and a 99 Flake. I'd always wondered who was crazy enough to buy ice cream from the vans on the moor in winter and now I had the answer. It was ponies.

Every popular and busy part of Dartmoor is close to a quiet part of Dartmoor that can feel totally your own. If you follow the stone rails of the old quarry north the back of Haytor, everything gets peaceful and boggy very quickly. In the 1800s, granite was transported from here, all over Britain, and was used in the building of several famous London structures. If you have walked across London Bridge, or through the British Museum, you have walked on some of Dartmoor. The tor itself also has its empty times. Early in the autumn of 2017, I got into the habit of climbing its rocks on a succession of cloudless, lilac weekday evenings. Only a smattering of people were around, the waning moon was thin and clear and I felt loose and as connected to all the geology beneath me as I ever had, comfortable with the idea that I was just another layer of it, to eventually be broken down and absorbed. Nightfall in this spot brought less, not more, isolation, as you looked south and saw the electricity of Bovey Tracey, Newton Abbot and Torbay begin to lick at the bottom of the hill. I remember first noticing this the previous winter, as I failed to watch the Orionid meteor shower on a much cloudier night up here under a blanket. There was a stronger, more ominous, sense of civilisation than you got in daytime, and when you looked at all the lights you realised how many people there were for each of them, and that this was just the tiniest fraction of the UK, and that the UK was just the tiniest fraction of the planet, and that every one of those people had problems and worries which they often made bigger than they really were, and then you started to think about the shooting stars and globular clusters taking part in the celestial event above, hidden by the cloud cover, who were all those light years away, and the people in other centuries, now dead, with all their problems and worries which they often made bigger than they really were, and then all you could do was pull the blanket more tightly around you and accept the tea your friend Roy was offering you from his flask and try not to get a headache.

A couple of years ago a friend's friend's dog fell off the back of Haytor. The dog broke its leg but survived. A vet in Bovey Tracey told the dog's owner that it was not an unusual event: they got about twenty dogs a year in the surgery who had been injured or killed as a result of falling off the tor. People I speak to who know Dartmoor only by reputation often think that I am putting myself at risk with all the walking I do up there: that I will slip off a tor, fall down an old mine shaft, sink into a peat bog without trace or get bitten by an adder. I have yet to fall down a mine shaft or off a tor on the moor but I have stepped into two large, concealed holes: a slightly jarring experience in both instances, but not resulting in any injuries worth mentioning. I have only encountered two adders on the moor, in all my hundreds of miles of walking up there, and it was very obvious that neither one of them wanted any trouble.

On the whole I feel that Dartmoor is far more likely to be responsible for the improvement of my health than the decline of it. In the days directly before my fortieth birthday, I was feeling a little run down, and a large sore spot appeared on the end of my nose. I had hired a room for a sizeable party and although I felt sure that nobody I had invited to the party would like me any less because I had an enormous red nose, I would, given the choice, have preferred it not to be a dominating feature of the night. In the preceding days I dowsed the nose in all manner of tea tree oils and antiseptics, to no avail. Two days after the party, with the spot – which, if I was looking myself properly in the face and being frank, could perhaps be labelled more officially a boil – still raging, I walked on Dartmoor, from Postbridge to Fernworthy Forest, through rain, wind and unseasonable breath-sapping hail. A cuckoo sang through the deluge, undaunted. When I returned to the car, the spot was gone, leaving not the smallest blemish in its place. I should have known: the moor cure was the way to go. Dartmoor had successfully, emphatically exfoliated me. Had the spot been one or more warts, the moor could have helped out too, if old lore was to be believed: all I'd have had to do was put some stones in a bag and leave them by the side of the road to be picked up by another traveller, who would subsequently inherit my warts. Had I made a small detour to the north-east on my walk, I could also have passed through the Tolmen Stone – a large rock overhang-ing the North Teign river, with a smooth hole in its centre, alleged to possess magic healing properties – and guarded myself against the future possibility of rickets or infertil-ity. Having already been through the Tolmen twice in the last six months, however, I figured I was insured in both departments. At one point, the village of Chagford was well-known for its population of faithless wives who, having cheated on their spouses, were sent to the Tolmen for purification. When you arrive in Chagford from the direction of Waye Barton in summer, the foliage obscures the 'C' in the sign, and I have always wondered if the decision not to prune around it is intentional.

Dartmoor has a strong tradition of women failing to be well behaved at times in history when good behaviour was expected of them. Climb the hills above Belstone, and you can visit the Nine Maidens, where a group of female villagers were turned to stone for the crime of dancing naked on the sabbath. Even in death, they continue to rebel, since they in fact total seventeen, not nine. At night, they are said to still have a little dance around, and sometimes swap positions. Great-Grandma Kathleen liked to drink and she liked to go to the bookies. When Kathleen and her family moved from Dartmoor to Nottinghamshire, her mum, Ellen, caused a stir by being the first woman in the local village who had the temerity to visit the pub on her own. Apparently this was standard practice for the progressive women of Dartmoor, while still frowned upon in much of the rest of the country. The moor always feels a little outside the rules, outside of Britain, even. It has not been the scene of any major historical battle, nor closely associated with any king or queen. It is its own small, squelchy, non-conformist country. I am sometimes surprised by how much knowledge I have gained of this small country in little more than half a decade, but I am more frequently overwhelmed by how much there is to know of it, and all that I will never know of it, no matter how many walks I take or books I read or people I meet or questions I ask.

My main soundtrack for the recent trips I have taken to Dartmoor has been the late, non-conformist country singer Townes Van Zandt – particularly his album *Our Mother the Mountain*, and an anthology that came out a few years ago. There's a very shocking moment on the anthology when it jumps from the songs Townes wrote in the early seventies, directly into 'Marie', a ballad he sang with Willie Nelson in 1990. The first time you hear it, you wonder when Townes will start singing, and then you realise he *is* singing. That deep burnt sound, like ash cleared out from a grate and compacted into song, is him. I cannot think of another musician whose voice changed more dramatically in the space of less than two decades. He sounds as old as a tree in Wistman's Wood, as old as some moss-coated clitter in a ravine below the shadow of a tor. He is, in fact, at this point, close to his forty-sixth birthday – just seven years from his tragically early death. I will be the same age in three years, but when I walk on Dartmoor, I often feel considerably more youthful. It's something about the intoxicating quality of the air up there. It's air that creates lichen and makes wooden foot-path signs and boulders look old but makes people feel young. I don't know that it actually makes people look any younger. Probably, if I spent enough time up there, my face would end up covered in lichen too, just like a wooden footpath sign or a boulder. I find that I do not fear this. I would enjoy stroking the lichen on my face, while deep in thought. I feel so young and bouncy on the moor, it makes me wonder what it would be like to be immediately transported into my seven-year-old self, when I was possibly at my most bouncy. How shocking would it feel? How amazing would it be to find out how far, how gradually, you'd leaked away from who you once were? I suspect that if the forty-six-year-old, ash-voiced Townes Van Zandt was translocated into his seven-year-old self, it would be even more shocking, were it not for the fact that Townes Van Zandt appears to have been a very unshockable kind of person.

The fact of Townes' Texan heritage does not stop his music being perfect for Dartmoor in winter: it has just the right level of devilry, just the right amount of mountain and hill obsession, just the right whiff of eternity. One Townes song I listen to a lot is 'Waiting Around to Die', in which the narrator, embodied by Townes, has trouble with his violent father, a duplicitous woman, trains, wine and prison, before finally finding a friend he can trust, in the form of codeine. My mum, who also likes the song, thought it had a much happier ending, not having realised that Townes was saying 'codeine' and thinking he was just talking about a man with an American name who was quite nice. The other Townes songs I listen to most regularly are 'Lungs', 'Snake Mountain Blues', 'Our Mother the Mountain' and 'Kathleen', which is about the imminent prospect of being reunited with someone called Kathleen, who is almost certainly dead.

People who trace their ancestry are always telling you they're related to someone historically significant. From what I can work out by tracing a little of mine, most of my Devon ancestry were historically significant too, since agricultural work and serving the needs of the aristocracy are very historically significant professions. The line clusters around the Moretonhampstead and North Bovey area at least as far back as the mid-1700s. Where did my people roam, I wonder, as I walk the moor. Which bogs and basins and earthworks have their feet and mine both trodden? Were our womenfolk some of those who fought in the North Bovey rectory and damaged the beleaguered clergyman's crockery? As she reached the cusp of adolescence and explored the moor, did Kathleen ever tramp and stumble north from Fernworthy Forest to the bubble in the earth where the Dart originates, as I did in summer 2017? Did she ride there, maybe? Was her love of gambling on horses in later life a result of growing up in such an equine place? Did she ever ride or walk anywhere near the cabin and the stable of the horse who wasn't Willow?

Back then, both buildings would have been just a field, probably: the trees wouldn't even have been planted, the smaller proto-cabin perhaps not yet even built. My neighbour's parents would still be four decades away from purchasing the accompanying farm buildings and lake. But Dartmoor's weather would still have been hurtling down the south side of the Beacon and landing on everything. The winter before I arrived, in the biggest storm of the year, all but the largest of my neighbour's chickens blew away, never to be seen again. Now the lone survivor pecked around the wild ground next to the cabin, hoovering up the wildflower seeds I'd thrown down. The loss of the seeds to the hen's appetite would turn out to be moot, since one day in May, when the wildflowers were reaching their apex, one of my neighbour's Boys would strim them down to nothing while I was out. 'My Boys' was what my neighbour called the younger men he paid to fell and mend trees, drive his tractors and maintain his land. The cabin's heating and cooker ran off bright red LPG bottles. The bottles were heavy but the gas in them lasted no time at all and when it was gone it was my job to let my neighbour know and pay him for a new bottle, which he would ask one of his Boys to wheel over from the shed and install. 'I'll get one of my Boys onto it dreckly,' he would say. 'Dreckly', I had gathered, was a word used by Devonian and Cornish folks which meant 'in a period of time that will take precisely as long as it takes'. But that was OK. I didn't do much cooking while I was living at the cabin and the weather soon warmed up.

Outside on the dirt and wood shavings, the lone hen, who now had a new hen friend, pecked about. Behind the hens, my neighbour's three-legged terrier powered around the communal lawn with great determination, driving forwards with her one unusually muscular front leg, and behind her my neighbour's son, the sister of Willow who wasn't a horse, powered around on a motorised go-kart. My neighbour's PA's husky, which had killed one of the chickens last year, depriving the chicken of the chance to blow away, stood guard over the whole scene from the doorstep of the PA's quarters, narrowing its eyes in my direction as if permanently at work on the equation of how easily and effectively it could take me down. The go-kart buzzed along the track leading behind the pen of my neighbour's two pigs, whom my neighbour would soon put on the enormous outdoor grill beside his lake, cook and eat. The pigs oinked excitedly when I came out of the cabin, having learned to see me as a daily bearer of culinary gifts. I tried, and failed, not to love the pigs. I fantasised about kidnapping them and taking them to my next home and permitting them to just be pigs.

During periods of forgetting to make the cabin work in various ways, my neighbour, whose love of giving and

receiving gifts was as large as his more general love of pleasure and luxury, kindly brought me glasses of gin and the occasional record. 'Do you have The Doors? Put The Doors on!' he asked, arriving at the cabin door one night, with gin. I put The Doors on and my neighbour danced around my living room to The Doors. When I clinked glasses with my neighbour but failed to look him directly in the eye, he told me off, and made me do it again. I became increasingly aware of my disappointing inability to be one of my neighbour's Boys; an inability that made itself most apparent by the fact that I did not drink enough gin, plus the fact that I was not technically any-where close to being an actual boy. 'You're forty-two?' my neighbour said, sounding shocked and saddened, after asking my age a few weeks into my tenancy. He had not read the part of my contract where my date of birth was listed. He took a literal step back as he said it and lost three or four inches of balance and his look was so profoundly forlorn that I almost put an arm on his shoul-der to comfort him. He would not tell me his own age and if this was a ploy to encourage me to think of him as a person who didn't have one, it was wholly successful.

One day I emerged from the cabin and a man – older and in possession of more gravitas than my neigh-bour's Boys – was wandering through the trees, running his hand along a branch here and there. The canopy was in full leaf now and formed a tight dark ring around my impostor-tree home. The man introduced himself as a business associate of my neighbour, and said he was an arboreal consultant. He told me about the ways trees communicate with one another underground, via their roots, and alerted me to a couple of personal crises that these trees were going through. He said trees can teach humans a lot about the best way to deal with problems: that the answer is not running away to places where our problems will ultimately only follow us, but is to remain rooted solidly in one spot and face up to our problems honestly. I absolutely saw what he was saying, and concurred with a lot of it, but my six months at the cabin were coming to an end and I was already excited about where life might take me next. After he had posited his theory, the arboreal consultant examined the trunk of a eucalyptus and, apparently finding it to his liking, unzipped his trousers and blessed it with a torrent of steaming urine.

When I moved from the cabin, I saw no reason for any major emotional farewell to the moor, since I knew I would be back regularly and would not be moving any huge distance from it. But on the day prior to my departure I felt moved to retrace, and slightly rework, one of my favourite Dartmoor walks, along the River Erme, on the high bit of the moor directly above the cabin. It was a much cooler, overcast day after weeks of uninterrupted heat, but as I squeezed through gorse and bracken on a

barely defined path and reached the riverbank, the sun started to push through. By the time I drew level with one of my favourite swimming spots, the clouds had totally given way, and I felt overdressed, over-hot and niggled by undergrowth. From somewhere deep within the sweaty tangle of my hair, a flying insect, possibly feeling even more hot and bothered than I did, protested angrily and I shook it free. At this point of the Erme, the water slowed and the banks widened, forming a natural twenty-metre-long pool with a deep central shelf. I hadn't brought my trunks but I was totally alone and the lucid, coppery temptation of the water was too strong. I stripped naked, leaving my clothes scattered along the bank, and swam twenty glorious lengths. I had never skinny-dipped on the moor before so this was effectively the first time that there had been no barrier between the two of us. I was Dartmoor and Dartmoor was me. 'What on earth are you thinking, leaving here?' said a voice in my head. 'I can't wait to be somewhere new!' said another voice in my head. The voices were equal in strength and volume. As I pulled my trousers back on, I regretted getting out of the water, and could easily have stayed in for the rest of the day, were it not for the packing I still had left to do. A party of eight female walkers, all in their fifties and sixties, but collectively sounding much younger than that, passed by on the footpath above me, the vantage point of which, had they arrived at it two minutes earlier, would have given them the clearest possible view of my naked form against the coppery surface. Struggling to get a sock back onto a damp foot, I shouted a hello, then watched them fade into the grass, the cheerful mess of their noise lingering long after they had vanished.

OLD FAT BUM

(2015–19)

As I drive the roads, I watch the hills. I always notice the interesting ones, and none of them aren't interesting, so I notice them all. I notice them like some other people notice types of car or dog they are enthusiastic about. If there's a hill that particularly catches my attention, I'll look it up on the map when I get home, find out if there's public access up it and, if there is, feel the excitement rising in my chest, and make my plans: loose plans, usually, that I have no need to trouble anyone else with. Society isn't ever going to buy you a drink for climbing a hill. A hill is not a mountain. You climb it for you, then you put it quietly inside you, in a cupboard marked 'Quite A Lot Of Hills' where it makes its infinitesimal mark on who you are. One I'd had my eye on for a long time was Brent Knoll, beside the M5, a little north of Burnham-on-Sea. I wouldn't go so far as to say I couldn't stop thinking about it, but every time I drove past it, on my way somewhere else, I would ogle it and make a mental note: 'Climb the big hill near the motorway that looks like a fat squashed onion with the stem sliced off.' But then I'd forget. It was always freshest in my mind when I was on my way elsewhere with no time to spare. Before I experienced its various moods intimately, I got to know them from a distance: the Easters when it had a wooden cross on its summit, the days when, in the very localised mists you got in this part of the Mendips, it appeared to have its own halo. Then I did the unforgivable: before we'd even properly met, I went on a date with its rival.

In my defence, when I climbed Crook Peak, on the opposite side of the M5, I did not know the fraught history between it and Brent Knoll. In the time of King Arthur, giants lived on top of each hill and would throw large stones at one another across the valley. If you stand on the summit of either hill, a rivalry remains apparent. In Severn Coast terms, they're the two tallest kids in class. As they vie for supremacy, Crook Peak comes across as the more pouty and petulant of the two, and is the highest, by a larger margin than is obvious from the road. From its trig point you can gaze down at the six-lane carriageway snaking between the Quantocks and the Blackdowns in the south and briefly appreciate the beauty of motorways, until you realise it's not the beauty of motorways you're appreciating but the beauty of what a

274-metre outcrop of Carboniferous limestone and the
setting sun of a sharp, bright winter's day has briefly
bestowed upon a motorway. Motorways are still motorways: functional scars in the land, which I am not quite
allowed to hate since they permit me to more easily reach
walking routes in the places they haven't yet destroyed.

The M5 wasn't here prior to 1962 but an indication
of its topographical dominance is that when I first read
about the fifth-century giants and their missiles, I imagined the vast rocks flying over six lanes of traffic, while
police blocked the road and the drivers of important
Sports Utility Vehicles paced the hard shoulder ranting
into their phones, until the giants tired of their rock
throwing and fell into lengthy giant sleeps that made all
of the West gently vibrate. I bought a very beautiful
1930s guidebook to Somerset published by the Great
Western Railway company, and it was only while reading
this that the force with which the M5 slices the county in
two properly hit me – or, rather, I'd already known it
sliced the county in two, and it had already made me
mentally divide Somerset into its more rugged west and
softer east, but what properly hit me was the fact that it
hadn't always been that way. Once, as you tootled
through it in your Morris Minor, not getting anywhere
quickly, Somerset was much more of a cohesive whole. I
found myself returning again and again to a photo in the
book of a craggy hollow near Wellington, a lost, fairy-
tale place. Did it even still exist? How many others of its
kind had been destroyed during the motorway's construction? The M5 is now the hollow. It's the West's great
unnatural valley, and as such has become the king of all

hill-watching roads. While I'm on it, my excitable hill surveillance goes on long past Somerset's northern border, past the Tyndale Monument at North Nibley in Gloucestershire, to the Malvern Hills and the mountain ranges of Wales.

Having been repeatedly beckoned by the dark high shapes on the skyline to the west while taking the motorway from Devon to visit friends and family in the Midlands, I caved in to pressure, cancelled some practical stuff I should have been doing to earn a living and booked into a B&B in Hay-on-Wye, on the Herefordshire–Wales Border. I had an ulterior motive: Hay is full of books. More books per square yard, perhaps, than any other town on the planet. Before the first of my walks, I shopped for a few, showing great restraint by stopping at a total of seven. The purchase I was most pleased with was a first edition of *Coming Down the Wye*, the 1942 memoir by the naturalist engraver Robert Gibbings. The pages had some foxing, but I didn't mind. That's one of the many things I love about buying old books: even the negative jargon sounds attractive. Who wouldn't want a nice bit of foxing?

In the early 1940s Gibbings set out from his home on Plynlimon, the Cambrian mountain where the Wye's source is found, and travelled down the river, past Hay, all the way to its mouth, near Chepstow, gathering folklore, creating a vivid picture of farming communities and trout-tickling fishermen in wartime, making a before-its-time plea for ethical meat consumption, and recording conversations with locals in pubs, sometimes in a fashion pleasingly divergent from the main narrative. At one point he goes totally rogue, telling us, apropos of apparently nothing, about an attractive young lady who – he claims – gives him the eye on a train. This is perhaps a telling insight into Gibbings' state of mind at the time of writing, when you learn that he subsequently got off with his wife's sister, who was his typist for the manuscript.

There are two eerie stories about hares in the book. The first concerns Gibbings' neighbour Bill who, with his friend Evan, tries in vain to catch one at night, but it keeps darting through the arms and legs of the men, until Evan decides that the hare is in fact an apparition. The second is of a hare in the valley that cannot be shot, until a wise man recommends that a hunter uses a sixpenny bit instead of a cartridge. The hare, wounded on its flank, retreats in the direction of a cottage, where, upon entering, the hunter finds an old woman on the floor with a broken leg. I've found versions of this story in numerous books of folklore: a hare that is 'not right' being shot with silver or herbs and transmuting back into a witch. Another version is told in 'The Hare and the Harbourer', an old Herefordshire story collected by the folklorist Ruth Tongue in 1962 from a Welsh WI member: here, the hare – giant and with glowing eyes – is attacked in the throat by a dog and screams out in pain in the voice of a human female.

On my Herefordshire walks, I got the sense of being in a forgotten dragon-green space, much bigger than it appeared on the map. It's worth remembering that, until 1969, Herefordshire wasn't even on the National Grid. My most abiding memory of the county was a childhood holiday in an isolated riverside cottage without electricity, where water came from an outdoor pump. It was the spring of 1985, but it felt, to a nine-year-old used to hot baths and nightly viewing of *Blue Peter*, like the winter of 1885. As soon as we blew the candles out each night, we heard mice scampering around us on the flagstones. The guest book, largely filled with the eloquent observations of fishermen, stretched back to the 1920s, and my dad took it to bed to read each night as a person might read a work of literary fiction. Mayflies abounded above the small adjacent tributary to the Wye: a paradise for trout and their oppressors. My mum chose to clean the toilet, since apparently nobody else had bothered since the end of the Jazz Age, and in doing so had to make a super-human effort not to throw up. In the local pub, I was offered hare for the first time in my life, and declined, unable to conceal my horror. In the living room there was a copy of *Masquerade* by Kit Williams. There always seemed to be, in living rooms, in 1985. I stared and stared at the illustrations, feeling pleased with myself when I found the hares Williams had hidden in them, and getting whisked away to the rolling, greener than green English countryside of their setting, which – not totally unlike the place we were staying – appeared to be in a permanent state of spring and had a touch of the pagan and the gro-tesque about it.

I drove south from my plusher and less interesting twenty-first-century guest accommodation in Hay to the Black Hill and saw a hat-trick of pleasing village names: Cockyard, Vowchurch, Turnastone. Local lore says the latter two were named after two sisters who built com-peting churches. One sister vowed she would complete hers before her sibling had the chance to turn a stone of hers, then went ahead and completed the task. Not far on, the Black Mountains loomed and the road ended, in a way that suggested it could signal the end of everything, not just the road, or England. I paused midway through lacing up my walking boots, mesmerised by the shadow of the clouds tracing across the mountain on the opposite side of the valley; a giant ghost curtain being drawn, again and again, for all of eternity. Another book had brought me here: the 1982 novel *On the Black Hill* by Bruce Chatwin, whose descriptions of eight harsh decades in the life of two farming brothers on the border had frozen themselves inside me. The reality was no letdown. According to the forecast, the weather wasn't doing anything particularly unpleasant to anyone anywhere in the UK, but I still got the sense that anything could happen here, that it was slightly outside the rules.

As I climbed to the Cat's Back, the long, aptly named ridge at the hill's summit, I saw bits of sheep everywhere: sometimes just their wool, sometimes other bits of them, rotting. It was a dominating theme of all of my Herefordshire walks: sheep here seemed to leave more traces of themselves than sheep elsewhere, as if they were constantly walking into trees and bushes, drunk. Later, on the climb up to Arthur's Stone, a Neolithic chambered tomb above Dorstone between the Golden and Wye Valleys, I saw a whole tree entirely festooned with sheep's hair, as if, not satisfied with merely bumping into it, the inebriated sheep had tried to climb it too. Jim Capaldi of the band Traffic once lived in a farmhouse in the Black Mountains, until he left and the place was turned into a wreck by squatters. On the cover of his poorly titled but mostly excellent 1974 solo album *Whale Meat Again* he posed with a local sheep-farming family. The harder you look at the expressions on the faces of the sheep-farming family, the more vividly you can imagine the conversation that led to the photo shoot.

Farming family: 'Us? Why?'

Jim: 'Come on. It will be cool. You can pretend to be me band.'

Farming family: 'OK, if you say so. But how long will it take? There's a ewe gone lame in the back field.'

I could quite easily imagine leaving bits of myself up here, like a sheep. At the top, after I'd crossed Offa's Dyke into Wales and scaled the easternmost Black Mountains, January took place, undaunted by the fact that it was legally still six months away. Hail and rain drove into me until I leaned like the wooden prop of a washing line. Through the deluge I saw tall piles of stones, a trig point and another ewe carcass. All three looked like signs of some abstruse future mountain religion. Something about you might change, dramatically, noticeably, up here, if you lingered too long. 'What *happened* to that guy in that place?' they might say of you, down where normal people hang out, when you returned. On the descent, a looped monster bramble, unquestionably possessing full awareness of what it was doing, closed its long arms around my neck. I ripped myself free, drawing blood, gaining a deeper understanding of what the sheep around here were going through on a daily basis and feeling bad for insinuating that they were wreckheads. The ghost-cloud curtain closed on the mountainside, then closed again, then again. When I got back to the Wye, it was July again. If I'd told the river what I'd just seen, it probably would have said it didn't believe me. But the water knew, because it had been up somewhere similarly lofty, earlier in the day. It was a trickster of a river, always telling you one thing when it meant another. People often compared it to a snake but what it reminded me of most, with all its loops and feints and zigzags, was the movement of a hare across a field.

I missed watching that unique dash, living in the west. It had now been nearly three years since I'd seen a live one: an unthinkable gap, back when I lived in Norfolk and came to view the sighting of hares as a standard part of my week. In spring, I'd peeked over hedges and seen pairs of them boxing. It was like looking behind a curtain where animals who thought they weren't being watched stood vertical and played out various human activities. But hares could do all sorts of stuff humans couldn't, such as run at speeds of over forty miles per hour and get pregnant when they were already pregnant. Later in the year, hurrying the finale of walks where I'd overstretched my daylight allowance, I'd disturbed them in their furrows, watching them scatter and zigzag ahead of me. I'd had high hopes that Herefordshire would break the recent dry spell, but when I returned from my four days there I remained hare-less. Even a stop in Gloucestershire on the way home to explore Painswick Beacon and Nailsworth – the homeland of Kit Williams, which had directly inspired *Masquerade* – yielded no results. But that is the nature of hares: they're liminal, edge dwellers, mercurial, non-conformist, always in the corner of the picture of the British countryside, or more likely just outside it. That was the idea Williams had explored in *Masquerade*, both with the hares hidden in his illustrations, and with the riddle he embedded in the story which would lead to the location of a golden one he had buried in the actual countryside, in Bedfordshire.

I'd been lucky enough to meet Williams in 2015, through a friend who'd modelled for him. It had been a time when I had been just starting to become more hare-like myself, less imprisoned and predictable in the way I spent my time, more free, more me. When newspaper editors got in touch and asked me to write a piece reacting to something that I didn't have a reaction to, I said no, and went out and circled a hill on foot instead. People told me the sensible steps I should take for the benefit of my career and my profile, and I did the opposite. I know Williams would have approved. I had rarely met a more hare-like man, sinewy, long-looking without being tall, with piercing eyes full of occult knowledge, and mostly covered in a thick layer of hare-coloured fur. The way he had behaved after *Masquerade*'s success, and the publication of its follow-up, *The Bee Book*, was the way a hare would probably have behaved if a hare had ever created books that sold millions of copies, suddenly found itself discussing them on primetime TV with Terry Wogan and received thousands of fan letters a week. When his publisher asked him to write another 'puzzle' book that he didn't in his heart want to write, he vanished from public life, continuing to live at the base of a hill in rural Gloucestershire and make the art he had always been compelled to make. But in truth Williams had always been hare-like, and the high-profile period around *Masquerade*'s publication was the aberration. The publisher Tom Maschler had first discussed the idea for the book – or one not unlike it – with Williams in the mid-seventies, to not a massive amount of enthusiasm on the part of Williams, and the project had, in Maschler's mind, been forgotten, so he was more than surprised when Williams got in touch three years later to say *Masquerade* was complete, then turned up with a trunk containing the illustrations, all painted on wood, sewn into individual blankets for protection and insured for £100,000. This, you feel, is exactly what a hare would do if it wrote a book. You probably wouldn't have even met the hare beforehand. 'Hi,' the hare would say, arriving at your office. 'The book is complete.' 'Who are you? What book?' you would ask the hare. 'I am a hare, and this is the book I have written. Also, I have some big news for you: I am pregnant. Also, I have some more big news for you: I am pregnant again, even though I am already pregnant.'

The scene from the top of Painswick Beacon was much like a scene in *Masquerade*, a book where all the landscapes were rolling and soft. The Severn Estuary sparkled to the west, an upturned full-length mirror rested flat on the ground. I peered at it. Was the hidden hare in the water? Or was it in the trees below, or the clouds, or on a Stroud rooftop? Earlier in the day I'd been reading about Phyllis Barron, the early twentieth-century Painswick-based textile designer, who made indigo dye using urine and used to hold what she called 'piddle parties' to obtain it. I could see her, too, in the distorted Williams version of the scene in my head: a lady in a 1940s dress, taller than any tree, sitting at the foot of the hill holding a giant bucket, preparing for her latest piddle party, surrounded by patchwork fields.

The Beacon allowed me to track the corridor of the M5, the hill road, from a new angle. It offered a fresh appreciation on the shape of the country, the closeness of everything, the true size of the quilt we live on. There is nothing like climbing hills for perspective. Only a face full of sea rivals it. Perhaps this is why I climb so many hills: to make up for thirteen years of living in inland Norfolk and having no perspective. I'd had hares, but I'd not had perspective. Perhaps that was the choice you had to make in life: hares or perspective. You could never have everything. I'd loved Norfolk, and I loved here, but no place is without drawbacks.

I think there is another reason for my hill obsession that goes beyond just the perspective they offer and the intoxicating thrill of reaching the top of them: I am afraid of heights. But my fear of heights is weirdly selective and goes hand in hand with my unending fascination with heights. I'm the person who watches planes coming into Heathrow with his mouth open in uncomprehending wonder, yet who, for the last seventeen years, has done everything in his power to avoid getting on one. I still dream about the plane I was on that was struck by lightning over the Channel in 1998, but sometimes I sense the dreams are less PTSD and more a Netflix of the mind. I was a satchel of nerves by the time I'd got scarcely more than halfway up the Eiffel Tower but I will dangle my feet off the edge of the Golden Cap, the highest point on the country's south coast, as casually as a child on a swing. On visits to Bristol, I go to great lengths to incorporate the Clifton Suspension Bridge into my day, because of the beauty of the Avon Gorge, but also because I don't fully believe the bridge exists and have decided the matter needs properly investigating. When I see it lit up in the mist, I am perfectly prepared for it to vanish. How does it meet in the middle, and stay up? It all seems very fishy. I have visited the small museum just beyond its western extremity – the M5 side of it – numerous times, looking for evidence of black magic. I have not found the black magic, but I now know a fair bit about the bridge, whose architect Isambard Kingdom Brunel died five years before its completion and only narrowly escaped death much earlier in its construction, in 1843, when he had to have a tracheotomy to remove a coin he'd swallowed while performing a magic trick for a child. When the bridge was finally complete, the first person to cross it was twenty-one-year-old Mary Griffiths, an impressively hare-like runner who – after paying the one penny toll, and lifting up her skirts – raced and beat an unnamed young man to the other side, by several yards. The toll is now a pound and you don't have to pay it if you are not a car. Weirdly, considering that it's 331 feet above the river and man-made, the bridge doesn't frighten me, apart from when there's a very high wind, and it starts to shake. In his 2017 BBC documentary about wind, the writer and producer Tim Dee tells a very moving story of the time in his youth, while doing his paper round, that he saw a man commit suicide off the bridge, and believed he had flown away on the wind. According to my parents, when I was a toddler I asked their Irish friend George why we can't see wind. I think it is still a very valid question, especially when I am on the suspension bridge in a minor gale.

My attitude to heights could be viewed as the ultimate manifestation of a trust in nature and mistrust of man: the same outlook that means I am far more at ease with the idea of being eaten by a tiger than being put to death by lethal injection. But it's about more than that. Heights,

even those that would be viewed as non-spectacular by any daredevil mountain climber or skydiver, are a drug for me, and like all drugs, a dependency on them can cut in and have a detrimental effect on the rest of your life. You put it ahead of responsibilities – to work, to the people you care about. I have climbed a lot of hills when I should have been filling my time more sensibly. I suppose this is my completist side coming out. I've never been a puritanical completist, though. I don't need to own the inferior albums a great musician made, just because I like the great musician's great albums. But hills are always good. Hills don't make bad albums. Put a hill on a song on your album, and the album will almost certainly be better for it. 'The Hills of Greenmore', on the first Steeleye Span album, is already fundamentally great because it's about a hare, but is further enhanced by featuring not one but several hills. Where were these hill hares that folk bands sang about, and why wasn't I seeing any of them? It isn't as if hares are exclusive to flatlands. One of the sixty-nine ancient monikers for the hare, mentioned in *The Names of the Hare*, the poem written on the Welsh border in the late thirteenth century, is Ring the Hill, and presumably that doesn't come from nowhere. It's one of my favourite hare nicknames, along with Old Fat Bum, Dewflirt, Stag of the Stubble, Woodcat and The One Who Does Not Go Straight Home. The last is presumably a reference to that indirect, mazing run hares are prone to, but it's suggestive of something else too, a secret after-dark activity. The hare's extra business, which it will never stoop to reveal to us.

In the opening illustration of *Masquerade*, field mice build their nest in a tangle of weeds at the perimeter of a field under the light of a full moon. On the horizon, you can make out just a sliver of sea. There's a farmhouse whose foundations lean with the slope it's built on to the extent that, if you laid out a meal on a table in its kitchen, every last plate of food would no doubt slide off it onto the floor. Behind the farmhouse, obscuring the rest of the sea, is a hill that looks like a buttock, which, when you look more closely, turns out to be the answer to the illustration's puzzle: the hare, its ears pinned back in alertness, its eyes focused on something unseeable in the stubble pasture ahead of it. A hare hill. Old Fat Bum. To me it is the most Dorset scene in the book: it's the combination of the particular kind of green, the angle of that farmhouse, the precise depth and shallowness of spaces between the hills, and the shape of that buttock mound. It's a hill that's patently an individual and has just a touch of the man-made and prehistoric about it. If you got a bit closer, the grass at the top would appear tightly stretched across the chalky topsoil, as it does on many Dorset hills. It reminds me of Colmer's Hill, just outside Bridport, another lone Dorset mound, although Colmer's is a little too tall to be a buttock, and boasts a rockabilly quiff of trees, allegedly to assist the ships of centuries gone by with navigation. When I climbed it in late 2018, on Remembrance Sunday, a bright red carpet of artificial poppies had been laid over its eastern slope, which seemed entirely fitting of its VIP status in the landscape.

I was at the beginning of a phase of being seduced by Dorset's hills in much the same way as I'd been seduced by the ones that provided the walls for the M5's corridor. Growing brave, I forged farther along the Jurassic Coast, into the east of the county, throwing aside my preconception that everything over there was essentially an outer suburb of London. On one of several coastal walks on the Isle of Purbeck in the first half of 2019, I spotted another hare, my third live one in total since moving to the West Country. It was just a brief sighting on a ridge above Kimmeridge Bay, where for an amazing half an hour before sundown I felt like I'd stumbled on the exact spot where all of Purbeck's wildlife congregated. Before I'd seen the hare, I'd turned a corner to find myself ten yards away from a fawn who'd looked me directly in the eye before hurdling a fence and bouncing away across the field ahead in the most cartoonish, fluffy-tailed way. I realised I was grinning. It was early April and the lambs were tiny and just as cartoonish and for many yards in every direction southern England had the deceptive appearance of having recently been born. I'd not even embarked on this walk specifically for the wildlife; the day's mission had been to see Tyneham, a village a few miles west along the coast, last inhabited in 1943. Tyneham's 225 residents left their homes during the Second World War when it was repurposed as a military firing range. The villagers expected to be allowed to return but the military decided to hold on to the land. The houses are now ruins, largely roofless, but there is something untarnished about them, which adds to the feeling that you are tumbling through time. The spaces hold you and tell you their story, which is one where the twentieth century made only the lightest of marks. In 1940, the farm here was still tractor-less, with no running water or electricity. Milk churns were kept in water overnight as a rudimentary form of refrigeration and the lorry driver who collected them would dip his head in the churn to test the freshness.

The general public aren't permitted to walk through Tyneham and along this part of the Jurassic Coast except on certain dates, and you need to check the firing range timetable before you try to do so. In *Nuts in May*, Mike Leigh's 1976 TV play about a Dorset camping holiday, the holidaymakers Keith and Candice-Marie fall foul of the in-use firing ranges. *Nuts in May* is still, for my money, the greatest thing Leigh has ever done, even more subtle and clever than his better-known *Abigail's Party* from the following year. Alison Steadman stars as Candice-Marie in *Nuts in May* and as the patronising party host Beverly in *Abigail's Party*. The dizzying, impossible fact that these brilliant and entirely different performances could emerge from the mind and body of one human was what, when I was in my early teens, first made me aware that acting was an art form. As Candice-Marie and Keith drive around Dorset, Keith mansplains rural England to her, lectures her about how crucial it is to chew your food seventy-two times, tells her off for picking stones off the beach because 'if everyone did that there wouldn't be any pebbles left' and reminds her of the importance of his 'schedule'. Down from Croydon, on hiatus from their respective jobs in social services and a toy shop, Keith and Candice-Marie make up naive folk songs together, clash with noisy yobs on bikes and stick to a health-conscious vegetarian diet. Their treat, when they feel like they've earned it and really want to kick back and let go, is raw mushrooms. At the time, *Nuts in May* was part of a growing tide of anti-hippie piss-taking that helped invent the 1980s, but now Candice-Marie and Keith come across as a little ahead of their time with their eco-awareness and simple, sustainable lifestyle, and Candice-Marie's inventive, knitwear-heavy, jumble-sale wardrobe seems less goofy, more stylish. A subplot of the play is Candice-Marie's rebellion against Keith's despotic governance of their relationship. This could have been conveyed in a much more heavy-handed way, with Candice-Marie yearning to leave Keith for a Hell's Angel and drop litter in bluebell woodland, but the central genius of the story is that the rebellion is a subtle one: Candice-Marie loves the planet, loves birds and trees and mushrooms and history, but she'd prefer to get away from Keith's schedule, and not have to worry about getting mud on the floor of their Morris Minor. In the final scene, on a new campsite, Keith heads off into the woods with a toilet roll in his hand and we see her alone with her guitar, singing the play's one non-twee song: a dark eco-ballad about what humans have done to ruin the earth. A vision emerges of her shaking off some of her rabbit-like aspects, discovering her inner hare, and breaking away from Keith to forge a successful song-writing career as a politicised songwriter: Wessex's answer to Joan Baez.

Purbeck remains spotted with *Nuts in May*-style campsites, barely pimped up farmland with not a hint of glamping, whose barbecue smells drifted over as I walked. On a bridleway through one, a sartorially flawless female camper emerged from a gate. Her wide-brimmed hat and floral dress seemed straight out of a 1969 fashion-magazine photo shoot, and I felt no less transported than I had in Tyneham, earlier in the day. Behind her in a field, a man juggled with oranges beside a campfire, an activity suggestive of a life without a spreadsheet. I headed farther east and ordered a post-walk pint from the Square and Compass, a pub with a serving hatch for a bar and which doubles as a fossil museum, in the village of Worth Matravers. No county in Britain names its villages more inventively, and less predictably, than Dorset. I see Worth Matravers as a reclusive billionaire, a William Randolph Hearst figure, who, after making his fortune in the US, came to the south-west of the UK to stare at the sea, grow his fingernails long and collect books on the golden age of sailing. His half-brother, Langton Matravers, who always mimicked his business methods and tailored suits but with less success, now continues to live in his shadow just a few miles farther along the coast. Head inland and a little west from here, and you soon reach Wool, where I can picture Candice-Marie settling after breaking away from Keith. Farther inland you soon reach the tightest concentration of villages in the world to have been named after pools of potentially tainted liquid: Puddletown, Piddlehinton, Briantspuddle, Affpuddle, Tolpuddle, Piddletrenthide. It won't be long until you also find a Caundle – Purse, Bishop's or Stourton, probably – which is an old Dorset word meaning 'conical hill'.

I'd been reading about a caundle I particularly wanted to visit: Round Knoll, above the village of West Milton, near Bridport. When I did, it was just as commanding as I'd been led to believe: another, more pert, buttock, crowned with a lichen-splashed storytelling tree. Margaret Morgan-Grenville, who owns the converted mill at the foot of the knoll, told me that everyone always thought the tree was an oak but it was an ash. Margaret had kindly invited me over for lunch, after I'd written to her and told her I was interested in the mill's former owner, the writer Kenneth Allsop. During the fifties and sixties Allsop was best known as a TV presenter, but he was also a restlessly eclectic author and, during the early seventies, when he moved to West Milton, became west Dorset's most prominent and active eco-campaigner. In his 1972 book *In the Country* – originally a collection of columns published in the unlikely context of the *Daily Mail* – he railed against agribusiness and its pesticides, and created a vivid picture of the tranquil and hidden triangle of land between West Milton, Powerstock Common and

Eggardon Hill, an area he called 'The Last Place'. With the help of his new neighbour, Brian Jackman – a fellow nature writer, several years his junior – he drummed up local support and prevented the Common, an atmospheric ancient woodland teeming with wildflowers and marsh fritillary butterflies, being turned into a deadened conifer plantation. Jackman and his wife Annabel, who still live next door and own donkeys called Punda and Toto, joined Margaret and me for lunch at the mill. Jackman recalled his first meeting with Allsop, which came about after Jackman spotted a hen harrier above Eggardon Hill and called Allsop to tell him, after looking up his number in the phone book.

At the time of writing, there are only two clips of Allsop available to watch online: an interview with John Lennon and an episode of *Points of View* where Allsop's Soho hairdresser is interviewed, in response to a viewer's

letter criticising the presenter's 'flash' new haircut. Few
people under the age of sixty-five know of Allsop now
but in the 1960s he was a famous man who enjoyed a
very glamorous lifestyle. A few weeks after my lunch with
Margaret, Brian and Annabel, I met Allsop's son Tristan
in The Three Horseshoes in Powerstock, and he remembered how Ken would walk along city streets, very focused,
and erect invisible walls at the sides of his face, so ready
was he to be recognised and stopped by members of the
general public. At their house in rural Hertfordshire, where
the family lived before moving to West Milton, they
threw parties attended by the likes of Dudley Moore,
Cleo Laine, Johnny Dankworth and other celebrities of
the day. 'Robin Day broke my pogo stick at one,' remembered Tristan. 'But he paid for a new one.' Lennon,
another of Ken's friends, would later cite a conversation
with Ken in the green room before a TV performance as
a major catalyst for his decision to leave The Beatles.
Tristan had once met Lennon and recalled how he had
introduced his sister, Amanda, to the singer, 'This is my
sister.' 'Well, I didn't think it was yer brother,' Lennon
had replied.

Ken had whipped along the tiny lanes around West
Milton in an E-Type Jaguar, which might seem at odds
with his environmentalist beliefs, until you remember that
the early 1970s were not the late 2010s. 'He was very
concerned about pollution, pesticides, oil,' said Tristan.
'But he had no knowledge of global warming. Nobody
did, back then. I suspect if he was alive now he'd feel very
guilty about it.' Tiny West Milton, which many decades
before had been in possession of the comically large

number of three hostelries, was pub-less by the time the Allsops moved there, so The Three Horseshoes had been Ken's local. As I'd sat in the bar waiting for Tristan, I'd known by all logic that I was meeting a man born in the middle of the previous century, but because I'd been reading *In the Country* and the posthumous collection of Allsop's letters to his daughter, Amanda, my head was in 1973, and I was half-expecting a fresh-faced university graduate to walk through the door, not the smiling, dignified, silvery man who did. Tristan Allsop was sharp and eloquent, with a crushing handshake and his dad's excellent hair and clothes.

Some of the fans of Allsop's TV work might have known of his simultaneous existence as an ornithologist and nature writer – his debut novel *Adventure Lit Their Star*, took the breeding of the ringed plover as its subject and won the John Llewellyn Rhys Prize in 1950 – but almost none would have been aware of the chronic pain he lived with every day. Allsop only had one leg, as a result of an injury sustained on a battle training course during his time in the RAF in the 1940s. He took medication for the pain of his phantom limb, walked with a limp – 'More of a kick than a limp, really,' recalled Tristan – and while on screen was almost never filmed below the waist. Despite his disability, he walked miles with his binoculars, observing Dorset's birdlife. In the spring of 1973, he'd recently been fitted with a new suction prosthesis, which had been giving him even more trouble, and had fallen off while he was walking through King's Cross. He was also having various troubles with his employers, and envied his neighbour Jackman's carefree life, away from the pressures of celebrity.

Jackman thinks it wasn't one overriding factor that prompted Allsop to take his own life via an overdose of barbiturates on 23 May 1973. That month in Dorset it rained, almost constantly. The mill is a beautiful building and the day was clear when I visited, but its rooms do not let in a large amount of light and, in the middle of a sequence of unrelentingly dingy days, I could see how the darkness might get to a person. Allsop's suicide note, addressed to his wife Betty, was exceedingly well-written, right up to the moment where his pen visibly trails off the page, as he loses consciousness. 'He was a consummate professional, right to the last,' said Jackman. Margaret says two of her guests have seen his ghost wandering around the mill, although she has never seen the ghost herself, and feels it's a benevolent building that's always been good to her.

Before Margaret and I walked through the valley to Powerstock church to visit Allsop's grave, she and Jackman and I wandered around the back of the mill, beneath the shadow of Round Knoll, to a wild pond. Jackman found some otter scat and identified frog bones in it. Margaret tuned in to the call of a kingfisher down on the river below, but Jackman said his hearing could no longer pick it up. It was the same with a lot of birdsong. It was, he said, one of his least favourite aspects of getting old. He was now three decades older than Ken had been when he died. I asked him whether he thought Ken would have been pleasantly surprised or saddened by the state of Britain's wildlife today. Jackman said he thought it would be a mixture of the two, that – and this was echoed by

Tristan – he'd be deeply saddened by the diminishment of birdlife, but he probably wouldn't have expected to see the resurgence of otters in places like this, or the peregrines who'd defied the odds to come back and nest on virtually every cathedral in the UK. Just before his death, Ken had seen a peregrine while on holiday in Wales and been convinced it was the last he or anyone he knew would ever witness.

A week later, I walked from Powerstock, through the Common to Eggardon Hill, and was surprised to find it still much the way Allsop had described it: 'The Last Place' remained a fitting description. I explored the old railway line, a late survivor of Beeching's axe, among the branch lines, where trains had still been running at the end of Allsop's life. Back then, cows would step out onto the line from time to time as the trains went to and from New Malden and the driver would stop the train, getting out to shoo them away. Now the disused cutting was made almost solely of primroses and atmosphere. The Common, just beyond it, felt like a mindbendingly old place. Under Eggardon, farmhouses nestled on the lower slopes, like the one in the *Masquerade* illustration, albeit probably with kitchen tables that did not slant quite so severely. The hill itself, over 800 feet high, was wide and weird and stark with spiky totemic-looking trees and a sky that made me feel dispensable. Cars were known to cut out along its dome, for no scientifically explainable reason: three at the same time, on one occasion. The mud as you descended was wet and hot, as if underneath the surface layer upon layer of matter was fermenting.

*

I continued to tick off the hills, failing to stick to the schedule, often not going straight home, getting mud on the floor of my car, treating myself to the occasional raw mushroom when I decided I'd earned it. Hambledon and Hod, with the nightingales, jumpy cows and chalky Neolithic causeways. Ashmore, the highest village in Dorset, where I watched the annual festival, The Filly Loo, in which villagers danced in slow motion wearing antlers to elegiac flutes playing the Abbots Bromley Horn Dance beside the village pond, which is said to be inhabited by Gubbigamies who gibber in the night. The only mention I can find anywhere of Gubbigamies is by Michael Pitt-Rivers in his 1935 book *Dorset: A Shell Guide* and I still am in the dark as to precisely what they are. Pitt-Rivers, grandson of the legendary archaeologist Augustus Pitt Rivers, also reports that, beside the pond, 'a Mr Hare failed to win Miss Rabbits, so he married instead Miss Bunny' but doesn't expand on the matter. Were these actual animals, people with amusingly coincidental surnames, or liminal creatures of the crepuscular hours? In Ashmore, on a summer evening, with the sun slipping behind the old hunting forest of Cranborne Chase, all explanations seemed possible. I chased another spectacular sun into the sea behind the Golden Cap, not quite making it in time. In the pub below, I got talking to an Australian man, who asked me what music I liked. He said his name was Michael and he had been in the industry but was now retired. His wife had recently passed away and he'd felt the need to escape, because back home his friends were doing something he described as 'killing me with kindness'. He had a bittersweet air about him that suggested an intersection of sadness and freedom. He was staying very flexible for the remainder of his trip, he said, and asked me for West Country hill recommendations. He was obviously not somebody who stuck to the schedule and I liked him instantly.

If you drive north from the Cap, you'll find yourself in some quiet valleys, where, if it's night-time, you have no satnav, your phone has run down and you can't charge it because crisp crumbs or beach sand or maybe both have clogged up the cigarette lighter socket behind the gearstick, you can get lost for well over an hour. If it's daytime, and you navigate more successfully, you'll eventually hit the Blackdown Hills, and you'll know the moment you have because that's when the mounds and mumps and buttocks start to act less like individuals and the person who paints the landscape adds a bit of black to the green on their palette. In the Second World War fires were lit on The Blackdowns, to lure German bombers away from Bristol, and when I walked in them they always seemed a bit smoky – never more so than in November 2017, when I climbed through Prior's Park Wood.

As I emerged from the wood, feeling sure I had reached the top of the hill, I was surprised to find another sharp incline ahead of me, and another crown of mist. Out of the silence I heard the heavy thump of hooves, and through the mist I saw the hot breath of three stallions who were chasing in circles around a field at the summit, violently, as if conjured out of a secret hole in the earth by a spell. Their size and power was awe-inspiring and the ground shook underneath them. What I was seeing had a flavour of America's Old West, a shocking reminder that men and women rode and tamed these animals, nonchalantly, but a flavour of something very English too. I wanted to watch them but also – despite being shielded by a fence – to move away, and as I did, a larger than average dog of unspecific breed leapt at me from behind a hedge. It bounced beside me as I walked, like a toothy punk in a mosh pit, and nipped at my jacket – not exactly vicious, and certainly not quite friendly, just . . . possessed. 'Don't worry, it's OK,' I told the dog, again and again, before I realised that my instructions were aimed not at the dog but at myself. It was as if the whole fifty-square-yard circle of land was possessed and I would not have been surprised to find a large ancient stone at its centre, glowing.

Afterwards, I walked along a fast road, dodging cars driven by people that, like the horses and the dog, seemed more untamed than most of their breed, and was glad to get into calmer country: first a fallow field behind a barrier of beech trees with exposed roots, then gold-carpeted paths through thick evergreen woodland, and an even deeper locked-in quiet. Even through this calmer part of my walk, some of the energy from that invisible circle on the hilltop carried over. I passed a bare witching tree with sharp prongs reaching towards an orange crack in the sky, and then a child's toy panda trapped in dying brambles, which from a distance resembled an esoteric hedge spirit, then along more quiet paths with mist sinking down onto them. I finally reached a village pub, where I stopped for a drink and to make some notes. The countryside in the approach to the pub was somehow simultaneously savage but rigorously organised: a neat but very Gothic church, a bonfire set up two days in advance for Guy Fawkes Night, with a scarecrow trapped inside, dressed sensibly ahead of a potentially cold night. The inside of the pub was raucous and cramped, alarmingly so for 4.30 p.m. on a weekday in a scenario that did not involve a stag or hen party. I was hot from walking fast to beat the dark, so I took my pint outside to the deserted beer garden, and began to write about my walk in my journal. After a couple of minutes, I became aware of a shadow looming over me. 'What are you doing? Writing in your *diary*?' a voice asked. The tone was not totally unfriendly but had dashes of School Bully and cider in it. I looked up and saw that it belonged to a wide shouldered bald man. I initially put him at about forty-seven, which, after talking to him for a few minutes, I revised down to a hard-lived thirty-eight or thirty-nine. We chatted a little while, and a few of his friends joined us, smoking roll-ups. They observed that I didn't come across as someone from round there, and I told them they were correct, and that I lived in Devon, not far from Dartmoor.

'I've been to Dartmoor,' said the bald man. 'Fucking horrible place.'

'What took you there?' I asked.

'I was in the prison,' he said.

'That prison used to get its food from my great-grandma's family,' I said.

'Well, tell them it's shit,' he said.

The bald man's friend told me about the birds of prey

he had seen in the woodland above us: huge hawks. 'You haven't asked him what he was in for,' he said, pointing to the bald man.

I told him that I thought it would be a bit impolite of me to do so.

'Go on!' the avian enthusiast told the bald man. 'Tell him.'

'Stealing women's knickers. I got three years.'

'He's not right,' said the avian enthusiast.

'If he's right,' said another, older man, who had joined us, 'I don't want to be.'

A middle-aged woman emerged from the bar and made our party larger, and the bald man started to engage in flirtatious chat with her. I noticed a sign next to us, which advertised the area as a 'Man Creche', offering women the chance to 'go shopping' or 'relax'. What about the women who didn't want to go shopping, and who preferred to relax by getting pissed up? Were they welcome here? And where were these shops of which they spoke? I'd just walked ten miles and hadn't seen a hint of so much as a petrol station. You get these ideas into your head, when you're in the West, that everything gets more raw and empty the further you probe away from the middle of the country, down towards the bottom of the sock of the peninsula, but that isn't the full story. Rules like that are unwise generalisations. They are for the Keiths, not the Candice-Maries, of the universe. This was a raw place: much rawer than the place, over an hour farther west, where I was living at the time.

*

That same autumn was the one when I ended my long dry spell and saw my second West Country hare: three years after the one I'd seen near my house in Devon, and a year and a half before the one I saw on the Isle of Purbeck. It happened on the day I finally got around to climbing Brent Knoll. I'd been going straight home, on my way back from another steep walk, then changed my mind and decided that my investigation of the big stemless onion by the M5 was long overdue. All I'd seen was a flash of brown in the stubble field below, nothing like as clear as my East Anglia hare sightings, but the movement, the zigzag, as it ringed the base of the hill, was unmistakable.

Ring the Hill: the phrase had good connotations. I liked the idea of a hill as something you might get in touch with in a crisis, big or small . . . at a point when you needed perspective: 'Dial 999 and choose option 3, "Hill", to speak directly to a hill.' 'Fun hills are waiting to chat just with you. Calls cost 60p per minute peak time!'

Brent Knoll was everything I'd hoped it would be and more. It was a more sociable companion than its rival, Crook Peak, and despite the shortfall in height the view from the ancient fort on the top was somehow better. I realised the corner of the Bristol Channel, the moment where the north coast of the South-West Peninsula begins, was much closer than I had thought. I'd realised this before, but obviously needed to re-realise it for it to totally sink in. There was some very strange, flat land down there: mudflats, pillboxes, sunken boats daubed with graffiti. It was a small fenland with various geographical laws of its own. SLURRY LAGOON. TOXIC GAS. NO ENTRY. DANGER OF DROWNING, a sign had warned me at the beginning of the six-mile walk I'd done down there, which kind of set the tone. The sea became a thing gradually, out of miles of flatness, without seeming to know it had become sea. Down in that corner at West Huntspill I'd walked up Plymor Hill, which, at just two feet high, has been acknowledged as the smallest hill in England. I had tried to notice the ascent, but I might have tried too hard and merely imagined it. From my vantage point at the top of Brent Knoll, I turned to the east, where I could see Glastonbury Tor, fifteen miles away. South of that was the Wellington Monument, where I'd walked through more strange Blackdowns Mist, more like steam than mist, just above Popham's Pit, named after the corrupt Speaker of the House of Commons and Attorney General who allegedly perished there in 1696, having been flung violently from his horse. The pit purportedly leads directly to Hell, where Popham's spirit was held on probation until, after some hard praying from his widow, he was permitted, at the meagre rate of one cockstride per year, to return to Wellington Church, four miles away. Above the pit is a tree that two foresters tried to cut down in the 1860s but had to stop, after hearing 'pitiful cries' emerging from a disembodied voice in the trunk.

I am not sure how many cockstrides it took me to get to the bottom of Brent Knoll, but it didn't feel like many. I kept my eye out for the hare on the way down. At the bottom, before I left, I decided to have a look inside the church. Its neat and friendly exterior was juxtaposed with a series of gruesome medieval carvings on its bench ends,

depicting the trial and execution of a fox by hanging. It was an unexpectedly sombre end to a pleasant day and it prompted my thoughts to flick back to a walk I'd taken with a friend over the corner of the water, deep inside the peninsula, when the friend had told me about the time he and his brother had been taken fox hunting as a child, and, as the youngest member of the party, he'd been anointed with the blood of the murdered animal. He was a quiet and reclusive character, sensitive and gentle, a slower walker than me who took time to listen to the countryside and was always having intense encounters with animals. We'd been walking up to Bowerman's Nose at the time, a tall pile of rocks on east Dartmoor, not unreminiscent of a stack of pale sheep dung, but which people also said was the effigy of a medieval hunter, transformed to stone by a coven of witches after upturning their cauldron during his pursuit of a hare. Talking about this hare folk tale led the friend to recall his one West Country encounter with a hare, which had happened on a deserted Devon lane at night, on his route home from the pub. It had not lasted long, but long enough to be a little different to his other encounters with wild animals, and he said it would probably stay with him forever. The hare, crouched in the middle of the lane, had locked him in its gaze, and both of them had frozen. In that position, for over a minute, they had both remained – until the hare finally turned and zigzagged away. And for just a second, before the hare made its escape and got on with its unknowable business, the friend had been certain he had been stared at by the eyes of a man.

THE LION, THE WITCH
AND THE DRESS CODE
(2014–17)

If I'm going to speak in depth about the Magic House, I
should probably begin at the railway station. There are
persuasive arguments for starting on the riverbank, or on
the wildflower path leading down to the back gate from
the top of the hill, or even in the pub, but I think the
station is the place, because that was the walking route I
took back to the Magic House most often, and the direction I was coming from when I first set eyes on the Magic
House, which is a place where, in the nicest possible way,
you cannot escape an ambience of rail travel. The station
is also where you might say The Compound starts. That's
what I would announce to friends who were visiting for

the first time, when we passed through the old stone gates of the estate: 'We are now entering The Compound.' It was a joke, a reference to the place's otherness, its illustrious yet flawed past as a social experiment, and the idea that, once within its boundaries, you might not be able to escape, but now, with the perspective that comes from having been back on the Outside for eighteen months, it seems more like a plain statement of fact. The Dartington Hall estate in south Devon is a mixture of many things and isn't really like any other place on earth. Once you've been part of it, you never entirely leave.

What is interesting to me now is that I remember walking past the Magic House on my first visit to Dartington in late 2011, noticing it from the pavement on the opposite side of the road – which a surprising amount of people don't – and wondering what its function was. I don't think I even realised it was a residential building, less still the kind I would ever want to live in. It looked dark and unwelcoming and Gothic, possibly a former chapel, and I was finished with dark old buildings and was now utterly under the spell of the light, functional living spaces of the mid-twentieth century, some of which – designed by the Swiss-American architect William Lescaze – I had come here specifically to see. What I didn't know was that the Gothic front was a disguise. The Magic House was a sweet old grandma in a Dracula mask.

Sweating profusely in weather that was November's only in name, I lugged my heavy bags on up the hill and did not give the building another thought for well over two years. Because I'm me, I had decided not to take a taxi to the estate from the hotel in Totnes where I'd stayed the previous night, and instead to walk with my suitcase and rucksack two miles from the far end of town to the hall, passing the station where I'd arrived for the first time two days earlier. Between March 2014 and the end of 2017 I would do the same walk – or at least the latter two thirds of it – close to a thousand times. By then I would be familiar with the shortcut: you nipped through the car park beside the westbound platform, down a small alleyway behind the disused Dairy Crest plant, whose huge chimney dominated the skyline of the town no less than its Norman castle or medieval hilltop grid of merchant houses and jumbled terraces. You passed graffiti and penitential-looking hoops of barbed wire, rounded a bend, then hit some trees, which brought you out at a junction of paths beside the river.

There is a shockingly dark spot in those trees, so dark that I find it hard to believe that there could be a darker spot of countryside within half a mile of a town in the whole of the UK. You're still within a hundred yards of residential streets at this point, which makes the darkness all the more unfathomable. Soon you will be properly out of town, into the untrammelled countryside of the estate, but you will find nothing as inexplicably dark on the paths there. On the nights when I had no phone battery or torch and walked back from town and hit the dark spot, I would often lose my sense of direction entirely, realising I was walking back the way I came, as if the dark spot itself had spun me around. And I am generally a person with a good sense of direction. On one occasion, I hit the dark spot, fell over and grated an amount of skin on my arm that would have not been viewed as a frugal addition to an Italian meal, had it been parmesan and not skin. I was a little drunk, but I don't think that was the reason I fell; it felt more as though the dark spot had been in a particularly black mood and had dashed me to the ground. The official entrance to the estate was another couple of hundred yards on from the dark spot but I began to think of the dark spot as a curtain in the land, a partition where you became briefly invisible – the unofficial entrance to The Compound.

I had only been dimly aware of it at the time, but during my initial visit Dartington was going through a period of transition. The legendary Arts College there had been shut down a year before as part of a drive to save money, and a rebranding process was underway which would involve the vans of estate workers being emblazoned with inane, airy slogans such as 'Driven By Ideas', and the beautiful, cosy White Hart pub in the fourteenth-century Hall being relocated to a bigger, adjoining room and laid out in a manner that my friend Jay once memorably likened to 'a 1980s German techno bar'. By 2014, when I arrived as a tenant, the estate was in a quiet, sluggish period. There was a lot of resentment in Totnes regarding how far it had strayed from the original vision of Dorothy and Leonard Elmhirst, the couple who'd bought the estate in 1925 for £30,000 and had turned it into a charitable trust, a school, a working farm and an arts venue, generating hundreds of jobs in what was at the time, largely as a knock-on result of the Industrial Revolution, an extremely deprived area of the British countryside.

Anyone who had lived in the TQ9 postcode for more than a few years remembered a time when you could wander along the River Dart and into the woods of the 1,200-acre estate on a summer evening and stumble on an impromptu piece of theatre or live music. They could not help but notice the drop-off in attendance at gigs in town since the college had closed and the students had gone, and many were saddened that the estate had turned its focus towards corporate weddings and other functions and away from community and creativity. But all of life is relative. Not being saddled with the comparisons that having known Dartington in its heyday entailed, I simply marvelled at how amazing it all was. My first spring and summer were one long dream where, while being regularly told how terrible it had all become, I wondered what administrative error had allowed a scruffy ill-educated northern oik like me to live in a place so pictur-esque, historically esteemed and spiritually untarnished. TOTNES: TWINNED WITH NARNIA announced the defaced sign at the bottom of the lane. But the sign was facing in the wrong direction. Everybody who knew Dartington and Totnes knew the real Narnia was through the gate-posts and up the hill.

In late 2013 and early 2014, I had been looking unsuc-cessfully for a place to rent in south Devon. Because I was doing my hunting from my home in Norfolk, at a 350-mile disadvantage, everything decent in my price bracket was snapped up before I got chance to see it. Then the happy memory of my visit to Dartington three autumns earlier popped into my head. 'They had lots of buildings on that estate,' I thought. 'And people probably live in some of them.' I wrote to the Trust, who put me on a waiting list for their rental properties. The houses were thin on the ground and Dartington employees got first refusal, but timing was in my favour; just as my contract was coming to an end on the bungalow I'd been renting as a stopgap in Norwich, a terrace on the northwest side of the estate became available. Better still, it was one of the flat-roofed modernist Lescaze buildings that I'd been fetishising on my earlier trip: the smallest one on the estate.

People think they can get the hots for a house solely from seeing its photographs, but that's not true: it's ultimately all about a house's pheromones. You need to have a chat with a house in 3D and see if there's any chemistry. When I met the Lescaze house in person, I liked it, but not nearly as much as I'd imagined. As she showed me out, the Property Manager announced that by sheer chance a detached cottage had also become available that very day, on the opposite side of the Hall, and we wandered over, through the courtyard and a little way down the hill. Because we entered the garden through the rear gate, I didn't initially realise I was looking at that same Gothic building I'd spotted a few years previously. It oozed charisma instantly from every brick. It was, like Dartington itself, a mix of many apparently disparate elements that somehow coalesced into a mellow coherence: classic inky Devon granite, 1920s Crittall windows, a touch of arts and crafts, a cottagey extension, that ecclesiastical front. It appeared very substantial from the back but much of the bulk came from the depth of the walls. 'It's like a Tardis!' is the King Cliché Phrase of house viewings, an observation made so often, and often so inaccurately, that all meaning has been beaten out of it. This was a rare instance of the opposite, a house that was much smaller than it looked from the outside: the Anti-Tardis. Its core felt deeply old, but not spooky, with the sole possible exception of the understairs cupboard, which my cats would give a wide berth or gaze into in wide-eyed terror whenever I opened it to fetch a screwdriver or the vacuum cleaner. The house was only dark in summer, which ultimately wouldn't matter because in summer, at Dartington, you always wanted to be outside. Close to the centre of the building was a second doorstep, an arch and a huge old painted hinge: evidence of a former main door, a suggestion of a solid, squat edifice dating from long, long before the Elmhirsts arrived here, when the estate belonged to the Champernowne family. In winter, the almost-hilltop location and lack of double-glazing resulted in draughts that slithered under the hedges, through the gaps in the doors and windows and up the legs of your pyjama bottoms. On the hottest days of July, every room remained a benevolent, slatey sort of cool. In four months' time, returning shivering from the estate's unheated outdoor swimming pool, I would dash up through that slatey cool, and warm myself in a hot bath, still feeling the buzz of the cold and the exercise, watching the purple gradually drain from my fingertips: a new kind of bath experience, better than any previous bath experience I had known.

What I remember most about my first weeks at the Magic House is the growth, all around me, a crescendo of it, building and building until it finally broke, in early July, and the universe momentarily attained total perfection. It was evident even in the alleyway near the station with the graffiti and the hooped barbed wire, where the walk to Narnia began; in a small patch of waste ground under a wall, red valerian, ox-eye daisies and St John's wort formed a gang to suffocate broken bottles and crisp packets. That path to my new back gate, my favourite approach to any house I had ever known, was a waking dream of speedwell, forget-me-not, fleabane, wild strawberry, crocus, snowdrop, celandine, primrose, bluebell and teasel, if never quite all at the same time. Part of this could be attributed to early 2014's particular combination of weeks of flooding followed by weeks of fierce sunlight, but partly it was just south Devon. When the Elmhirsts began to restore the gardens of the estate in the 1920s, they discovered it was possible to grow numerous sub-tropical plants there that they wouldn't have been able to grow in the east or north. Horticulturally, and in several other ways, if felt to me like a different country, after almost four decades spent entirely on the other side of England.

In April and May, below Nellies Wood – a wood without an apostrophe, so presumably an area where you might once have found several Nellies, rather than one Nellie who lorded it about the place – not far from the entrance to The Compound, the bank of bluebells always raged, but I have never seen it rage quite like it did during that period in 2014. The colours were like colours only normally seen on old postcards, or under the influence of drugs, or in a mid-twentieth-century Powell and Pressburger film with cinematography by Jack Cardiff, or in your vision of spring as you always assume it looks in your grandparents' saturated memories. On the lane here someone installed a BEWARE FROGS sign. I never saw any frogs near it but as I passed I would often spin around, a little wired, vigilant for frogs in every way. I soon learned on my walks back from the station that the best way to the house was not to continue up the hill, but take a half-right shortly after this, along the footpath that runs parallel to the river and into a meadow. From April until summer's end you found small rings of lolling teenagers here letting their river-damp hair dry in the sun, listening to the techno hippie music all Totnes natives under sixty bafflingly seem to love. Young cows with big eyelashes rubbed their sharp cheekbones ecstatically on the low-hanging branches of the oaks closest to the bank. Near the mainline station, the two trainlines of the area inter-sect: the more functional one running between London and Cornwall and the one used by the steam train that chugs down from Buckfastleigh. After that, the pair part ways and the steam train rejoins the line of the river. My dad was so excited when he first walked along here with me and saw the train make its gentle way through the valley that he ran alongside it for a little spell, cheering. If you were to turn the soundtrack of the Magic House's garden into an LP, 'Steam Train Whistle' would be one of the essential tracks, along with, 'Woman In Tunic Learns Flute Under Distant Mulberry Tree', 'Woodpecker', 'Bat Wingbeat', 'Newly Besotted Lesbian Couple Discuss Bio-dynamic Farming While Resting On A Navajo Blanket', 'Upmarket Dog Gets Lightly Scolded', 'Sudden Jackdaw', 'Industrious Bee' and 'Randy Owl'. From dusk, the tawny owls were a constant in the oaks near the river. My friend

Nathan helped restore the crumbling eighteenth-century wall of the estate's medieval deer park and was adamant that, during winter, not long before the end of his day's work, he would hear the owls calling back to the whistle of the train, perhaps mistaking it for a giant owl, the Master of All Owls, an all-seeing Owl Deity.

After reaching the end of the meadow on my walk from the station, I passed through a gate into a wooded, often boggy area, where huge gale-blown tree trunks snoozed in the shallows, some horizontal and dead, some looming at impossible angles over the water, like tall hung-over executives who'd fallen asleep leaning on the desks

in their office. A red setter once chased a fox past me close to this spot, and I worried for the fox until it found its extra couple of gears, leaving the dog in a pleasing, literal cloud of dust. Of its ilk, if it has an ilk, which I'm not convinced it has, the estate is virtually unrivalled for public access, a wish of the Elmhirsts that is still upheld to this day. Dog walkers are encouraged into the compound but asked by numerous signs to keep their dogs on leads. While I lived there many ignored the signs, unable to believe their coddled, perfect dogs could possibly do any harm to another living thing, until – as happened with depressing regularity – their dog killed one of Dartington's sheep. It was always when the dog walkers weren't around that you'd see the best wildlife Dartington had to offer: the foxes, the badgers, the kingfishers, the cirl buntings, the otters.

You can continue along the Dart here and, as a newcomer, be under the impression you're walking far, far away from the Hall, not realising that the river forms a semicircle around The Compound, keeping you safe, looking after you, never putting you in danger of re-entering society. That was the way I went on my walks in the early mornings, when I was looking for wildlife or mist, often still in my pyjama bottoms. But when I was coming back from town I left the river here. After a few more yards in the boggy area, I took a gate on the left and doubled three quarters back on myself, before taking a right turn up the hill, past a compost cradle set up by the estate to encourage Dartington's adder population. A grass corridor, where rabbits hopped about sweetly oblivious to the narrowed eyes of stoats and weasels in the undergrowth, led to the long, rising meadow in front of my house, a deceptive steep place where I would always feel the ache in my calves and shoulders, especially if I was carrying the paraphernalia of a supermarket trip or train journey, and would yearn for the respite the Magic House offered as it came into view up the hill.

The meadow changed character drastically from season to season. During my second summer at Dartington, satisfying curved paths were mown into the meadow and the remainder was left unkempt, for the benefit of pollinating insects. On my lawn, on the opposite side of the lane, I mowed paths mirroring those in the meadow, leaving much of the rest long, and not just to get out of some of the giant job of mowing the massive, temperamental, wrap-around collection of grass patches that came with the Magic House. Corvids were always circling above the dead trees in the meadow, a 300-yard-long rectangle of ground where small moments of aggro occurred strangely often. In spring, obnoxious bullocks crowded and shadowed walkers who crossed the meadow, as if jeering at them in the way sailors might as they followed antisocially close behind a girl walking along a pier. Dogs quarrelled. Dog owners attempted to adjudicate, often without success. Here is a five-way dog and dog owner conversation I transcribed after witnessing it take place in the meadow in November 2016:

Pooka the Dog: 'Ruff!'
Rufus the Dog: 'Ruff Ruff!'
Pooka the Dog's Owner: 'POOKA!'
Rufus the Dog's Owner: 'Rufus.'
Pooka the Dog: 'Ruff Rawgh!'

Rufus the Dog: 'Ruff Ruff!'

Pooka the Dog's Owner: 'POOKAAAA! NO! POOKA! Nooooo. POOKAAAAAA.'

Rufus the Dog's Owner: 'Rufus.'

Wilson the Dog's Owner: 'Don't even think about it, Wilson.'

You couldn't see a person approach the front gate of the Magic House from the meadow, due to the screen formed by a huge leylandii, my garden's least interesting plant. So it was baffling to me how my cat Shipley was usually already three quarters of the way down the long path to greet me by the time I'd got through the gate. Shipley, a wiry, strutting cat whose meow wasn't so much a meow as a swear-yap, was late into the autumn of his life by the time I moved to Dartington, but still had tip-top hearing and presumably could distinguish the sound of my footsteps from those of the postman, friends, the boiler repairman, and Ian the Dartington plumber. This is more than could be said for my even older cat The Bear, who, by the time I'd been renting the Magic House a year, lived in a soundless world and could frequently be found curled in a happy slumber, 2,000 leagues below consciousness, as I mowed the grass two feet from his tail. The total degeneration of The Bear's hearing had robbed Shipley of his favourite pastime of creeping up on The Bear then blasting him with thuggish profanities. The pair had, in their respective old and older age, become friends of sorts, and ultimately Shipley's swearing had always worked a little bit like the swearing of many of the people I'd grown up with in the East Midlands: calling you a colossal twat or prime bellend was his own special way of demonstrating that he liked you. As I climbed the path to the side entrance to the house, he'd hit me with a volley of salty anecdotes and affectionate slights on my character and appearance.

'Squirrels pay me to take my collar off and twerk when you're not here!' Shipley would say to me, as I climbed the path, being careful not to slip on a damp mossy patch.

'Why don't you get your hair cut?' he would ask, as I diverted diagonally across the lawn to the back door, past a tulip tree whose canopy contributed to the house's darkness – and the garden's lightness – in summer. 'You

look like one of the three crap Irish wolfhounds I ruined last night.'

'I've been going around some local bungalows, shitting in bins,' he would add, following me into the house.

'You bought a job lot of this last month,' he would say, as I hurriedly spooned out some expensive new cat food I'd bought, in an attempt to keep his life interesting. 'I pretended to eat it then sold it online to some Russians.'

In the middle of any day outside the boundaries of winter, and quite a few within, you'd be able to lift petals and fronds in the Magic House's garden and almost certainly find at least one cat snoozing beneath them. It gave the impression that cats were just another product of the rich earth, another element of all that rampant growth. In addition to Shipley and The Bear, there was Shipley's sun-loving hippie brother Ralph, and, for a brief spell, George, a ginger and white stray I lured in from the nearby foliage for a summer before sending him off on a permanent spa weekend at my mum and dad's house in Nottinghamshire. Finally there was Roscoe, my CEO, an industrious feline strategist who was attacked by a dog in one of the mostly strictly dog-free zones of the estate, brought back from the vet half-bald and covered in deep scars after two huge life-saving operations at Christmas 2015, then, over spring and summer, flourished against all odds into an even more dynamic version of her former self. The bald patches from her operations stayed bald for four months, then, in April, grew rapidly, as if her fur worked like the copper beech hedge in the garden, and had just been waiting for the right amount of warmth and sunlight to restore itself.

That same February, while Roscoe was recuperating, I was told by the vet who'd saved Roscoe's life that a scrawny Shipley was experiencing chronic kidney failure and had a maximum of two months left to live. By April, he had gained several pounds and was greeting me at the front gate more saltily than ever. The Magic Spring at the Magic House had done its work, again. I was told, repeatedly, that I'd had 'bad luck' with cats since moving to Dartington, but my take on the situation ran to the contrary. If you had several cats, three of whom were past the age of fourteen, it was likely you were going to have problems to deal with, and I felt lucky to be dealing with those problems here, rather than elsewhere. I lived with the increasing belief that this place had extended the lives of two old cats, one extremely old cat, and one cat who'd suffered critical injuries. No, it was not Cat Paradise – as what Roscoe had been through proved – because Cat Paradise did not exist, but it wasn't far off.

One of the first ever photos of the Dartington Estate that is still in circulation – maybe *the* first – features a cat. It's lurking in the background, through the archway near the then derelict-looking courtyard, in what is thought to be 1925. Although the photo is faded, you can see the cat is staring the camera down punkishly, possessive of its rich territory, eager to be in on the action. The spot, close to what is now the entrance to the Barn Cinema, is in more or less what was known to me as the outer northern limit of Roscoe's roaming territory, about 400 yards from the Magic House's back gate. But who can say for sure? She might well have regularly wandered much farther. She became the latest in a long line of cats who'd flirted their way into the Dartington culture, regularly sidling up to summer drinkers on the Great Lawn, climbing on the leaning sepulchres of the ruined church and beheading shrews beside the walled flower garden. During Dartington's annual classical music festival, in late summer, I would walk through the Gardens and frequently witness her jumping coquettishly into the outstretched hand of a flautist, life coach or kinetic healer.

Once you climbed the wildflower path behind my back gate you were effectively in the Gardens: a vast area where people drank, kissed, practiced t'ai chi, sang, played didgeridoo, sensitively dissected their diets and friendships, and my smallest cat took on an ambitious second CEO position. And why should Roscoe have distinguished between our garden and the bigger one beyond? Both had been inextricably linked for a century, probably much longer. It was even there in the Magic House's real name: Gardens Cottage. Before the Magic House had undergone a spell as cramped student accommodation then been tenanted by a string of Dartington employees and me, a succession of the estate's Head Gardeners had occupied it, beginning with William Percy, the first ever gardener employed by the Elmhirsts upon their arrival in 1925. So much that was going on horticulturally at the Magic House echoed what was going on just up the hill. The two clipped Irish sentinel yews, beneath which The Bear liked to take his long deep naps, were scruffy siblings of the dozen at the back of the Great Hall, overlooking the Tiltyard. Fleabane self-seeded in my wall, just as it did in those beside the paths leading up to the White Hart pub. For decades, tiny flecks of magic had been blowing over the copper beech hedge that separated me from the Gardens, downsizers looking for a more humble home. A crackhead clematis spread its long ungainly legs all over my paving stones. In its spidery shadow, euphorbia danced in ever-decreasing circles. Behind that, bees violated a gangly buddleia, under the shadow of two trachycarpus, a magnolia and a pink hawthorn. In more senses than one, I lived in the place where the renegades and misfits escaped to make a new life.

The Elmhirsts, with the help of several experienced British and American garden designers, including Edith Wharton's niece Beatrix Farrand, made the Dartington Gardens the magical combination of wild and neat, relaxed and formal, that they are today, but a vast garden of sorts had existed behind the Hall for centuries. The clipped Irish yews, known as the twelve Apostles, had been planted in the early 1800s to provide a screen between the old nursery and an area traditionally used for bear-baiting and dog fights. When the Elmhirsts first found it, the tiltyard at the Gardens' heart was – besides being vastly overgrown – relatively unchanged since the fourteenth century, when it had been used for jousting matches. In the 1940s, a reclining Henry Moore sculpture was installed above its huge, restored terraces, beneath which I once saw a lone woman in a black leotard dancing very tenderly with a feather on a stick, as if it were her partner, rather than a feather on a stick. This was all in particularly sharp contrast to the area directly behind my previous house, in Norwich, which was used for the disposal and compacting of county council waste and was not associated with any known history of jousting, interpretative dance or modernist sculpture.

It was for John Holland, the half-brother of Richard II, that the Hall had been built, in 1398. After he was beheaded for his attempt to assassinate Henry IV, the Crown took hold of the estate until the reign of Elizabeth I, when it came into the possession of the Anglo-Norman Champernowne family, where it remained for the next three and a half centuries. The last Lady Champernowne to live at the Hall was known for riding her horse down to Dartington village and rapping impatiently on residents' doors with her horse whip when she required their services. When the Elmhirsts arrived in 1925, the whole estate was near derelict, having been abandoned by the Champernownes four years previously. The Great Hall, where the main events at Dartington's music and literary festivals now take place and where I once ended up talking about vaginal glitter in front of over a hundred pensioners, was missing its hammer-beam roof. On his first visit, Leonard Elmhirst had to fight through rampant brambles, bracken and rhododendrons to get a look at many of the buildings, but excitedly pronounced to his wife Dorothy that Dartington was 'a fairyland'. Fortunately, funds to restore the buildings were not a problem. Due largely to an inheritance from her father, a financier who had been the Secretary of the American Navy, Dorothy was one of the richest women in America. During her first solo trips into Totnes, she often walked out of shops without paying for what she'd bought, since she was used to being accompanied by a purse bearer who handled all her transactions.

Leonard, whom she'd met at Cornell University five years earlier, was from a more humble but still far from ordinary background, being from Yorkshire's landed gentry. Dorothy's belief that her wealth entailed social responsibility, combined with Leonard's interest in rural reconstruction, gained from the work he'd done in India with the poet Rabindranath Tagore in the early 1920s, led them to utterly transform not just the Dartington Estate but the surrounding area, creating hundreds of new jobs and a vast cultural overhaul. The school they founded was a small revolution in itself, being anti corporal punishment, anti uniform, pro freedom of expression, anti segregation of the sexes, with teachers who were intended to be friends, not authority figures. Within a few years, artists, writers, poets and musicians were flocking to Dartington. Ballet director Kurt Jooss and his dance company escaped Nazi Germany to make the estate their home between 1936 and 1940. Michael Chekhov, nephew of Anton, set up Dartington's Theatre School. The legendary ceramicist Bernard Leach founded the estate's Pottery School. In his autobiography, Ravi Shankar cited his visit to Dartington in the summer of 1936 as the moment when he realised he wanted to devote his life to music. It was on the estate that the social innovator Michael Young – a former pupil at Dartington – would draft the original proposal for the Welfare State and NHS.

The local feeling during my first couple of years living in the Magic House was that the Dartington Hall Trust, tasked with continuing the Elmhirsts' legacy as the money finally dried up, wasn't making nearly enough of all this esteemed history, having become lost in a swamp of branding and corporate functions. Many of the Hall's public information signs looked tired and sad. Cranks, the legendary 1960s vegetarian restaurant on the village side of the estate, had been purchased by Nando's. A couple of nearby villages made quite a big deal of the thousand-year-old yews in their churchyard, but the one at Dartington, which was at least 500 years older, sat in the shadows behind the Hall, unadvertised. A timeline of significant Dartington events had been stencilled on the 1980s German techno bar at thigh level but, rather ominously, left no room for the illustrious future. A lot of the community – particularly the older residents of Totnes, Staverton, Littlehempston and Dartington village – felt deeply protective and passionate about Dartington. The place and its history could make people shake with emotion. Not long after I'd moved there, my mum saw an old friend, who asked after me. When the news that I was living in Dartington was delivered, the old friend surprised my mum by spontaneously bursting into tears of happiness. It turned out she had been to school on the estate in the 1960s.

When, in the Barn Cinema, across the courtyard from the Great Hall, I watched found footage of the Dartington Foundation Day celebrations from 1969 – a lone Leonard presiding over them, in brown bowtie and yellow shoes, beneath the courtyard's gigantic swamp cypress, a few months after Dorothy's death – the swell of nostalgia was more powerful than any collective emotion I've ever known in front of any recorded entertainment. Gleeful shouts emerged from the dark, as older audience members recognised themselves or their friends. Such strong local affection had not come quickly to the Elmhirsts, though. In the twenties they won little favour by refusing to let the south Devon hunts ride on their land. By agreeing to pay agricultural workers the minimum wage, which most farmers in the South Hams region steadfastly refused to do at the time, they sparked a minor Devonshire rerun of the Peasant Revolt that had famously taken place across England around the time of the Hall's construction. Reverend Martin, the village rector, felt personally attacked when the Elmhirsts did not attend his services. He wrote to Leonard, complaining of nudity he had witnessed on the estate, including 'a young woman, thought to be in her twenties, very well-developed, wearing nothing but the scantiest pair of drawers'. By the late sixties, the Trust's public relations officer had amassed a bulging file of anti-Dartington comments in the local and national press, including 'a sort of nudist colony, free love and all that', 'it's run by the BBC' and 'Communists trained in Moscow'.

Here, on top of a hill in Devon, 230 miles from the capital, twenty miles from any major population centre, the counterculture had been happening, decades before the counterculture was even a thing. Those loose hand-made outfits I was always seeing worn up the hill, behind my back garden, those hushed conversations I heard about foraged diets, self-exploration and spiritual well-being? They didn't begin here in the twenty-first century, or even during the era of the Flower People; their association with Dartington stretched right back to the interwar period and Dartington's links to the Fabian

Society. When my dad visited on one of the first hot days I experienced at the Magic House, and insisted on sunbathing topless, I worried a little, protective about my tenancy, and keen to be on my best behaviour in every way. I didn't need to. Dartington's association with nudity was long and illustrious. After a new CEO took over in late 2015 and began to slowly inject new life into the estate, one of the sure signs of Dartington moving back in the direction of its former self was that the following summer the amount of skinny-dipping in the river markedly increased.

Even in the 'quiet' period of those first couple of years, there was plenty of stuff going on in the Dartington Gardens: meditation, frightfully well-spoken nocturnal teenage rapping sessions, martial arts, dance, yoga, throat singing, post-foraging summits, tightrope walking, squatting, blanket-based plots to reinvent society. One day I ascended the hill and took up a stranger on his offer of a Korean massage, which involved him freeing my upper body of toxins by karate chopping me about the neck and shoulders while performing a kind of beatboxing that sounded not dissimilar to the noises my friends and I made while playfighting when we were eight. Afterwards, I felt loose and relieved, although much of the relief possibly came from no longer having to stifle a giggling fit.

During my time at the Magic House, my mum, who is such a keen gardener you assume she'll leak pure green blood when she cuts herself, taught me a new horticultural term: 'garden escape'. As well as the scarlet pimpernels, clematis and euphorbia that had blown over the hedge from next door, I inevitably experienced other, different kinds of garden escapes. Faded when I first moved in, the PRIVATE signs on my gates were more striking after I went over them myself with white paint, but strangers still occasionally wandered through the garden of the Magic House – sometimes because they didn't spot them, or sometimes just because they were nosy, or belligerent. One May weekend when my friends Rachel and Seventies Pat were staying, Pat and I popped out and left Rachel in the garden playing her guitar on the step in front of the Crittall windows. Coming out of a creative reverie, she looked up to find a fey man in a kaftan standing in front of her. 'I'm ever so sorry,' he explained. 'I seem to have wandered off course and lost the rest of my t'ai chi class.' One winter, a boy of sixteen or so living on the estate repeatedly walked through my garden on his way to school, in clear view of the living room window, without any apparent inhibitions. 'But it's really muddy over there!' he protested when I gently explained to him that it was, like, y'know, my house and stuff, and that it might be an idea if he fucked off and didn't do it any more. As annoying as it was, here his trespass seemed somehow less of a violation than it might elsewhere. At Dartington, after all, the earth was a common treasury for all.

The under-25s who had grown up in the Totnes and Dartington bubble often had a particular anointed aura about them that I'd not quite seen anywhere else. Their life surely had many of the usual agonies of adolescence, but from the outside, from April to October, it came across as one long, hugging and drug party, alternating between the river, the woods and the beach. They were as extremely sheltered as any extremely educated and unusually worldly young people can be. If they came across as arrogant, which they frequently did, it was usually in the politest, gentlest way, although things got marginally edgier down by the skate park on the other side of the station. 'You look like John Lennon!' a youth once shouted at me there, strutting a bit and showing off to his mates as I walked past – an observation that warmed my heart not just with its high level of in-accuracy but with its civilised nature, especially when I compared it to remarks I'd received in the corresponding area of the previous market town where I'd lived, such as the memorable 'All right Poncey Scarf, I bet you take it up the arse' and 'SHOES!'

All of this could, of course, be seen as the cultural contrails of the Elmhirsts: a direct result of the people they'd initially attracted here, those who'd settled here permanently, the people who'd been influenced by those people, and the offspring of both. The alternative Sands School in nearby Ashburton was founded in 1987 by ex-pupils and -teachers from Dartington. According to the parent of a pupil there whom I met, the school had only one rule, which was that nobody was allowed to throw a fridge out of a tree. This was apparently in con-trast to the period prior to the day when a pupil had thrown a fridge out of a tree, at which point there had been no rules at all. In one piece of fairly well-known Dartington folklore, a Sands pupil had reportedly phoned Childline to complain when her parents had forbidden her from going to a rave in Haldon Forest, near Exeter.

These were the same children who listened to drum'n'bass behind my garden hedge on summer nights, which I did my best to drown out with records by Funkadelic, Buffy Sainte-Marie, Bonnie Koloc, Buffalo Springfield and Tim Buckley. One quiet, flawless night in 2016 I was standing on the opposite side of the Gardens, the best part of a quarter of a mile away from my record player, on which it was still possible to very clearly hear Buckley's *Happy Sad* album playing, and watching a badger scuttle into the undergrowth just as a hot-air balloon eased overhead through an unblemished sea-blue sky, when my phone rang in my pocket. It was a friend from town and he sounded excited. He asked me to walk farther up the hill, from where, he assured me, I'd be able to see the crop circle he'd just made in a field on the opposite side of the valley.

'But don't aliens make them?' I said.

'Noooo,' he replied. 'That's far-fetched nonsense. The aliens just send down psychic waves to me so I can make them on their behalf.'

For years, I'd had a yearning to write fiction about alternative societies, hippie life, communes and the occult, but on my best day, with all the will in the world, I could not have made a fraction of this life up.

Yet I hadn't really come here *for* any of this. A central factor in the distilled nature of life around Totnes and Dartington is that for the best part of a century it has been a place people relocate to not just because of what's there but because of the lifestyle it promises, which of course then makes it even more distilled. But I hadn't moved there for the culture; I'd moved there because I'd fallen in love with the surrounding countryside and was going out with a girl who lived less than half an hour away. I spent a lot of my time at Dartington feeling like the biggest garden escape of all, something a bit ragged around the edges that had blown in on the breeze then grown, a weed amongst wildflowers. I didn't talk the talk and I didn't wear the cultural uniform. 'So are you working for Dartington?' more established residents of Totnes would typically ask, when they found out where I lived. 'So how come they let you live there?' they would often say, when I told them I wasn't. 'I don't know: it's a mystery!' I'd reply. The monthly rent of the Magic House was beyond my original budget and, because of this, I'd initially imagined I'd only be able to stay there a year at most. But somehow I managed to keep going. A year passed. Then another. Then another. I realised the House had changed me: I felt calmer at my core. I was a never-going-back vegetarian, as opposed to the slightly half-arsed one I'd been when I arrived. I'd finally taken the plunge to go independent and give up writing for the national media, rather than just telling myself I would, and had begun to enjoy my work more than I had in my entire life. I looked different to when I'd arrived and felt more me, physically: browner, wirier, greyer in the beard, but happier, on the whole, with my appearance. I began for the first time to be beamed a very vivid psychic picture of my distant future self, still here in four decades' time, even browner and wirier and greyer and calmer, still walking back down the wildflower path shivering from the river or the cold lido, no longer just a ragged northern blow-in but as much an integral part of the furniture as the lady who rented one of the semis on the other side of the Hall and knew everything there was to know about bookbinding and unicorns. Would the estate have finally decided to replace the Magic House's terrible, repeatedly malfunctioning boiler by then? I hoped so. My future vision was not set in stone, but it was a definite path that appeared eminently possible. 'The Gothic House? That's where the very old man lives, in the middle of all the plants. They say three of his four cats are now in their late forties. He has had them since the time when polar bears and phones still existed.'

On the evenings when I walked up into the Gardens, the cats would often follow me: not The Bear, who knew his limitations and did not leave the boundaries of the Magic House's garden, but invariably Roscoe and usually Shipley and Shipley's brother Ralph. If you were going to get away with looking normal walking a cat anywhere, it was here. Shipley and Ralph would stick close by my side, but when we headed back Roscoe would typically stay on without us, looking for a clarinet player or sha-manic healer to cop off with. If it was August or late July, music would float over from the studios and offices behind the house, where musicians were rehearsing for the Dartington International Summer School, the classical festival that had been held annually here since 1953. In the same buildings could also be found the studio of Soundart, the experimental community radio station where, once a fortnight, or once a month, or sometimes just when I felt like it and there happened to be a slot free, I broadcast a two- or three-hour radio show. The first time I made a show for Soundart, I was directly preceded by the station's beekeeping show, presented by a beekeeper called Dick who, when I arrived, was making a heartfelt apology on air to his bees, having decided he had spoken unkindly about them earlier in the show. During the subsequent month I was scheduled after a very youthful man who was hosting a Scotch-egg-eating contest. I asked him how long he had been DJing on the station. 'About a decade,' he answered.

'So how old were you when you broadcast your first show?' I asked.

'I'd just turned ten,' he said.

After moving to a much bigger studio as part of the new Dartington regime in 2017, Soundart also briefly broadcast live wildlife discos where the audience danced, or more often sat, to old archive sound-effect records and other, more experimental sounds. At the one I attended, the fire alarm in the building went off, but we all took well over a minute to realise this, having thought the noise was just part of the set. My position at the radio station was voluntary but if I was lucky I received payment in fruit and veg. Locating my diary from 12 June 2015, I see that for that week's show I was paid the impressive sum of one apple, one large broccoli floret and two courgettes, which I deemed to be more than fair.

Eventually, irresistibly drawn in by the innumerable greens and yellows and reds and oranges I saw every time I walked past, I enrolled on one of the introductory horticulture courses at School Farm, the organic allotment down the hill on the other side of the Hall. Here I learned how to delicately handle cotyledon leaves, puddle in a bed of leeks, tie the correct knots in the string holding up climbing tomatoes and not choke at the rotting nettles in our organic feeds, which everyone agreed smelled like used nappies. I ended as barely less of a bumbling novice than I had been at the beginning but it was pleasing to think that some of the tomatoes and lettuce that turned up at The Green Table, the estate's phenomenal new cafe, later that year had been given their first nudges towards adulthood by me. I had gardened before I went to Dartington, in the most basic sense, but being there made me want to do so more creatively. I made myself part of my garden, enjoyed getting its grass and soil and seeds and weeds on me, reshaped it, used its wild mint to make tea. I stopped going to the hairdresser's. I didn't have a hairstyle. I had hair. On some days, it had zero caterpillars in it. That was about as good as it got. I planted foxgloves and cordylines and ivy-leaved toadflax. Enhancing the green circle around the house for the benefit of a future I might not be part of never occurred to me as a waste of time; I was just being good to the Magic House, in a way that seemed only correct, since the Magic House had always been good to me. Friends began to refer to the house as if it was a person, easy-going and selfless, a positive influence to be around. Two couples who looked after it for me while I was away separately reported that they'd not been getting on beforehand but felt easy and harmonious after their stints there. Wildlife flocked to the house's goodness through the gaps in its edifice. Educated moths seemed to view it as an exclusive gentlemen's club. I arrived downstairs one morning to find a song thrush casually perched on a picture frame, unperturbed by my presence. One evening a colony of several hundred flying ants moved into the boiler room and the entrance hall. I dealt with the situation by leaving the back door open to the night, putting Neil Young's 1969 debut album on the turntable, and letting them get on with being flying ants. By the morning, they were gone. The boiler remained just as faulty.

The abstract painting my mum did of the Magic House during my final year there says a lot about the place's character. She chose to focus on the Gothic, ecclesiastical-looking side of the building, but there's nothing dark or ominous about what she came up with; it is orangey and earthy and verdant and welcoming, redolent of the finale of winter when lots of amazing events are happening just under the surface of the soil. There is something very optimistic and progressive about it, very 1925, very Dartington. I wanted to write about the house's unique personality, and Dartington's, but something was stopping me getting directly down to it. The place hadn't quite had enough time to ferment in its spot inside me. I also had the additional concerns that come with living with a minor celebrity: something which I'd been in denial about, but had recently been forced to face up to more honestly. Around a year before my move to Devon, I had started a Twitter account for The Bear called Why My Cat Is Sad, which had taken off, gaining him around 330,000 followers, and more than twice that number on Facebook. Intended to support the books I'd written about his life, it played on his wide-eyed soulful looks, every tweet featuring a new photograph I'd taken of him accompanied by a new, preposterous reason why he was sad. For example, to accompany a photo of The Bear looking small and sweetly forlorn next to a camp bed, some toilet rolls, a pack of Uno cards and a ukulele,

I used the caption 'My cat is sad because he has been sitting here trying to hitchhike to Glastonbury for hours but nobody will pick him up.' The Bear's placidity and stillness, and the fact he spent a lot of the day following me around and staring deep into my eyes, made photographing him in a variety of scenarios an easier task than it would have been with 99.9 per cent of other cats.

I enjoyed being creative with the tweets but saw the whole enterprise for the bit of nonsense that it was, as did the majority of the people who followed The Bear's daily adventures online. A minority, however, took it more seriously. People sent me photographs of cats that had been run over by cars, and messages announcing that they were coming to my house to kill The Bear. A group of young journalists discussed the party they would have when The Bear died and was no longer on Twitter. Some people told me I was exploiting The Bear, by putting his photographs on the Internet, as if they viewed The Bear as a cat who had strong moral views – which, admittedly, in the patently absurd online persona I'd invented for him, he was. A man in Eastern Europe wrote to ask if he could pay me several hundred pounds for his girlfriend to spend an hour with The Bear. I said no, just as I did to other ways to make money from The Bear, besides selling a small amount of cards and calendars featuring his face, which enabled me to buy him even more cooked chicken than I already did, which was a lot. I was careful on the Internet not to mention precisely where I lived, or photograph the Magic House in a way that made it instantly recognisable, but even so, to my knowledge, by 2016 at least three sets of people had come to the Totnes area to try to 'find' The Bear. The Bear himself remained bliss-fully ignorant of all of this, sleeping much of each day away beneath the sentinel yews, having the occasional cuddle with Roscoe and slurping up the stagnant, mossy water in the old grey can near the back door, which I could only conclude was some kind of elixir for eternal life.

The Bear was a cat who peaked in old age, becoming more mellow and plump after an anxious and scraggy early life. Looking back at photos from his seventeenth and eighteenth years, I am startled anew by his amazing plushness, his neatly packaged, compact bulk. It had only been during the months directly prior to my move to Devon that he had begun to look his age, his fur getting less sleek, his spine feeling more brittle, his eyes losing their brightness. I'd worried he wouldn't survive the six-hour drive to his new home, but Dartington soon made him young again, or, at the very least, young-old again. I have no doubt that the Magic House extended his life, although I'd feared it would do precisely the opposite. He'd been mutating into an indoor cat prior to the move but his new habit was to stay out in Devon's frequent rain, coming through the cat-flap with sparkling eyes and a drenched coat, then delighting in the ritual of having his back towelled dry by me and warming up next to the log fire. Some suggested his new love of rain was a mark of senility; I thought he had merely got wise to the way the liquid that poured from the south Devon skies could make him flourish, like everything else in the garden. By the time the trees were fully green in 2016, as The Bear approached his twenty-first birthday, Roscoe's fur regrew over her scars, Shipley made his unfathomable recovery from kidney disease, and the now almost fifteen-year-old Ralph lounged among daisies and buttercups looking not a day over five, I had arrived at the conclusion that I was living with four Miracle Cats, in a Miracle Place.

It is only now, looking back at my diary, that I realise how many genuinely trying events had taken place in my life in the short space of time between December 2015 and March 2016. As well as Roscoe and Shipley's narrow survivals, I'd lost the entire 23,000-word manuscript of the book I was writing. I'd thought I was over the relationship I'd left the previous year, realised I wasn't, met a couple of blatantly wonderful women who liked me, got thoroughly irritated with myself for not being capable of liking them back in the same way. The sky was oppressive and full of coal. But spring re-dignifies you, especially at Dartington. Inspired by The Bear, I put a lot of rain on my own fur, and it appeared to work. Myopic checkout operators sometimes asked me for ID. By May, the whole of the TQ9 postcode looked young again. In town, I played a game I called 'Old Person or Young Person'. This involved me trying to guess whether the person in front of me on the street was an old person or a young person. I frequently got the answer wrong. Teenagers around Totnes often dress not dissimilarly to their parents, who are often more than a typical generation's span older than them, but – to further confuse matters – tend to look younger than they are. People in their fifties and sixties often had long, thick manes of hair and look slim and toned, so it was only when you saw their healthily lived-in faces that you realise they were no longer in the prime of youth. Billowy skirts, tie-dye, chunky jumpers and ponchos abounded. Even in summer, everyone looked cheerfully woven. It was a look that went beyond just clothing. In the post office, I queued behind women wearing big fishermen's jumpers full of leaves and burrs who answered the verbose existential questions of small children tugging on their yoga pants. 'HUGGING HOUR!!' announced a sign in the market-place. 'Have you had your fourteen a day?' Another poster advertised an upcoming course for the niche, devil-may-care sector of the population who had always yearned to learn meditation and archery simultaneously.

'Lick my organic cheese!' shouted a rejuvenated Shipley at the front gate, as I arrived home, weighed down with bags of food and cleaning products from the supermarket, which, if I was fully committing to the Totnesian lifestyle rather than just being an accidental garden escape, I would have boycotted. I worked hard and rewrote what I'd lost. But also, in the refined, easier picture memory creates, my friends and I did nothing but swim, watch bats, listen to folk rock and burn logs in my fire-bowl in the Magic House's garden. October arrived. 'Trick or twat!' shouted Shipley, at the gate. November elbowed its way in behind it. 'All the leaves are brown, and the sky is an overwhelming bulbous cock!' shouted Shipley, at the gate. A few yards behind him, as fat rain fell, The Bear, now finally legally old enough to drink in America, slept soundly, in a plant pot.

In my heart of hearts, I knew that what had happened to The Bear and Shipley that summer could only be an encore, albeit a glorious one. The Bear was seriously old now, and seriously deaf. He weighed little more than a parrot and spent long intervals meowing at walls. I drew his Twitter account to a conclusion, not wanting to turn it into a picture board of his decline. In autumn, he developed a large and putrid abscess in his ear. He recovered, but not long afterwards the vet found a tumour between his jaw and eye socket. Yet The Bear did not seem unhappy. He retained a good appetite and, from time to time, still permitted Roscoe to sleep on his back. His unretractable claws and dainty posture made him appear to tap dance through the three rooms of the Magic House that were carpetless. Sometimes, he'd try to scratch an itch with his back leg but, due to his arthritis, not be able to reach, scratching thin air instead. If I was around, I'd try to find the spot and scratch it for him. I never quite got the right place. Every time he woke up he looked even more wide-eyed than the time before, as if pulled by a finer and finer thread back into reality and increasingly bewildered by his continuing hereness. I'm pretty sure I know the exact moment he died because at about 2.40 a.m. I woke with a full-body jolt that felt like a benevolently intended electric shock and the Magic House felt very different to how it had ever felt before. A few hours later, as the lazy winter sun was finally beginning to rise over the line of bare trees overlooking the Magic House, I arrived downstairs and found him on his side in the hallway, lifeless. It was 16 December 2016: a year to the day since the second of Roscoe's life-saving operations. I wrapped The Bear in the towel I'd recently been using to dry him after cleaning his increasingly matted fur, and buried him in the garden. I wanted to dig a grave for him under the one of the yews he'd like to sleep under so much, which would have suited The Bear, what with the folkloric links between yews and immortality, but this winter had not yet been as wet as the previous three and the ground was too firm. Instead I buried him on the opposite side of my house, near my shed, close to some

self-seeded verbascum. I dug the hole deep, recalling that badgers had made their setts near here in the past, then remembered that there were virtually none of them left now, because they'd been culled by sorry excuses for humans.

I had been alone during the final hours of The Bear's life, and – although I had friends nearby whom I knew I could look to for support – opted to continue to be alone during the few hours that followed. I struggled, as I knew I would, with an emptiness in the house, where a small comical, loveable and apparently deeply thoughtful presence once was. There was a part of me that felt that by burying him only mere hours after I was stroking him in his favourite spot on his chest and making him purr, I had in some way thrown The Bear away. I knew it was an irrational thought but also, in the circumstances, probably not an unusual one. Also not unusual, perhaps, was the way my mind tended to dwell on its more upsetting final images of him. In fact, maybe it was an important part of acknowledging what had happened. Mixed into the ache in my chest, there was a feeling that, above all, something here should be celebrated: a longevity so extreme and death-defying it made you laugh, a unique character, and an end that could have been far worse. Many would argue that kindness isn't in a cat's nature but if there was ever such a thing as a kind cat, it was The Bear. To my knowledge, he had never killed or even attacked another living being. When other cats – and, on the odd occasion, seagulls – appeared keener for food than him, he willingly moved aside. When I was poorly or sad, he seemed to know, and would move in closer. After seeing the poorly state he was in on the night before his death, I had steeled myself and decided that the next morning I would take him to the vet to be put to sleep, that it was the best course of action for him, the only course of action. But I utterly, utterly dreaded it. That he saved me that particular agony might be viewed as his final act of kindness. I was compelled to match it with one of my own. Experiencing tunnel vision, with soil from his grave still on my hands, I grabbed every bit of cat food in the house and garage, loaded it into the back of my car, drove to the pet-food shop in the village and then the supermarket, bought enough sacks and sachets and cans to fill the remainder of the boot, then drove the whole lot to the Animals In Distress shelter, five miles away, in Ipplepen.

The relationship between Shipley and The Bear had changed markedly in their last year together, Shipley no longer his tormentor, but undergoing a transformation into a tolerated, mouthy sidekick. In the weeks leading up to The Bear's death, I often found them sleeping in the same spot, sometimes with light fur-on-fur contact. From the moment The Bear died, Shipley's health went dramatically downhill again. He stopped swearing at me when I entered the gate, no longer followed Roscoe and Ralph and me up the hill into the Gardens, drank and drank and drank, picked at only the squelchiest parts of his food, and soon became as scrawny as he had been the previous winter when he'd been kept in on fluids at the vet's for several days. One Saturday in February I returned home from a misty walk on the Dorset coast to find him unsettled and agitated, struggling to support his back end. Despite his obvious discomfort, he managed to greet me with a hoarse swear-yap, and I fed him, gave him two of the five pills the vet had advised he should take every day, and treated him to a cuddle in his favourite position: on his back, on my lap. He purred and air-padded in a faint way but felt a little limp. Half an hour later he vomited and started to act more unusually, walking in constant circles, unable to settle. While I was on the phone to the vet's out-of-hours emergency line, he collapsed on his right-hand side on the carpet in front of me, his eyes glazing over. I placed him gently on a blanket in a cat carrier and rushed him to the surgery, fearing he might no longer be alive by the time he arrived there. The nurse attached a catheter to him and got him settled in a kennel and we waited for the vet to arrive, which took just over twenty minutes, although at this point I had lost almost all sense of time as a concept. The vet told me that Shipley was still alive, but his heart rate was very fast, his temperature was very low and he was unable to get up.

Two options were open to me: treat Shipley's condition very aggressively with fluids and medication and hope it might help; or the other one. The vet asked me about Shipley's behaviour before his collapse and, with the extra evidence of my answers, said it was likely he had suffered an embolism. I asked the vet several questions about the likelihood of Shipley having a good and comfortable life, if they were able to lift him out of his current pain. Upon hearing the answers, I made the choice to have him put to sleep. He was brought into the examining room so I could say my last goodbye to him. I kissed him on the head several times and told him how much I loved him. He looked directly at me with apparent recognition and seemed far more aware of his surroundings than he had half an hour earlier, which made what was happening both worse and better: worse because I suddenly questioned, again, whether I was doing the right thing, and better because I wanted him to be conscious enough to be aware of just how much he meant to me. I wanted what he saw at the very end to be someone who'd adored him every day since he first saw him leaping boisterously over a garden pond in Essex in autumn 2001. He died at the exact moment that dusk turned to dark. As I drove away from the surgery, I burst into proper tears – full, uncontrollable tears, that barely allowed me to see the road ahead – for the first time in years.

I had anticipated that Shipley's death would hit me harder than The Bear's, and I was correct. I have loved all the cats I've lived with in varying powerful ways, but the line separating Shipley in the period immediately before his death from Shipley not being here any more was much thicker than the line that separated The Bear in the period immediately before his death from The Bear not being here any more. The Bear was never very cat-like, a little furry island of Almost Cat who did his own thing, and in his final months that island had drifted farther out to sea. Shipley, though clearly in pain, was still shouty, demanding, boisterous, right up to the very end. He was a cat who seemed to need me much more than The Bear did. Much like Ralph, Shipley would be always seeking you out in the house, wanting to know what you were doing and whether he could join in. The space he occupied was huge and I was going to notice that space for a long time.

Many cats love boxes but Shipley's love for them was more ardent and impatient than most. Any time I brought one home and emptied it – and very frequently before I'd had chance to empty it – he'd be inside it within seconds, swearing his head off. Even if he'd been in a deep sleep somewhere in the bowels of the house when I opened the front door, his boxdar would kick in and he'd quickly locate the cardboard. Before I went back to the vet's to collect his body, the vet nurse on duty, Catherine, had asked me over the phone if I wanted to bring his carrier to put him in. That might have seemed more dignified to some but I don't think Shipley would have viewed it that way. I asked her if, instead, she had a cardboard box she could put him inside. We probably tell ourselves all sorts of nonsense about our pets' thoughts in order to feel better in times of grief but I had a strong belief that, with his particular predilections, Shipley would have preferred this method of transport. After I refilled the hole with earth I noticed the slogan on this box: 'Understanding your needs. Innovating the solutions.' If Shipley was a person, he'd no doubt have been the kind who wouldn't be able to resist remarking on the idiocy of a slogan like that. 'Corporate cock sponge!' I could almost hear him meow, in typical insurrectionary disdain. I buried him behind the pond, on the opposite side of the house to The Bear, just on the off-chance Shipley decided to become his tormentor again in the afterlife. Both would fertilise the good Dartington soil and spend eternity in this place of culture: the intellectual and the punk poet.

A week after The Bear's death, during our Christmas meal at her place, my friend Hayley found a potato – almost certainly grown at Dartington – with a mark on its skin bearing an uncanny resemblance to a small, neat cat. It was a quick turnaround, but we decided it was The Bear anyway.

I had spent a large amount of time looking after, and worrying about, both of these cats, ferrying them to and

from the vet's, medicating them, cleaning up after them, waking up in the early hours to check on them, cancelling trips because of them, which meant that, after their deaths, life became more carefree, but also didn't, because of the guilt that I felt about their deaths making life more care-free. Another vibrant, technicoloured spring was in motion. Daffodils then primroses then bluebells grew around Ship-ley's grave. One of the cordylines I'd planted less than two years before had already grown as tall as the ceiling of the Magic House's ground floor. Roscoe was fully recovered. Ralph was about to turn sixteen but still looked five and had hair like a young Kurt Russell. More was going on in the evenings at Dartington: gigs, courses, talks, tightrope walking, conversations. My friends and I took glasses of wine and beer back from the White Hart to the Magic House's garden and lit outdoor fires. Singing and guitars happened sometimes. Phoebe, one of Dartington's employ-ees, came down from the Hall with a shruti box, an obscure instrument from the Indian subcontinent whose miniature mournful bellows soundtracked our friends Emily and Seema's solemn burning of some phone bills, payslips and insurance documents from 2013. Skinny-dipping stats were up again on the previous fiscal period. The deer-park wall restoration was completed and deer were reinstalled beyond it. The giant owl that made steam and travelled in a line at ground level called out into the evening and some-times the smaller mortal owls called back. The new cafe, The Green Table, was rarely less than heaving, full of deli-cious, locally grown food, and contained beautiful 1960s furniture salvaged from the student canteen. Dartington's new CEO, Rhodri Samuel, not only had good ideas and obvious passion for his job, but a detailed and respectful knowledge of the Elmhirsts and Dartington's past. One of his upcoming projects was to restore High Cross House, the biggest of the flat-roofed buildings on the estate designed by William Lescaze in the 1930s, which had been sitting empty and damp for almost half a decade. I got talking to a printmaker in the cafe and ended up learning printmaking in a studio behind the Hall on printing presses older than the Elmhirsts. I swam and walked and consumed beer and cider and crisps and local salad in the sun and rain and didn't lose 23,000 words of a book.

It was exciting to live in this revitalised Dartington, but I was still entranced by the estate's more neglected corners: Aller Park, the old, empty school building, right at the head of the valley, with the phantom swimmers of its abandoned outdoor pool; the arcane ruin in the woods above School Farm. When I walked around Foxhole, a vast empty early twentieth-century building which had once been student digs, faded, peeling gig posters were still on the walls and the images of the pupils I'd seen larking around on silent early 1970s Super 8 films felt close enough to touch. For each of my summers at Dartington, part of my standard playlist had been Mark Fry's *Dreaming With Alice*, a little-purchased, now very rare acid folk album from 1972, which sounded, at times, like a less needy Donovan, and struck me as a very Dartington record. To my delight, I discovered it actually *was* a Dartington record: Fry – now better known as a painter – had recorded the album in Italy, but written much of it as a teenager living in one of those very rooms I'd peered into at Foxhole, on a guitar he'd made himself in a Dartington carpentry class. All of

Dartington's ghosts struck me as very benevolent – well-meaning spectres who still loved the earth, even in death. There was a legend about a Woman in White, who would only appear to presage the demise of a resident at the Hall. This worried me slightly, as there were no longer any residents at the Hall, and it could be argued that the nearest thing to one was either me or the tenants of the cottages on the other side of the courtyard. I don't think I ever saw her, unless her sartorial penchant was for kaftans and her favourite habit was to play the penny whistle in broad daylight under a swamp cypress.

In late August 2017, I woke at 3 a.m. to the sound of church bells drifting through my open bedroom window. I sat bolt upright, with a little shiver. There were two churches on the estate: the 'new' St Mary's, close to the main road at the bottom of the hill, built in the late nineteenth century, and the old St Mary's, behind the Hall. I'd got to know the bells just a little at the new St Mary's lately, pulling on one of the ropes attached to them during an introductory campanology lesson I'd been given by the church's head bell ringer. There's an addictive rhythm to bell ringing, an elusive sweet spot to be hunted out, and soon you begin to see the bells turn over in your mind's eye. It dispelled a notion that I knew was untrue yet had always lingered in my mind, that a church is a bit like a wound clock, or even a sentient being, and is able to ring its bells all on its own. In campanology you also get a new appreciation of the size and power of the bells. Even so, I knew there was no way that even at their loudest, with the wind blowing in the right direction, the bells of the new St Mary's could possibly be so audible in my bedroom, a mile away. The old St Mary's, meanwhile, was now only a ruined thirteenth-century tower, a church which had not rung out its song for a 140 years or more. The night felt thick and deathly still. 'The witch is coming through my window,' sang Mark Fry, in my head. I sat up for a while, listening to unidentified creatures rustle behind the hedge, behind Shipley's grave.

I discovered a disappointingly logical explanation a few days later: some drunk members of the Dartington Summer School had managed to get access to the tower above the Hall that night, discovered there was a bell up there, and decided it would be a shame not to check it was still working. I rang the same bell a week later, in broad daylight, having been given a tour of some of the lesser-seen parts of the Hall, including Leonard Elmhirst's old study with its secret door, which it is said he put into use when he was feeling antisocial and Dorothy had visitors. I also got chance to go up to the top of the tower of the old St Mary's, where before I'd only seen jackdaws and three trumpet players who'd serenaded me the previous August as I walked past leaning gravestones which stood against a wall, like chairs pushed to the edge of the room to make way for an event. From here, the highest viewpoint on the estate, you got a new appreciation of just what a vast project the Elmhirsts had undertaken here in the twenties, taking all the ruined buildings and overgrown green spaces around and transforming them into utopia. I looked for the Magic House off to the south, but the dense leaf canopy of high summer gave the impression that it had used its magic to totally vanish.

Everything became a little ragged and feral after that; summer had shed its belt and stopped tucking in. Nature's wisdom teeth started playing up again. I'd been friendly with many of the Dartington cattle, often stopping to let a Jersey or two lick my palm as I walked through their green and gold playground, but one day in September when I was passing through the field leading down towards the Magic House from the old badger setts, a herd of assorted breeds charged me. I turned to face them and ran a little at them and they backed off, before redoubling their efforts, and I leapt the wall at the end of the field, inches out of the reach of the leader's horns. I had an idea for a new book swimming around my head: a different kind of book, not a very Dartington book. Hares – so rare in Devon – were one of its underlying themes. I was trying to decide whether to write this book, or a different one that I also wanted to write. I was on the phone to a friend, talking about this precise dilemma, when I walked out onto my wet autumn lawn, tatty with dead wildflowers at its edges, and found a freshly dead hare at the lawn's exact centre. Shortly after, I heard a rumour, first from a tree surgeon friend, then from Mary, the lady who lived on the other side of the Hall and who knew all there was to know about unicorns, that part of the new redesign of the Gardens was likely to involve the repurposing of my house. 'You need to tell them how important you are, so they'll let you stay,' she advised me. But I wasn't in the business of telling anyone how import-ant I was. It had never been my style. Besides, I was the blow-in, the accident. A week later, I opened my front gate and found another hare, as dark as the sky above, dead, on the tarmac.

I am now struck anew by just what little time there was between me enjoying the best summer of all in the Magic House, and my departure in December of the same year. Months later, people were still asking me why it hap-pened. That rumour about what the estate were planning to do with the house is not sufficient explanation. 'I'd take that with a pinch of salt if I were you,' a long-time Dartington affiliate had cautioned me. 'They're always proposing stuff like that, and it usually doesn't happen, or takes years to.' Eighteen months after I left, the Magic House remained tenanted as a residential property.

Imogen Holst, the legendary composer who lived and taught on the estate in the 1940s, summed Dartington up as a heaven on earth you felt you could live in for the rest of your life, before you realised that to go on learning you had to leave. I lived in utopia and would surely never live in another place so sublimely removed from the everyday yet so rich in culture and community spirit. But the word utopia comes from the Greek word 'outopia' which translates as 'no place'. Did I want to live in utopia all my life? Wouldn't that be a little like living a life without mistakes, where every decision you made was tediously and mind-numbingly correct? I had become a big fan of mistakes over the years and headstrong, impulsive behaviour had worked out pretty well for me. One of the problems of getting older, though, is that Experience happens and, no matter how much of a headstrong, impulsive person you remain, it will insidiously begin its work on that side of you: in the back of your head where resides the chorus of voices that disapprove of your headstrong impulsive behaviour – individual and real, or nebulous and societal – this choir of sensibleness will be joined by a new voice, which you might recognise with some dismay as your own. This can be frustrating. By late 2017 it felt like a long time since I'd made a major headstrong and impulsive decision that could be widely criticised by others. So I decided maybe it was time to do something about that.

Snow began to fall on the day I left: the first I had experienced in all of my nearly four years at the Magic

House. That was a weird thing about *this* Narnia: it was almost never white. An icy wind blew the ashes from my last, monumental fire-bowl fire over the garden. It looked messy, but they would do it good, in the long run: more fertiliser in the land of magic growth. For a fortnight I had been experiencing that same tunnel vision I'd experienced on the day The Bear had died when I took the cat food mountain to the shelter. It made me hyper-efficient and stronger than my strength. The previous day, I'd carried a king-size bed frame, alone, down to the car, gaffer-taped it to my open car boot then driven it to the charity shop, who refused it on the grounds that it was missing a safety sticker, then to the recycling centre. By 4 p.m., I had burns on my hands – from the fire, but also from an absent-minded moment with my kettle earlier that morning – my sweater was covered in ash and soil, and I was trying to find Roscoe, who was missing, while also instructing my movers on which of the outside plant pots did and didn't need to go into the van and trying to remember how many sugars they had in their tea. In twenty minutes the Property Manager was due to arrive and do her final inspection, and I needed to clean up the last of the glass from an internal window I'd smashed with the corner of the bed frame.

As I was coming down the stairs carrying a full-length mirror and an aloe vera plant and the edge of the mirror was digging into the angry blister that was forming on the worst of the burns on my wrist, I noticed that a well-bred-looking stranger was standing in my hallway. 'Oh hello,' said the well-bred-looking stranger, who sounded even more well-bred than she looked. 'I noticed you were moving out and wondered if that meant the house is up for rent again, and I was wondering if it would be a convenient time to look around.' Somehow restraining my inner Shipley, I told her that no, it would definitely not be a convenient time to look around. Outside, weather fell, seeping down through dead brambles and soil towards Shipley and The Bear. 'The witch is coming through my window,' Mark Fry had sung on my stereo the previous night. 'The winter snow upon her hair.'

The moment I know I've moved out of a house is usually when I start to pack the multi-sockets. They're always one of the very last things you remove: part of that collection of straggling, uninteresting essentials that appear to take up no space in the final illusion of emptiness but in fact fill a few boxes and bring your car dangerously close to capacity. After that, all that's left are spiders, a five-pence coin, lines of dust-fur ghosting where bookshelves once stood, a couple of screws and elastic bands and the lost lid from the beloved dried-up pen you reluctantly threw away five months earlier. Leaving the Magic House was different. The moment I knew I moved was when I shut and locked the doors: not the big front door on the Gothic side of the house, but the Crittall-style French doors, likely installed in the 1920s, on the side facing the Gardens. They made a different noise to the one they usually made, louder and more reverberant, and I heard it in the chamber of my chest as well as my ears, and it was now that I realised on a greater level that you don't live in the Magic House twice, and it was over. I felt like a man leaving a building for the last time in a film, and that somewhere in the dark empty room beyond, which looked bigger than it ever had when it had been mine, there was already a ghost forming of another version of me who had stayed here forever. No longer in possession of the keys to any house on earth, I walked to the car where the cats – the two who weren't staying behind with my ghost – were waiting. The freezing sky was full of good and bad, and I blew up the lane.

ACKNOWLEDGEMENTS

Illustrators are too often unacknowledged or barely acknowledged presences in books, so I'll start by thanking Clare Melinsky for the wonderful psychedelic jacket design of this one – which turned out to be everything I'd imagined it could be and more – and my mum, Jo Cox, for the thirteen prints you will have found inside. Jo has contributed linoprints to my latest three books, despite finding the process of cutting the lino very difficult, due to the arthritis in her hands. More recently, the pain has got to a point where it's impossible for her to continue, so the linoprints in these pages will probably be her last in that medium, but what a grand and special finale they are. Knowing such beautiful images were going to be sitting alongside my writing was an extra motivating force to try to bring my own work up to scratch. Thank you to Imogen Denny, Katherine Ailes, Mathew Clayton and the rest of the team at Unbound for helping to make this book exactly what I wanted it to be. Thank you Jenny Porrett for the help researching my ancestry, Wes White,

Johanna van Fessem and Steve Leighton for the Avalonian expertise, Ed Wilson for the top agenting, my dad for the top dading, Matt Shaw for the website help, Dave Holwill for the top typo-spotting on my website, Tristan Allsop, Brian Jackman and Margaret Morgan-Grenville for helping me with my Kenneth Allsop research, Rob and Donna for the soup, Charlotte Faulkner for the ponies, Allen Cotton and Jane Allen for the info on Teapot Lane (Worms Lane), Justine Peberdy and Phoebe Wild for the secret tour of Dartington Hall, and Sara Benham for the prison tour. Finally, I'd like to thank coffee and swimming. I couldn't have done it without either of you, or at least not in the same way.

Unbound is the world's first crowdfunding publisher, established in 2011.

We believe that wonderful things can happen when you clear a path for people who share a passion. That's why we've built a platform that brings together readers and authors to crowdfund books they believe in – and give fresh ideas that don't fit the traditional mould the chance they deserve.

This book is in your hands because readers made it possible. Everyone who pledged their support is listed below. Join them by visiting unbound.com and supporting a book today.

Linda Abelson
Ludovic Abrassart
Yvonne Aburrow
Natasha Aburrow-Jones
Kathleen Ahearn
Adrian Ainsworth
Elisa Aitchison
Kathleen Alexander
Sheila Algeo
Ben & Jane Allardyce
Catherine Allen
Judy Allen
Kelly Allen

Nicola Allen
Kathy Allso
Becca Allsopp
Gina Alven
Ariane Amann
Becki Amborn
Lynda Andersen
Fran Anderson
Misha Anker
Jenny Anslow
Becky Appleton
Sandra Armor
Julie Arnold

Diana Arseneau-Powell

Kay Arthur

Sue Arthur

Dawn Ashford

Fiona Ashley

Jamie Ashmore

Louise Ashton

Dawn Atherton

Rose Auerbach

Danielle Auerbach-Byrne

Chloe Aust

Nick Avery

Carole Backler

Laura Ellen Bacon

Duncan Bailey

Hannah Bailey

Edward Baines

Katharine Baird

Susan Bakalar Wright

Matt Baker

Susan Baker

Emma Ball

Phil Ball

Ali Balmond

Nicola Bannock

Jenny Barnard

Rosie Barr

Jenny Barragan

Christine Barratt

Sara Barratt

Norma Barrell

Brett-Michel Bartlett

Sarah Bartlett

Lisa Barton

Justin Bartz

Katy Barzedor

Paul Basham

Cameron Bashir

Laura Baughman

Leslie Bausback

Gisele Baxter

Emma Bayliss

Ally Beal

Henry Bear aka Bubi

Bob Beaupré

Sam Beaven

Kate Beazleyington

Ella Bedrock

Alison Beezer

Donna Bell

Christine Bellamy

Chrissy Benarous

Alison Bendall

Linda Bennett

Yvonne Benney Basque

Anita Benson

Claire Benson

David Benson

Janet Benson

Julie Benson

Sue Bentley

JoAnna Berry

Suzanne Bertolett
Darren Bertram
Tracie Bettenhausen
Mary Bettuchy
Suchada Bhirombhakdi
Rhianydd Biebrach
Heather Binsch
Maggie Birchall
Helga Björnsdóttir
Deborah Black
Rhian Blackmore
Amy Louise Blaney
Graham Blaney
Graham Blenkin
Bart Blomfield
Charis Blomfield
John Blythe
Meryl Boardman
Ali Bodin
Vickie Boggio
Jane Bolinger
Caroline Bolton
Alison Bonathan
Steven Bond
Christen Boniface
Nadia Bonner
Alex Booer
Ella Booker
Stephen Booth
Jeannie Borsch
Chloe Botting

Val Boud
Anna Boughton
Lesley Bourke
Judith Bowers
Neil Bowers
Teresa Bowman
Mary Ann Boyd
Kevin Boylan
Elizabeth Bradley
Jim Bradley
Aisha Brady
Carol Brady
Hugo Brailsford
Sira Brand
Vanessa Bray
Caroline Bray and Finn
Gill Brennand
Gemma Bridges
Margaret Brittan
Lindsey Brodie
Marianne Brøndlund
  Jensen
Alexander Brook
Eleanor Brooke-Peat
Andy Brown
Kathleen Brown
Richard Brown
Sally Browning
Sian Brumpton
Gilli Bryan
James Bryan

Nigel Bryant
Leslie Buck
Elaine Buckley
Gary Budden
Janet Bunker
Rachel Burch
Amanda Burden
Carson Burgess
Leanne Burgess
Julie Burling
Donna-Marie Burnell
Anna Burns
Arwen Burns
Chris Burns
Christina C Burns
Joanne Burrows
John Burton
Alex Burton-Keeble
Heather Bury
Ann Byrne
Joanne Cabannes
Vivian Cafarella
Victoria Cahill
Michelle Calka
Judi Calow
Donatella Campbell
Jane Campbell
Lara Caulfield
Toby & Ruth
  Canham-James
Rosanna Cantavella

Catherine Cargill
Sarah Carless
John Carney
Caroline Carpenter
Barry Carr
Jonathan Carr
Victoria Carr
Lorrie Carse-Wilen
Philippa Carter
Simon Carter
Philippa Carty-Hornsby
Denise Case
Susan Catley
Stephanie Cave
Heather Cawte
NJ Cesar
Justin Cetinich
Kathryn Chabarek
Sarah Chalmers Page
Lesley Chamberlain
Tamasine Chamberlain
Laura Chambers
Sharon Chambers
Caroline Champin
Liz Chantler
Patricia Chaplin
Zoe Chapman
Heather Chappelle
Jane Charlesworth
Ailsa Charlton
Gill Chedgey

Susan Chedgey

Paul Cheney

Nigel Denise Chichester

Joan Childs

Rachel Chilton

Happy first anniversary,
    Tim & Steph Chilvers

Jo Chimes

Charli Chmylowskyj

Kirsten Christiansen

Kellie Christodoulou

Linda Francesca Church

Amy Ciclaire

Lisa Claire

Mathew Clare

Adrian Clark

Anna Clark

Dee Clark

Heather Clark-Evans

Adie Clarke

Helen Clarke

Mandy Clarke

Katie Clay

Penne Clayton

Alison Cleeve

Julia Clement

Margaret Clement

Jess Clenshaw

Gill Clifford

Freyalyn Close-Hainsworth

Waving Cloud

Svein Clouston

Levi Clucas

Sophie Coffey

GMark Cole

Hannah Coleman

Gina R. Collia

Janet Collins

Sally Collins

Amanda Colnaghi

Jacki Connell

Paula Connelly

Trisha Connolly

Susanne Convery

David Cook

Jeff Cook

Denise Cooper

Fiona Cooper

Mark E Cooper

Sheryl Cooper

Christie Cope

Sue Corden

Rosie Corlett

Ellie Cornell

Amanda Corp

Caspar Corrick

Kati Cowen

Jo Cox

Robert Cox

Ann Crabbe

Duncan Craig

Melissa Crain

Julie Craine
Jacqui Crane
Sara Crane
Tessa Crocker
Nancy Crosby
Vivienne Crossley
Julia Croyden
Denise Cruse
Leah Culver-Whitcomb
Gill Cummings
Joanna Cunningham
Neil Currie
Matthew d'Ancona
Sorita d'Este
Nicole D'hondt
Beth Dallam
Patricia Daloni
Tracy Dalrymple
Jackie Daly
Claire Daniells
Elizabeth Darracott
Claire Davidson
Karen Davidson
Alison Davies
Bethany J. Davies
Harriet Davies
Heather Davies
Jim Davies
Meryl Davies
Rob Davies
Sandra Davies

Ariella Davis
Catherine Davis
Laura Davis
Sandra Davis
Donna (and Oliver) Davis,
    Shipley's Jizz Tree
Jeannie Davison
Mark Davison
Alexandra Dawe
Chase Day
Emma Day
Annie de Bhal
Jacco de Kraker
Nicole de Morton
Lydia Dean
Alison Deane
Michael DeCataldo
Joanne Deeming
Vicky Deighton
Nat Delaney
Jamie Dempster
Christine Dennison
Susanne Dent
Emma Dermott
Suzie Dewey
Sue Dewhirst
Mark Diacono
Miranda Dickinson
Claire Dickson
Peter Dimond
Christine Diorio

James Disley

Rachel Dittrich

Catherine Donald

Zoë Donaldson

Marina Dorward

Jill Doubleday

Katy Driver

Kathryn Drumm

Miyako Dubois

Eileen Ducksbury

Hilary Duffus

Julie Dunne

Sue Dunne

Vivienne Dunstan

Amanda Durbin

Susan Durrant

Pene Durston

Rachel Easom

Stephanie Eaton

Alex Eccles

Gabi Ecclestone

Sarah Eden

Roxanne Edgar

Julie Edge

Elizabeth Edwards

Sharon Edwards

Eirlys Edwards-Behi

Crystal Eilerman

Esther Ellen

Tom Ellett

Caz Ellis

Ember

Alice Anne English

Dawn Erb

Raelene Ernst

Jeanette Esau

Pascalle Essers

Amy Evans

Karen Evans

Kate Evans

Lynda Evans

Rachel Evans

Rachael Ewing

M.J. Fahy

Jeffrey Falconer

Liz Falconer

Shelley Fallows

Paula Fancini-Hooper

Gina E. Fann

Alison Faraday

Sarah Faragher

Charlotte Featherstone

Amy Feltman

Richard Fensom

Rozanne Ferber

Lori Ferens

Verity Ferguson

Peter Fermoy

Erika Finch

Jane Finnan

Andrew Fisher

Nick Fitzsimons

Sorella Fleer

Theresa Flynn

Aurora Fonseca-Lloyd

Joanna Forbes

Susan Ford

Anna Forss

Christine Fosdal

Fi Fowkes

Catherine Fowler

Matthew Fox

Tiffany Francis

Nancy Franklin

Christine Fraser

Sarah Freeman

Mary Freer

Jennifer Freitas

Abi Freshwater

Tim Friend

Rebecca Frost

Anne Fucaloro

Steve Fuller

Deborah Fyrth

Renee Gagnon

Mel Gambier-Taylor

Claire Gamble

Heather Gaona

Ian Gardiner

Laura Gardner

Sarah Garnham

Elaine Gauthier

Sam Gawith

Clare Gee

Sarah Gent

Elizabeth George

Claire Gibney

Candice Gilford

Vicki Gilham

Laura Gill

Gill & Ian

Joanne Gillam

Bruce Gillespie

Richard Gillin

Jayne Globe

Sharon Glosser

Dave Goddard

Jennifer Godman

Stephanie Goldberg

Susan Goodfellow

Paul J Goodison

Heide Goody

Mandy Gordon

Rachel Goswell

Alan Gowland

Natalie Graeff

Emma Graham

Jayne Graham

Kathryn Anne Graves

Darrell Green

Hayley Green

Elizabeth Greenlaw

Rebecca Greer

Caroline Gregory

Michelle Gregory

Amy Gregson

Jo Griffin

Louise Griffiths

Rachel Griffiths

Lisa Grimm

Sharon Grimshaw

Helen Grimster

Claire Grinham

Jane Grisdale

Juliana Grundy

Maria Gutierrez

David Guy

Laura Guy

Sara Habein

Terri Hackler

Julie Hadley

Madeleine Haighton

Anna Hales

Marie Halova

Lauren Hamer

Bryan Hamilton

Laura Hamilton

Karla Hammond

Sharon Hammond

Stephen Hampshire

Margaret Hand

Samantha Handebo

Lizz Hann

Kate Hannaby

Cathy Hanson

Mark Harbers

Jan Hargrove

Hilary Harley

Candy Harman

Lynda Harpe

Sue Harper

Tim Harper

Rachel Harrington

Charlotte Harris

Danielle Harris

Pete Harris

Stephanie Harris

Fran Harrison

Sharon Harrison

Greg Harrop

Nicky Hartle

E Ruth Harvey

Evee Harvey

Graham Harvey

James Harvey

Kay Harvey

Martin Haselup

Anya Hastwell

Luke Hatton

Michael Haut

Katherine Hawes

Emily Hawkins

Ruth and John Hayes

Kate Haywood

Rebecca Haywood

Elspeth Head

Bethan Healey

Gillian Heaslip

Emma Heasman-Hunt

Katherine Heathcote

Hambley Hedgehog

Cat Heeley

Anne-Marie Heighway

Richard Hein

Emma Helks

Vicky Hempstead

Cathy Henderson

Lynne Henderson

James Hendry

Heather Henry

Elizabeth Henwood

Amanda Heslegrave

Anneka Hess

Diane Heward

Eve Hewlett-Booker

Anne Hiatt

Jan Hicks

Jeremy Hill

Carlien Hillebrink

Charlotte Hills

Ann Hiloski-Fowler

Kate Hinds

Bendy Hippy

Beth Hiscock

Kahana Ho

Jackie Hobbs

Adrian Hocking

Emily Hodder

Becky Hodges

Jason Holdcroft

Rocki Lu Holder

Zoe Holder

Samantha Holland

Fran Hollinrake

Claire Holliss

Holly Holmes

Rachel Holt

Barbara Holten

Sam Hookem

Alan Hooppell

Lizzi Hopkins

Pamela Hopkins

Geoffrey Horn

Clare Horne

Antony Horner

John Horsley

Andy Horton

Peter Hoskin

Caroline Howard

Jacki Howard

Jacob Howe

Jo Howell

Nat Hudson

Clare Isobel Hughes

Crystal Hughes

Jennifer Hughes

Yvette Huijsman

Sandy Humby

Lewis Hurley
Marian Hurley
Claire Hutchings
Claire Hutchinson
Gisele Huxley
Kay Hyde
Alison Iliff
Greg Ireland
Hazel Ireland
Anna Jackson
Bex Jackson
Jess Jackson
Judith Jackson
Clare Jackson Spark
Lindsey Jackson-Kay
Michelle Jacques
Talula Jade &
   London Yerta
Jo James
Kellie James
Kit James
Sandra James
Melissa Jane
Nickie Jane
Linda Janiszewski
Marieke Jansen
Sarah Jarvis
Abigayil Jenkins
Christine Jenner
Lynds Jennings
Niki Jennings

Stinne Jensdotter
Paul Jeorrett
Lisa and James Jepson
Simon Jerrome
Deborah Joachim
Andrea Johnson
Kitty Johnson
Vicki Johnson
Emma Johnston
Helen Johnston
Pauline Johnstone
Allison Joiner
AJ Jones
Aliy Jones
Caroline Jones
Hollie Jones
Kate Jones
Mary Ann Jones
Meghan Jones
Myra Jones
Suzi Jones
Lesley Jones for Dylan
   and Marble
Alice Jorgensen
Sara Joseph
Melissa Joulwan
Alex Joy
Vickie Kakia
Paul William Kane
Matilda Karlsson
Lori Kasenter

Annette Katiforis

Lizzie Kaye

Jo Keeley

Maureen Keenan

Frances Keeton

Minna Kelland

Colleen Kelly

Danny Kelly

Gill Kelly

Tricia Kelly

Hilary Kemp

Rebecca Kemp

Denise Kennefick

Janine Kent

Debbie, Graeme, Rigby,
    Charlie & Dudley Kerr

Mary Kersey

Alice Kershaw

Audrey Keszek

Rosie Keszek

Ruth Keys

Dan Kieran

Jill Kieran

Stephanie Kilb

Peta Kilbane

Janet T King

Katja M. Kinkhorst

Jon Kiphart

Linde Kirby

Michelle Kirk

Jackie Kirkham

Kelsey Kittle

Carrie Knapp

Jules Knight

Jailbirds Knott

Mel Knott

Patricia Knott

The Bash Brothers Knott

Laurie Koerber

Sandra Kohls

Christy Kotowski

Helene Kreysa

Laurie Kutoroff

Kevin Lack

Mary LaCombe

Susan L. Lacy

Leslie Lambert

Peter Landers

Patty Langner

Teresa Langston

Simon Lankester

Joelle Lardi

Lorraine Lardi

Jessica Lasher

Ronni Laurie

Barbara Lavender

Terry Lavender

Michelle Lawson

Stephanie Lay

Catherine Layne

Sinead Le Blond

Kim Le Patourel

Morgan Le Roy
Katherine Leaf
Michael Leary
Capucine Lebreton
Claire Lee
Diane Lee
Helen Leivers
Kathryn Leng
Deb Lennard
Fiona Lensvelt
Sandra Leonard
Barb Lerch
Catherine Lester
Jill Lethbridge
Beth Lewis
Helen Lewis
Katherine J. Lewis
Marian Lewis
Pam Lewis
Bonnie Lilienfeld
Lois Lindemann
Susan Lindon-Hall
Diane Lindsay
Francesca Linton
Rachel Lloyd
Vikki Lloyd
Cassie Lloyd Perrin
Ellen Logstein
Anne Long
Kirrily Long
Catriona Low

Jennifer Lowe
Katherine Lowe
Kathryn Lowe
Sarah Lowes
Caroline Lucas
Rachael Lucas
Helen Luker
Elspeth Luna
Kara Luscombe
Katherine Lynn
Gill Lyon
Margo MacDonald
Zoe Macdonald
Karen Mace
Helen Mackenzie-Burrows
Yvonne Maddox
Laura Magnier
Nicki Maguire
Catherine Makin
Lynn Mancuso
Claire Mander
Caroline Mann
Alice Mannering
Keith Mantell
Jennifer Marang
Judi Marie
Hugh Marriott
Anne-Marie Marshall
Melissa Marshall
Sally Marshall
Wayne Marshall

Emma Rachel Martin
Mary Martley
Lucy Maskew
Catherine Mason
Frances Mason
The Mason-Laurence
    Gallery, Dartington,
    Devon
Louise Matchett
Suzanne Matrosov-
    Vruggink
Shannon Matzke
Vicky Maull
Shirley Mawer
Molly Mayfield
Wendie McBurnie
Cat McCabe
Yvonne Carol McCombie
Megan McCormick
Joel McCracken
Lauren McDaniel
Helen McElwee
Jane McEwan
Peter McGinn
Marcus McGowan
Ann McGregor
Samson McHandsome
Alison McIntyre
Cate McKay-Haynes
Colleen McKenna
Vanessa McLaughlin

Cate Mclaurin
Amanda Mclernon
Sue Yin McMahon
Peter McMinn
Leanna McPherson
Síofra McSherry
Denise McSpadden
Melanie McVey
Ffranses Medland
Stacy Merrick
Wendy Mewes
Ali Middle
Elgiva Middleton
Beth Milford
Eilidh Miller
Michelle Miller
Thomasin Miller Freeman
David Millington
Scott Millington
Chris Mills
David Minton
Laura Mitchell
Polly Mitchell
Stephen Mitchell
Susan Mitchell
Tina Mitchell
John Mitchinson
Deena Mobbs
Sebastian Moitzheim
Jonathan Moles
Gisela Møller

Karen Moloney-Lowther
Lani Momeyer
Faye Monaghan
Richard Montagu
Jennifer Montgomery
Kim Moody
Emma Moore
Kristine Moore
Natalie Moore
Sarah Mooring
Sue Morgan
Trish Morgan
Charlie Morley
Caroline Morris
LouLou Morris
Morgan Morris
Chantelle Morrison
Rowan Morrison
Sarah Morriss
Katrina Moseley
Sonja Moss
Sarah Mottershead
Judy Mould
Juls Moulden
David M. Moyer
Nicola Moyes
Florentina Mudshark
Donna Mugavero
Jean Muir
Suzy Muir
Ryan Mundell

Ellie Munro
Wendy Murguia
Ian Murphy
Jane, Parker & Mollie
    Murray
Meg Murrell-Peloquin
Mel Mutter
Laura Mutton
Benjamin Myers
Rich Mynett
Debbie Nairn
Victoria Nash
Samantha Nasset
Carlo Navato
Gemma Nelson
Kate Nelson
Tim Neville
Tamsin Newlove-Delgado
Colleen Newton
Sarah Newton-Scott
Lesa Ng
Ducky Nguyen
Laura Niall
Valerie Niblett
Nicoilín Nic Liam
Liz Nicolson
Andy Nikolas
Judi Noakes
Christine Nobbs
Claire Nodder
Anita Norburn

Esther Norton

Meredith Norwich

Hugh Nowlan

Artur Nowrot

Su O'Brien

Paul O'Donnell

Caoimhe O'Gorman

Liz & Ian O'Halloran

Mark O'Neill

Hannah O'Regan

Siobhán O'Shea

Dorothea O'shea

Sarah Oates

Sandra Oberbroeckling

Laura Ohara

Linda Oostmeyer

Hannah Ord

Mary-Ann Orr

Eric Ouellette

Deborah Owen

Emily, Jon and Axl Owen

Maria Padley

Earnie Painter

Kirsten Pairpoint

Pam Palmer

Janine Pannett

Imogen Paradise

Craig Parker

Lisa Parker

Rebecca Parker

Catherine Parkin

Alan Parkinson

Samantha Parnell

Kate Parr

Karen Paton

Trish Paton

April Patrick

Gill Patterson

Amanda Patton

Rob Paul

Pax & Bastet

Emma Payne

Stanislaw and Stefania Pazucha

Andrea Peacock

Mike Peacock

Melanie Peake

Ann Peet

Tiina Pelttari

Karie Penhaligon

Caity PenzeyMoog

Sylvia Perfetto

Bob Perry

Karen Peterson Fellows

Leslie Phelps

Chris Pickard

Lisa Piddington

Karen F. Pierce

Charlotte Pirrone

Awkward Pisswhiskers

Terri Platas

Shara Pledger

Jo Plumridge

Lucy Plunkett

Shannon Poe-Kennedy

Sue Polchow

Justin Pollard

Steve Pont

Jackie Poole

Mark Jarrett Porter

Becky Potter

Lucy Potts

Sheila Powell

Jo Power

Kate Power

Brooke Pownceby

Kristine Heidi Pratt

Alllson Prebble

Robert Preece

Virginia Preston

Laura Price

Sarah Price-Sinclair

Christina Pullman

Kate Pyle

Lisa Quattromini

Kate Quayle

Cheryl Quine

Bonita Quittenton

Zoe Radcliffe

Sue Radford

Helen Rainbow

Lucy Raine

Laura Ramos

Paul Randall

Peter Randall

Susan Randall

Tina Rashid

Laura Rathbone

Andrea Raymond

Angela Rayson

Kerie Receveur

Ceoltoir Redman

Victoria Reed

Alison Rees

Meg Reeves

Lynn Reglar

Louise Reid

Susan J. Reid

Vivienne Reid Brown

Peg Reilly

Chelsea Reimer

Steph Renaud

Marie Reyes

Debra Rhodes

Lesley Rhodes

Sam Rhodes

Julie Richards

Lizi Richards

Fiona Riddell Pearce

Lisa Riffe

Meryl Rimmer

Nikki Rimmer

Kerry Rini

Rachel Ritchie

Andy Roberts

Catherine Roberts

Nicole Robertson

Louise Robinson

Spencer Robinson

Patricia Rockwell

Jane Roe

Valerie Roebuck

Jeanette Rogers

Tom Roper

Vikki Rose

Jenny Ross

Matt Rowell

Rhona Rowland

Charlie Rowlands

Helen Rule-Jones

Sue Rupp

Gillian S. Russell

Ian Russell

Michael Russell

Sam Russell

Tony Russell

Angela Rutter

Elma Ryder

Karl Sabino

Sara Sahlin

Puskas Salts

Callum Saunders

Christine Savage

Keith Savage

Sherri Savage

Katie Sawyer

Nicole Schleicher

Julia Schlotel

Leslie Schweitzer

Anne-Marie Scott

Jenni Scott

Sarah Scott

Tracey Scott

Bill Scott-Kerr

Sara Scott-Rivers

Betsy Scroggs

Alison Scruton

Paul Scully

Jane Seager

Andrew Seaman

Louise Searle

Emma Selwood

Pamela Sentman

Belynda Shadoan

Mariese Shallard

  & Nimrod

Paul Shane

Lori Shannon

Sue Sharples

Geoff Shaw

Iola Shaw

Matt Shaw

Richard Sheehan

Tara K. Shepersky

Thomas Shepherd

Lesley Sherlock

Josephine Sherwood

Karen Shipway

Rachel Shirley

Alison Shore

Jo Short

Cyndi Simpson

Alan Sims

Melissa Sims

Heather Skull

Debbie Slater

Jane Slavin

Barendina Smedley

Smidgen of the Far Pavilion

Bec & Richard Smith

Carolyn Smith

Charlie Smith

Charlotte Smith

Eleanor Smith

Gabriella V. Smith

Hannah Smith

Lan-Lan Smith

Libby Smith

Mairéad Smith

Maria Smith

Michael Smith

Rosie Smith

LA Smith-Buxton

Julia Snell

Lynnae Sniker

Ingrid Solberg

Yve Solbrekken

Murielle Solheim

Roberta Solmundson

Soxx Claude Bernard
   Somersham esq.

sOOzworld

Julie Sorrell

Kit Spahr

Caroline Sparks

Lyn Speakman

Gem Spear

Maureen Kincaid Speller

Rosemary Spiteri

Mark Spokes

Rosslyn Spokes

Judith Stafford

Richard Stagg

Andy Stainsby

Pam Stanier

Rosheen Staniforth

Deborah Stanley

Elizabeth Stanley

Mandy Stanton

Hannah Stark

Rory Steabler

Amanda Stebbings

Andrew Steele

Sarah Steer

Karyn Steers

Angie Stegemann

Ros Stern

Nic Stevenson

Dawn Stilwell

Beth Stites

Mary Stoicoiu

Shelagh Stoicoiu

Carmen Stone

Emma Jane Stone

Gwilym R Stone

Julie Stonham

Stephanie Strahan

Leslie Kay Stratton

Brigit Strawbridge

Duncan Strickland

Rachel Stubbs

Barbara K Stuber

Nina Stutler

Nadia Suchdev

Richard Sulley

Sue Summerill

Helen E Sunderland

Adam Sussman

Judi Sutherland

Laurel Sutton

Kate Swan

Toni Swiffen

Russell Swindle

Kirsty Syder

Angela Sykes

Ian Synge

Peter Tags & Kim Jarvis

Angie Tanner

Rebecca Tanner

Kelly Tarrant

Alison Taylor

Andrew Taylor

Brigid Taylor

Dave Taylor

Lesley Taylor

Lusana Taylor

Sarah Taylor

Shereen Taylor

Jillian Tees

TeethingBeastie

Caitlin Tefft

Jennifer Teichmann

Sue Tett

Marthe Tholen

Nicole Tholt

Dave & Jan Thomas

Donna Thomas

Victoria Thomas

Pierrette Thomet

Claire Thompson

Fern Thompson

Helen Thompson

Mary Ann Thompson

Andrea Thompson
 & Alec Olah

Lynne, Kylie, Donna
 & Shelley Thomson

Alastair Thornhill

Mark Thornton

Carolyn Thraves

Donna Tickner

In memory of Tigellina

Adam Tinworth

Finest Titloaf

Sabine Titz

Joanne Todd

Delyth Toghill

Stacy Tomaszewski

Deborah Toner

Costanza Torrebruno

Angela Townsend

Emily Traynor

Carly Tremayne

Louise Treneman

Christopher Trent

Cherie Trounce

Rebecca Tuck

Kate Tudor

Cass Turner

Catherine Turner

Marie Turner

Russell Turner

Ruth Turner

Ben Tye

Lisa Undercat

Anita Uotinen

Clive Upton

Angie Vaites

Lorraine Valestuk

Sonja van Amelsfort

Anna van den Bosch

Robin Van Sant

Shane Van Veghel

Anne Vasey

Alexander Verkooijen

Sally Vince

Vivian Vincek

Paul Vincent

Rosalind Vincent

Shelly Vingis

Alice Violett

Nicole Vlach

Leslie Wainger

Allyson Wake

Tim Wakeham

Sarah Wakes

Anne Walker

Charlotte Walker

Mike Walker

Sally Walker

Stephen Walker

Sue Walker

Niki Walkey

Heather Wallace

Karen Wallace

Lucy Wallace

Linda Wallis

Mike Wallis

Declan Walsh

Robert Ward

Stephanie Wasek

Laura Watkins

Bj Watson
Rachel Watt
Catherine Watts
Tracey Waudby
Weaverbird
M. Webb
Susan Webb
Denise Webber
Lisa Webster
Daniel Weir
Julie Weller
Jane Werry
Casey West
Lyn West
Katy Wheatley
Andrew & Lucy Whelan
Pam Whetnall
Rebecca White
Susan White
Mark Whitehead
Richard Whitehead
Vicki Whitehead
Robert Whitelock
Miranda Whiting
Annalise Whittaker
Cat Widdowson
Kathleen Wieser
Badger Wild
Peter Wilde
Mary Wiles
Riki Wilhelm

Lorna Will
Anne-Marie Willard Jullien
Linda Willars
Caroline Williams
Christina Williams
Gillian Williams
Jenny Williams
Fran Willis
Laura Willis
Rosamund Willis-Fear
Derek Wilson
Fiona Wilson
Kirsten Wilson
Molly Wilson
Tracey Wilson
Oliver Wilton
Camilla Winlo
Kim Winspear
Amanda Winstone
Lucinda Winter
Rob Winter
Steve Winter
Caroline Winyard
Anna Wittmann
Howard Wix
Gretchen Woelfle
Laiane Wolfsong
Hannah Wood
John Wood
Judith Wood
Laura Wood

Lucy Wood
Matthew Wood
Rebecca Wood
Tabatha Wood
Techla Wood
Melody Woodall-Smith
Joanna Woodhouse
Mark Woodsford-Dean
Cate Woodward
Tim Woolcott
Brenda Wordsworth
Elizabeth Wright
Melanie Wright
Sue Wright

Jeremiah Wyke
Kirsten Wylde
Luke & Jo Wynell-Mayow
Theresa Yanchar
Jo Yeates
In memory of Pam Young
    and Pepperbox Hill
Lindsay Zaborowski
Donna Zillmann
Birgit Zimmermann-
    Nowak

21ST-CENTURY YOKEL

TOM COX

'Glorious – funny and wry and wise, and utterly its own
lawmaker. It makes me wish that Tom had been able to
go river-swimming with Roger Deakin, one of the other
great comic voices of British "nature-writing"'
Robert Macfarlane

'A rich, strange, oddly glorious brew' *Guardian*

21st Century Yokel is not quite nature writing, not quite a
family memoir, not quite a book about walking, not quite
a collection of essays, but a bit of all four.

It is intrepid in minor ways – thick with owls and
badgers, oak trees and wood piles, mystical spots and
curious objects – and its pages are haunted by the folklore
of several counties. Emerging from this focus on the detail,
though, are themes that are bigger and more important
than ever.

HELP THE WITCH

TOM COX

'Often unnerving, frequently funny and always original, the tangled roots of these haunted stories reach into deep, dark places to unearth an alternative England' Benjamin Myers, author of *The Offing*

'These stories are a delight' *Guardian*

As night draws through country lanes, and darkness sweeps across hills and hedgerows, shadows appear where figures are not; things do not remain in their places; a new home is punctured by abandoned objects; a watering hole conceals depths greater than its swimmers can fathom.

Help the Witch marks Tom Cox's first foray into fiction, collecting ten stories that broaden the scope of folk tales as we know them. Funny, strange and poignant, they elicit the unexpected and unseen to raise our hackles and set imaginations whirring.